# We Grew Up Together

# *We Grew Up Together*

## Brothers and Sisters in Nineteenth-Century America

ANNETTE ATKINS

University of Illinois Press

Urbana and Chicago

Library of Congress Cataloging-in-Publication Data
Atkins, Annette, 1950–
We grew up together : brothers and sisters in nineteenth-century America /
Annette Atkins.
p.   cm.
Includes bibliographical references and index.
ISBN 0-252-02605-5 (acid-free paper)
1. Brothers and sisters—United States—History—19th century.
2. Brothers and sisters—United States—History—20th century.
I. Title.
HQ759.96.A75      2000
306.875'3—dc21      00-008453

C 5 4 3 2 1

*To*
*Roberta Atkins*
*Judy Freeman*
*Linda Peterson*
*Susan Atkins*
*Michael Atkins*
*Peggy Devitt*
*Tom Atkins*
*Mary Atkins-Boe*
*Betsy Cartwright*
*Teresa Davidson*
*Steven Atkins*
*and, of course, our parents,*
*Bob and Betty Atkins*

# Contents

# *Acknowledgments*

One pleasure in bringing this manuscript to print is thanking the people who helped me turn an idea into a book. They are not responsible for the facts or interpretations of it but for its existence, for sure.

In the early stages of the process I was lucky enough to receive funding from the Huntington Library in San Marino, California (a researcher's paradise if ever there were one, especially a researcher from Minnesota in February), and from the Schlesinger Library at Radcliffe in Cambridge, Massachusetts. The commitment of the Schlesinger Library to collecting women's documents and making them available to scholars is truly remarkable and I thank them for that, especially. I received, in addition, a faculty development grant from the Canadian government that funded my research at the Glenbow Archives in Calgary and at the Ontario Provincial Archives in Toronto. None of this research found its way into the final book because the letters that I read there felt so different to me from those that I had read in the United States. I simply did not know enough then to make sense of the differences. I plan now to turn back to those letters as a separate project.

The staffs of these various libraries, and of the Library of Congress and the Minnesota Historical Society, were generously helpful, and I am grateful for their guidance, advice, and kindnesses, as well. These librarians and archivists often did transform the sometimes lonely process of research into a shared adventure.

The Minnesota Historical Society offered, in addition, something more valuable even than funding—space. Debbie Miller, the research supervisor, made me a home and at home in the Knight Research Suite at the MHS when I needed a research space again and again. Doing this book truly would have been incredibly more difficult without the Minnesota Historical Society, and I am deeply grateful to its director, Nina Archabal, to Ian Stewart, the deputy director, and to the staff for creating a community for and of historians.

At the beginning of this project I was fortunate to fall into the company of a summer seminar on family history sponsored by the National Endowment for the Humanities and run by Maris Vinovskis at the University of Michigan. They gave me lots of good advice, some that I stubbornly ignored, and we had a thoughtful and wonderful summer that I have not forgotten.

In my twenty years at Saint John's University I have been grateful to receive two sabbatical leaves, two leaves of absence, and two MacPherson Faculty Development Awards. The members of my department have been my best help. Norma Koetter, the departmental secretary and czarina, has been my friend, my ally, my software consultant, and my troubleshooter. If I thanked her a million times it still wouldn't be quite enough. My faithful colleagues—especially Dave Bennetts, S. Carol Berg, Ken Jones, and Martha Tomhave-Blauvelt—have not begrudged my time away and have picked up the extra work that my absence has occasioned. Then there is the legion of student workers who sorted, copied, tracked down references, made library runs, typed bibliographies, and generally eased the mechanics of the process. Among the most helpful to me have been Heather Butkowski, Sean Faulk, Nikki Stevenson, Becky Bunkers, Mark Schwob, Susan Efta, Matt Scheider, Doug Klapperich, Rachel Green and Rachel Ludowese, Craig Sevic, Jamey Tielens, Matt Ode, and the Reecy brothers, Greg and Jason.

I'm thankful too to the various people who read all or parts of the manuscript (some more than once): S. Eva Hooker, Ozzie Mayers, Les Bendtsen, Cindy Malone, Walter Nugent, Suellen Hoy, Martin Ridge, Ellen Abbott, N. Grey Osterud, and Jane Norbury. Their thoughtful, probing, critical attentions to my words always pushed me beyond where I could have gone alone, and the final manuscript is better—by far—for them. I especially want to thank Sally Maison for turning her professional psychologist's eye on the manuscript. She has helped me with this book in many ways.

And my writing group. I would have foundered long since without my writing group: Marcia Anderson, Debbie Miller, Carol Ryan, and

Anne Webb. We read aloud to each other, a practice that regularly reminds me that a book must be not the setting down of an idea but its communication. These four women offered their questions and criticisms directly, with good humor and grace.

I write these acknowledgments just after answering dozens of queries from Elizabeth G. Dulany and Theresa L. Sears of the University of Illinois Press and from the copy editor, Polly Kummel. I've heard other people tell horror stories of the process of their publications. These three women not only improved the manuscript but made the process a pleasure.

My friends are my greatest sustenance—in writing and in life: Kathy Paden, Les Bendtsen, Ozzie Mayers, Eva Hooker, Marcia Anderson, Fr. Ray Pedrizetti, Brian Horrigan, and Amy Levine; my Tacky Women Friends—Jane Curry, Gretchen Kreuter, Peg Meier, and Debbie Miller; the Tacky Auxiliary—B. J. Lovegren, Rebecca Lindholm, David Lund, and Bob Sutton; my London friends—Sanya Polescuk, Nigel Higgins, Jane and Robert Norbury, Meg Ford, John Stewart, Mark Wheatley, and Andrea Uphus. Then there's family: my parents and brothers and sisters, of course; Bart Sutter, who encouraged the first part of this project, and Tom Joyce—my dear only-child husband—who survived the second part. The small bit of space that listing them takes up belies the huge space they occupy in my heart.

Thank you, all.

# A Note about Method

Figuring out a methodology for this study took up most of the first several years of working on it. I knew early on that I wanted to use letters among siblings as my main primary source. First, I love reading letters. I wait for the mail (and check my e-mails now) with an eagerness rarely rewarded by the day's allotment of circulars, bills, and the occasional note or card. What am I waiting for, exactly? I wonder every once in a while. The coming mail always promises something new, something unexpected, perhaps magic, perhaps. . . . Of course I'd want to read letters. The letters that I read for this book proved to be the best mail that I've ever received. They contained so many surprises, so many fascinating stories, and revealed so many people intimately.

I also had a more strictly scholarly motive. I want to know about the interior of people's lives. I want to know how people actually thought and felt and behaved. Few documents offer that close a view. Moreover, I wanted to see people in action, not how they talked about their relationships but how they did them; not how they described what their relationships ought to be but how they were. The letter is the artifact of the relationship. In fact, sometimes the letter actually is the relationship. At the very least it shows us the person in a relational act. By reading a set of letters, it is possible actually to see how the authors presented themselves, what parts of themselves they showed, which they disguised, what parts they bent, and which they set straight. For a project in which understanding how people related to each other is central, letters are essential.

That was the easy part, deciding on letters. Then came the harder part: which letters? Whose letters? I depended heavily on Andrea Hinding's *Guide to Women's History Sources* (1979) in deciding which libraries and archives offered the largest selection of papers that might yield sibling correspondence (virtually never a category itself). There were more such papers than I expected. Lots of people have saved lots of letters over the years, and many of those letters have made their way into archives. (Thank you—all of you—who have saved and do save letters!) I settled finally on the Library of Congress; the Schlesinger Library in Cambridge, Massachusetts; the Minnesota Historical Society in St. Paul; and the Huntington Library in San Marino, California.

In selecting the families for this study, I looked for geographical distribution and have included families from New York, Massachusetts, Washington, D.C., California, Arizona, Wisconsin, Minnesota, Missouri, and Kentucky. Most moved around—which is why they wrote letters.

I sought as well a diversity of class within the confines that literacy in English allows. Moreover, class is a concept that fits only uncomfortably when applied to rural families in the nineteenth century. I have therefore included both rural and urban families, some with more resources and some with fewer. In any case, virtually all the families that I examined had the opportunity, means, and inclination to yield to the impulse (or the duty) to write letters. This means that most of my subjects are "middle class" in values, if not in income.

Some of "my" families are "famous"—the son and daughter of President Chester A. Arthur; Walter and Grace Stetson, who were related to Charlotte Perkins Gilman—some are well known enough for one or more family members to show up in the *Dictionary of American Biography,* and many were known only to their immediate neighbors and friends. I didn't search out famous or anonymous Americans but families that left rich collections of letters.

Because I have worked primarily with correspondence, we meet in this book families that generally stayed connected with each other. Correspondence does not often exist within families that are estranged, divided, hateful, broken. Nor does correspondence give us much information about or insight into families where incest and other forms of abuse occurred. We know that it did occur, but our certainty comes not so much from the written record as from extrapolation from the present. Evidence of parental abuse is relatively abundant today by comparison. In her biography of her father, *Old Jules,* Mari Sandoz relates in chilling and cool detail being beaten by him and watching (hearing) him abuse her mother.

But in neither the nonfiction nor the fiction of the nineteenth century can we find much about sister-brother, sister-sister, or brother-brother sexual abuse or even physical abuse. So the families here certainly underrepresent the violent and cruel side of family life, a side that we know exists and has existed.

Among the collections that I could have looked at, I aimed for letter sets that spanned at least thirty years so that I could look at changes over time. I also wanted letter collections large enough that I could get a real sense of the person writing as well as of the person or people being written to. I looked, in addition, for collections that included the letters of more than one person. I wanted to be able to look at exchanges of letters, if at all possible, and to see how more than one family member expressed himself or herself.

Because this is a book motivated in part by issues of gender, I sought out especially families that included both males and females. As a small aside, I also wanted to include a few families of only boys, in large part because historians have done a fair amount of work on sister-sister relationships that I did not wish to duplicate. As far as I knew, however, little work had (or has) been done on men's family letters.

I looked for letters too that fell roughly into the period between 1850 and 1920.

I started around 1850 because I wanted to get the lull before the Civil War, I wanted to see families during the war, and I wanted to look at the social effects of the war. I also wanted to end before the next war, World War I. As a social historian I have been inclined to reject historical periodization that is dependent on wars. Wars, however, have profound social effects. In the case of World War I, at least two effects seemed significant for this study. First, World War I speeded changes in modern technology. Many people had long been using the telephone or telegraph to convey important news. In most letter collections, announcements of births, deaths, weddings, and emergencies began to disappear in the last quarter of the nineteenth century. Clearly, they were communicating such time-sensitive news by means other than letters. Furthermore, as the telephone became more widely available, more and more news became more time sensitive. As it became increasingly possible to send messages quickly, more messages seemed to become urgent. Late in the nineteenth century, a change in job might merit a phone call. Today lunch plans warrant a telephone call or two. In any case, as people communicate by means other than letters, the value of the letters diminishes for my purposes.

I also wanted to stop around 1920 because letters in the 1920s feel

very different from those written in the 1890s. The more recent letters
have a kind of hard surface to them, a brevity. We might say that the
industrial values of speed and efficiency infected letter writing. Virtually
gone are the longer, ruminating letters. Fewer are the expressions of love,
of longing, of connection.

Do these signal changes in the family relationships themselves? I don't
think so. I don't believe that families in the nineteenth century were more
loving or caring than are families in the twentieth or twenty-first, but I
do think that the conventions and rhetoric of letter writing changed. The
decision about the beginning date I made rather arbitrarily and before I
started my work. My decision about the end date emerged from my reading of the letters.

The presence of only white families in this book is my most serious
concern. If women's documents were difficult for generations of scholars to locate, family letter collections from nineteenth-century African-
American, Native American, Asian-American, and Latino communities
were for me even more elusive. Such collections no doubt exist, and
perhaps if I'd adopted a different research strategy I would have located
them. One general consequence of using letters is that many people are
not represented in this book: all those who wrote letters that did not get
saved, all who wrote in languages that I cannot read, all those in repos-
itories that I never visited and in collections that I never saw. I acknowledge these as serious omissions and offer the families that I did include
as examples that suggest generalizations, and I look forward to other
scholars' work on other families.

Finally, having decided on the particular letter collections, I started
to read. I was looking first to get a feel for the genre, for the field. What
was going on in letters in this period? What seemed to be happening
between siblings? Now several years later, I've almost forgotten what it
was like not to have read thousands of these letters. I didn't know whether
they would be surprising or "normal." I didn't know that siblings would
be writing about a larger variety of topics than I'd expected. I didn't know
that they'd write virtually not at all about gender. I didn't know that
brothers would sometimes pour their hearts out and women would sometimes reveal nothing. I didn't know that I'd like some families and dis-
like others. Finally, I didn't know what the stories were that should or
could be told. So I read until I began to see the ground cover, the un-
derbrush, and the forest. I read until I could begin to see which families
seemed to be "peculiar" and which didn't and to recognize when that
peculiarity was about me and when it was about the letter writers.

In reading the letters, I took two paths. The first was simply reading them to find out what happened in the family. Who was where when, who did what, and the like. Sometimes I simply could not figure out all the details of a family's life in this way and had to draw on external records where possible—biographies, censuses, archival guides, librarians. Even then, sometimes I do not and cannot know. I have included with each chapter a rough outline of each family—siblings, birth, marriage and death dates, spouses, whether they had children. I have kept to this quite basic information because the more I tried to include, the more holes I found and, more important, what seemed appropriate was a way to keep track of lots of people. These do that, I hope. The big events go on off-stage. I am not overly concerned about the absence of information, in part because the patterns of interaction, not the particular event, are of primary importance here.

The second path was to read the letters until the family's story emerged. I'm one of the last people to believe that the data speak for themselves. They don't. The historian must always give life and shape to the information in the documents. Nonetheless, I was surprised at the resilience of the letters, their insistence on telling their own stories. They impose real limits on my ability to shape their tales. This is oddly comforting to me. I worried when I began writing that I would find the letters too malleable, that I would find in the letters what I presumed that I would find, thereby giving cause for worry about leading the documents rather than being led. I don't trust that I've found the only story that belongs to each family, but I do believe that the story I've found another historian could and would also find.

One serious problem in working with letters has to do with their completeness or, more accurately, their incompleteness. Collections always have gaps, and I often cannot identify the cause of gaps anyway. I don't know how often any of these siblings wrote to each other. Therefore, I don't take frequency of letter writing as a telling indicator of familial closeness. No doubt, families that wrote more often were closer than families that wrote less often; at the very least they would be better informed about each other and each other's daily lives. This is not always the same thing as love. One characteristic of sibling relations is that they often incorporate long periods of quiescence without deteriorating. Sisters and brothers can fail to write to each other for weeks, months, perhaps years and still find themselves with an immediate sense of intimacy on next contact. This is remarkable testimony to the power of family connections.

There are lots of methodological faults in this study. I have tried various ways of solving those problems. I took one swipe at content analysis of the letters. I took another at a kind of strict categorization of who gave advice to whom, who took advice, who offered help, who accepted it, and so on. I tried to count the occurrences of certain words and other factors. Where the evidentiary base is as intermittent as is the sets of letters that I am drawing on here, any such statistically based analysis finally seemed pointless. I can't do a random sample of letters or families. I can't do even a selected sample of letters and families because I don't know the universe. It would be like running regressions without knowing any of the numbers.

Finally, then, I decided to do what seems to work best: introduce the reader to some people I have met in the past, telling as much as I can about them and about their lives. I can offer the insights that my greater familiarity with their letters and lives prompts. I can put them into a context shaped, in addition, by my knowledge of American history. I have tried to draw into the work the commonsense psychology gleaned through an amateur's reading of contemporary literature on American families. Last, I have tried to tell about these families in ways that give us a larger field in which to see and tell our own stories.

# We Grew Up Together

# ONE

# Family History: Theirs and Mine

---

This is a book about adult sibling relationships, about how brothers and sisters in a variety of nineteenth- and early twentieth-century families lived with each other, how they understood and acted out their roles as siblings, and how those roles related to their gender. This story relates to women's and men's history, family history, and my history.

I grew up surrounded by siblings—eight sisters and three brothers. Today that's a peculiarly large family, but in Sioux Falls, South Dakota, in the 1950s it seemed normal. Nearly all my friends had a lot of kids in their families: the Shreveses had 11, the Connollys had 8, the Meyers had 9, the Elkjers had 7, the Grogans had 11. My best friend from kindergarten to college had nine in her family—five in high school at the same time. (To our minds *that* was a big family!) I felt sorry for those who had only three or four or, God forbid, no siblings. What did they do at Christmas and who did they play with? I knew who I was in part in relation to those siblings and was known in part by my relations with them. They provided the comparisons and the contexts. A few years ago a woman walked up to me in a grocery store—not in Sioux Falls—and said, "Aren't you one of the Atkins girls?" I stared for a minute, then recognized her as a Barnett. She was the age of my sister Judy; the woman's brother Tim was in my class in school. While I'd never actually met her, I felt in an instant that visceral knowledge that comes from knowing her family—especially her siblings—and she mine.

My sisters and brothers and I grew up in a home shaped by my parents' individual and family experiences and formed as well as by the larger context of midwestern, white, middle-class life in the second half of the

twentieth century. My parents set and enforced rules; they defined taboos and acceptable patterns. They taught me how to get along with
others, how to see myself, how to construct relationships, how to inter-
act with the world beyond the front door. So too did my siblings. My
childhood and teenage memory bank is full of family incidents in which
my brothers and sisters and their lessons loom large; real lessons too:
about sex from an older sister; about boys from my older brother; about
school and dating, anger, compromise, rebellion, and accommodation
from a whole bunch of them. Oh, yes, I learned about makeup, music,
clothes, and smoking too. I got and gave advice, reassurance, love, comfort, smart talk, and straight talk (and still do). They taught me how to
get along, how to use humor, how to get away with stuff, and what to
do when caught. I've told and tell secrets to various siblings that I have
never told my parents. I still want to grow up to be as sophisticated as
my sister Roberta and as beautiful as my sister Linda. My sibs and my
relationships with them are a central fact of my childhood and pivotal in
my sense of myself in adulthood. I've recently married a man who was
an only child. We often run up against differences that we attribute to
the differences in our sibling experiences.

Most people grow up with at least one brother or sister—about 85
percent, in fact. The average family size in 1800 was seven children; in
1900 it was 3.56. In 1890, according to federal census data, just under
20 percent of Americans lived alone or in a household with only one other
person. Eighty percent lived with three or more and almost a quarter of
those lived in households of seven or more. In the United States today
many people live in households of one or two, and more couples are
choosing to have only one child, but nearly 95 percent of adult Americans have had at least one brother or sister, by one estimate. In short,
the dominant experience of growing up in the United States involved
siblings.[1]

Historians of the family have written about families as if sibling relationships are largely incidental and certainly located primarily in childhood. I know from my own experience that neither is especially true, but
when I've looked for scholarship on siblings in the past, I've found instead a focus on parents and children, on the "invention" of childhood,
on changing norms for child rearing. First and foremost, then, this book
explores the nature of sibling relationships in ten nineteenth-century
American families. I'm focusing especially on those siblings as adults—
after they have left home, as they are establishing lives of their own, and
once their adult lives are established. How important are siblings and in

what ways? What childhood patterns persist into adulthood? How do relations within the family shape those outside the family? What are the phases of sibling relationships?[2]

A particular issue that I want to examine among siblings is gender. Bookstores these days are full of books about the differences between women and men. Those books range from serious scholarly works to popular how-to books for men from Mars and women from Venus and the like. Whether of the academic or the popular type, most of these books depict women and men as really different from each other. We see the world differently. We speak different languages. We handle emotions quite differently. These books are based primarily on adult relationships between women and men who are not related to each other—except by marriage.[3]

I don't discount gender. I know from my own experience that gender is really important—economically, socially, emotionally. I'm a woman teaching at a men's college run by a men's monastic order in the Catholic tradition. Raised to consciousness in the 1960s and 1970s, I recognize both subtle and overt expressions of gender discrimination. I know that women and men sometimes seem to each other as if we were born on separate planets of separate species. I often speak quite differently with men than with women and know that what many men of my acquaintance consider wrenching self-revelation, my women friends (and I) give away free to strangers. I prefer having both women and men in my classes because they often bring quite different dynamics to a classroom. As both cause and effect, I take gender seriously.

Gender was deeply important in my family, as I expect it is in every family. So long as gender differences exist in the world, they will exist in the home and have consequences for how children—and the adults they turn into—understand themselves and their circumstances, as well as how they are treated. In my family gender set various things. For example, it determined who did what kind of chores (brothers: yard, basement, garage; sisters: living room, bedrooms, kitchen). It also shaped familial expectations about jobs, spending money, college tuition (boys on their own, girls with parental help). And so on.

But gender wasn't the only thing that mattered. My older brother's gender may have given him freedom from the house-cleaning routine, but his age—three years older than I am—was what gave him authority over me at home, as age gave the same authority to all my older sisters. Conversely, I had female housekeeping tasks, but I had certain "bossing rights" over my younger siblings—males and females. My sisters (some of them) and I may talk more than my brothers (two of them), but we all talk in the same patterns. We tend to keep many of the same secrets and to get uncomfortable around many of the same subjects. We struggle with some of the same emotional issues and use the same vocabulary. On some issues we divide male and female, on others older and younger, on others by proximity and distance from our parents, on others by temperament.

Moreover, my sisters are not alike. In our work we range between full-time at-home mothers of many children to full-time, self-employed with no children and from deeply maternal to not very. We also vary in how comfortable we feel with intimacy and with assertion. We don't all fit into the portrait of "women" described in either the scholarly or the popular press. We don't all stand together across the great sex divide with our brothers on the other side—and they are not carbon copies of each other, either.

All this suggests to me that the family provides a rich setting in which to look at various gender issues, to locate where these issues seem particularly powerful and/or especially malleable. This could be helpful in understanding how such issues translate outside the family. If my first goal in this book is to examine adult sibling relations, my second is to see what those relations teach us about how gender roles work in combination form.

In this book I have also a third goal—to address the current conversation about the "traditional family." Politicians, journalists, and other social critics have adopted this phrase as if it has real historical validity. It doesn't. The picture shows a father at a decent-paying job, a mother at home tending her several well-cared-for and well-behaved children, with the grandparents, the church, and the school close by. These traditional families don't suffer from the problems that plague American families today: drugs, crime, mothers working outside the home, various kinds of abuse, sexual problems, various forms of defiance. The nostalgic glow around such a picture may warm us, but it also blurs the reality.[4]

I am therefore focusing on ten actual families (including two generations of one family), looking at them in enough detail that we can see inside their lives. Most of us know our own families. If we are of a particular temperament, we may also know something about the internal dynamics of a few other families. The societal strictures against speaking the truth about the internal workings of families, however, have made it difficult to breach the privacy walls constructed around virtually every family. We each have our secrets, our public persona. These show and conceal and serve as the basis for romantic notions of the traditional family. This book looks beyond the romance.

In thinking about and writing this book, I have made all sorts of assumptions. The first is that siblings are important relations who occupy a special and unique position for each other. They are not simply little parents or pseudo-children, they're not simply good friends (when they are friends), and they're not simply roommates or housemates. The sibling relationship partakes of all these others but is not the same as any of them.

Those of us who grew up with lots of siblings might from time to time have wished that we were only children (did my parents really have to have twelve children? Couldn't they have stopped at six—after me?). But these were the wishes of childhood. As an adult I love having such a lot of brothers and sisters. Some of them I talk to regularly, some I see only rarely. But I know that they're out there. They've made it easier for me to decide not to have children. I've known that I would have children around me as long as my siblings had children. They—my siblings— also make me feel safer, less vulnerable to the world, somehow.

Those who grew up with no siblings often feel that they have missed out on something. They are not only centrally and solely responsible for their parents (a responsibility shared among siblings—even when one or two usually take the lead) but without that special connection.

Girls who grow up with only girls often lament the absence of brothers. As one woman reported to me, she has never felt at ease with men, she thinks, because she had no brothers. She loved her sisters (most of them, anyway), but she regretted not having a childhood relationship with a boy who was not a "boy." A brother is a boy, of course, but not like other boys. Boys who grow up with only boys often feel similarly, that they would have learned better ways of getting along with women if they'd had sisters.

Siblings teach each other all sorts of things. Some of those things have to do with gender. Some have to do with getting along more generally. My friend Ray, who had a powerful (he would say bossy) older sister, has no trouble dealing with powerful women at work. Oh, I've met her type before, he'll say. I'm not intimidated.

I'm not suggesting—nor do I assume—that all siblings have good relations with each other. I know that's not the case. In the course of working on this book, I have heard dozens of stories from people about how they can't stand one sibling or another, how years have passed in which they have not talked, how strong a grudge they still hold about something. But even this testimony has convinced me of the larger point here, which is that sibling relationships are both powerful and special. The strength of those relationships does not depend on affection and seems in many cases to exist outside particular feelings one for the other. The bond of siblingship holds whatever we feel about it, whether or not we stay in contact, even if we reject each other. We're still siblings. We're still related.

The intensity of the loves, animosities, memories, and wrongs testifies to the power of the bond. Adult siblings often remember the disagreements or injustices or slights of childhood and continue to carry on arguments with siblings that were located in those childhood moments. At fifty-five one of my friends—an enormously competent and talented woman—is still trying to prove herself to her older sister and brother. Another friend still resents that her brother got more of the family's resources than she did. The Smothers Brothers made half their career on Tommy's line about Dick always being Mom's favorite. That line must have touched a responsive chord to be so popular for so long. Those sibling interactions continue to shadow dealings in the present. With siblings we learned how to face and live in the world, and we don't stop facing the world in those ways just because we've grown up and left home. We take those lessons with us into adulthood.

So the fact of our siblings shapes us, as does the order in which we come in that sibling string. Our placement in our family's structure matters in two ways. First, no matter how many children are born into a family, each is born into a different family. In other words, a family is different depending on time and its changing circumstances. My friend Peg was born the second girl in a family of two girls. By the time Peg was in school, her father had a different job than when her older sister (by eleven years) was young. In Peg's childhood he traveled around more, and her parents had more money and by then owned a house. Her mother was home more and may have been more lonely. These factors alone meant that Peg and her sister had quite different lives. Also, Peg's older sister was born into a family of no children, and Peg was born into a family that already had one girl.

Birth order also makes a difference in our development. There has been much argument and disagreement among psychologists about the matter of birth order and for good reason. Whenever we try to figure out why a person is the way he or she is, we are overwhelmed by the number of possible variables. One methodological problem in most birth-order research has revolved around exactly this issue: how to isolate the effects of birth order in the middle of the forest of other factors. I have paid attention to it through the course of this book, not in a rigid structural way but with the idea that paying attention to birth order can help formulate questions and focus our understanding of some issues with a family.

I've drawn mostly on the insights of Alfred Adler in thinking about how birth order might have functioned as a variable in the families in this book. Adler argues, and I'm persuaded, that "in the life pattern of every child there is the imprint of his position in the family succession." The nature of that imprint, he continues, follows some general patterns.

The oldest child, according to Adler, has many advantages. In cultures that practice primogeniture, oldest sons clearly benefit. More generally, firstborns have "an especially high evaluation of power"—their own and others'. They receive their parents' first attentions and initially don't have to share that attention with other children. This is also a disadvantage. Being for a time an only child, all firstborns who are followed by a second get "dethroned," their position usurped by another. The oldest, once the center of attention, must now share it with another. (Later children may also experience a version of this, but the effect is slighter because they had not been alone with their parents.) Adler further develops this idea of dethronement by arguing that in some kind of self-defense the eldest comes to "recognize any given authority as justified and to side with it." Historians might be especially interested to learn that oldest children—perhaps preferring how things were to what they became—have a special interest in the past. At the same time, an oldest may also "develop a striving to protect others and help them." In relation to their siblings they emulate and play the part of mother or father.[5]

The second-born (or middle) child is often threatened on both sides—by the greater power of the elder sibling and the more treasured status afforded the younger. They see themselves, according to Adler, as "constantly under steam." This can often make second children even more dogged in their attempts to achieve and perhaps more successful as a result, though they often feel more slighted and less recognized, no matter the success. Where the first child supports "natural" authority, the second is more inclined toward democracy, toward a leveling of people and the rejection of hierarchies. Where the first child might be the strongest proponent of law and order, the second may more often be the rebel.[6]

The youngest child in a family, Adler argues, experiences a warmer atmosphere than the older siblings because the youngest, smallest, and weakest is "the most in need of help," and has the most people around to help. In addition, youngest children might go in one of two ways: they might become bent on proving themselves because "no child likes to be the smallest, the one whom one does not trust, the one in whom one has no confidence, all the time. Such knowledge stimulates a child to prove that he can do everything," Adler notes. Another outcome of being the smallest is remaining the "baby" of the family for life. In some cases this means that the youngest lacks the self-confidence to achieve, having always been younger, lesser, not quite—always being done for by others who have more experience, knowledge, or priority of some kind.

The youngest might, however, take a separate path, casting a challenge for superiority not directly but indirectly by excelling at what the family has not done. As an example, Adler suggests that "if the family consists of business people the youngest becomes a poet or musician." Or the reverse.[7]

Adler was also quick to point out that these are hardly determinative factors. These are tendencies, inclinations. Much depends on other factors as well—the relationship of the parents, the spacing of the births, the timing, the talents and abilities of the siblings, even their looks. He also gives some consideration to gender, arguing that the gender of the child might sharpen some of these issues. A first-born boy might feel even more sharply the competition of the second-born girl, particularly because girls so often develop more quickly than boys. Or a second-born boy might feel more strongly the need to best his first-born sister—at least so long, Adler points out, as women and men do not occupy equal status in the world. His attention to the limitations on women's opportunities is quite modern. He argues, in addition, that the number and gender of the children is significant so that a boy who grows up in a household of girls will be either feminine or hypermasculine and a girl who grows up with boys will be either hyperfeminine or masculine.

These are what Adler posits as birth-order patterns. These patterns seem useful to keep in mind as we look at adult siblings. They suggest the extent to which sibling life is comparative. They suggest the power of family life in shaping our sense of our position in the world and in relation to others.

Brothers and sisters are not voluntarily joined. As a relationship of birth, rather than choice, siblingship is subjected to different pressures, tensions, and pleasures than is marriage or parenthood. Some of the same factors that favor egalitarian relations among sisters also encourage them among sisters and brothers. In addition, some factors that encourage hierarchy and inequality in other relationships between women and men may be mitigated by the nature of siblingship. Contemporary psychologists argue that the relationship of brother and sister is one of the most egalitarian between women and men—potentially, if not actually. Psychologist Michael Lamb points out that sibling relationships are the only heterosexual relationships outside marriage "in which Western adults can express affection and closeness without eliciting disapprobation and gossip." Moreover, not only is the sibling relationship unique because of its tendencies toward egalitarianism, its long duration, and its allowance of affection but siblings "share a common genetic and social heritage, a common cultural milieu, and common early experiences within the family." If these scholars are correct, sibling relationships stand in stark contrast to those between other pairs of women and men in society.[8]

Brothers and sisters are not necessarily related hierarchically—either linguistically or socially—nor are they essentially opposed to each other in any predictable direction. It is easy to imagine a brother *or* a sister as influencing, controlling, dominating, helping, confiding in, or supporting other siblings. It is easy to see and sense the enormity of what siblings have in common as well as what divides them. Moreover, although the words *brother* and *sister* take their definitions "relationally," neither is necessarily the "other," and neither derives its identity from the subjugation of the other.[9] Historians of women have for the last generation explored the extent to which women and men have occupied separate spheres in the past. This was useful and valuable work. It provided a way to take women's history seriously and to look at women in the past on their own terms. It lifted the study of women out of the era of comparisons with men. For that alone it proved of extraordinary value. In recent years historians of women and of men have been able to look with new eyes at the ways in which women and men have shared spheres. This book stands in that stream. Brothers and sisters—whatever separations and distinctions have, and did, exist outside their homes and even inside them between males and females—shared the private sphere.[10]

The rest of this book examines many dimensions of sibling life in the past, but let me preview here some of my conclusions:

1. Brothers and sisters play significant roles in each others' lives during growing-up years and afterward. The nature of those relationships may change over time but not their importance.

2. Families create a family culture, a set of rules that are shaped by the world outside the family but also powerfully reflect the particular values and identity of the individual family.

3. Families vary in the nature of their internal dynamics, in which emotions they express, how they express them, how they deal with conflict, resolve difference, and build lives in relation to each other.

4. Some families can weather conflict and discord, but sibling ties can and do break.

5. Families live in different historical contexts, but they seem remarkably the same over time. Siblings in the past expressed love and anger, jealousy and empathy; they complained about parents and each other; they gossiped; they told secrets and kept them (though not entirely because their preserved letters now tell some of their tales to us). In short, despite enormous changes in the United States from 1850 to 1920—urbanization, industrialization, internationalization—families' internal lives did not change much.

6. Families in the past were not completely alike, anymore than they are today. Siblings in different families dealt with many similar issues but not in the same ways. In some families the marriage of a brother or sister occasioned a widening of the circle to admit the new spouse. In others the siblings regarded the spouses as outsiders and resisted what they regarded as intrusions. Among some siblings rivalry predominated, among others cooperation. Moreover, life within a particular family was not the same for all members; the same family could seem warm to one member and cool to another.

7. Families in the past were quite similar to families today. In studying families in the past, I expected to find them quite different from families that I know. They weren't. Instead, their lives feel quite familiar. A time-traveler who landed a hundred years ago would certainly notice different clothes and furniture but would just as certainly recognize patterns and modes of sibling interaction. Siblings then and now face many of the same issues: rivalry and connection; allocation of family resources; marriages and deaths; and responsibilities for parents and for each other.

8. Gender mattered in how family members experienced life.

9. Sometimes family issues weakened the effects of gender differences. Where gender roles sometimes encouraged females to be more submissive, for example, the demands of family responsibilities could make submission impossible, even superfluous. Where gender roles might have dictated that a male take charge, the presence of older female siblings redefined that imperative for a younger brother.

10. Every family then, like every family now, had its story. Families may share some commonalities, but a striking aspect of the families that I studied is the intensely individual nature of each family's life. The particular circumstances, values, beliefs, and facts of each family make it surprisingly, remarkably, its own. This does not prevent us from generalizing about family life but does force us to acknowledge that a central generalization must be that no one kind of family exists.

Many in those families—like many people today—probably imagined a past in which people's lives were easier, with fewer pains and more clarity. But we must not mythologize just because we need or want the past to be different from what it was. To create a mythic picture of families in the past is disrespectful and will not really help us in the present. We shouldn't do it.

The past is difficult to understand in the best of circumstances. When trying to understand people's private lives, their hearts, we need all the help we can gather—scholarship, common sense, personal experience, and some imagination at least. So in this book I'm relying on conventional historical documents—letters mostly, hundreds of them. I'm also drawing on the psychological literature on families, especially on family systems. In addition, I'm taking cues from my own experiences of family, of my personal past and present. The result that I'm aiming for is scholarship tempered by common sense and personal experience broadened by historical evidence.

One pleasure of this research has been to look into the hearts of other people's families and the textures of other people's lives. I get to read their mail—mail not intended for the eyes of someone like me and barely imagined, I assume, by most of them. When I read their words, I can come to know other families in ways ordinarily denied the outsider. I learn their familial vocabulary and see them as they show themselves most intimately to each other.

Family history in general and sibling history in particular offers us the chance to look into people's hearts and lives at other times and in other places. When we can see clearly, we can define true continuities and point out real differences between then and now, between the "good old days" and the seemingly more complex present. Having a solid historical basis for making comparisons helps us to define our issues better, to diagnose our problems more accurately, and to imagine more fully what is possible. This is one grace of studying history and one goal of this book. Family history also invites us to look into our own hearts and our own lives. So read this with thoughts of your family too.

### Notes

1. U.S. Bureau of the Census, *Historical Statistics*, 42; Crispell, "Sibling Syndrome," 25.

2. See, for example, the following books of several kinds and from the last twenty years. Each looks at families and only glancingly or not at all at siblings, either in youth or in adulthood. Mintz and Kellogg, *Domestic Revolutions;* Coontz, *The Way We Never Were;* Drake, *Time, Family, and Community;* Degler,

*At Odds;* M. Gordon, *American Family in Social-Historical Perspective;* D. Scott and Wishy, *America's Families;* Demos, *Past, Present, and Personal;* May, *Homeward Bound;* Hareven, *Transitions;* and Hareven and Vinovskis, *Family and Population.*

There are several exceptions. See, for example, Mintz, *Prison of Expectations;* Stowe, *Intimacy and Power;* and O'Day, *Family and Family Relationships.*

3. The two best-known and most widely purchased are Tannen, *You Just Don't Understand* and *Talking from 9 to 5.* John Gray has created an entire industry from this idea that women and men are from separate planets. He has books, videos, audiotapes, and workshops. His best-known book has been on best-seller lists for years (181 consecutive weeks on the paperback lists as of November 1999 and for nearly as long previously on the hardback lists). See Gray, *Men Are from Mars.*

4. Two recent books do an especially good job of trying to rescue families from a sentimentalized history: Coontz, *The Way We Never Were,* and Gillis, *A World of Their Own Making.*

5. Adler, *Understanding Human Nature,* 152–53; *Social Interest* 232–35; *What Life Should Mean,* 142–55. See also Sulloway, *Born to Rebel.*

6. Adler, *Understanding Human Nature,* 153–54.

7. Adler, *Social Interest,* 238–39.

8. Goetting, "The Developmental Tasks of Siblingship," " 48; Lamb, "Sibling Relationships Across the Lifespan," 6. See also Bank and Kahn, *Sibling Bond;* and Kahn and Lewis, *Siblings in Therapy.*

9. Joan W. Scott, "Deconstructing Equality-Versus-Difference," esp. 36–38.

10. Various historians of women have found that within their separate sphere women created their own "female world" of language, values, meanings, behavior. In her book *Bonds of Womanhood,* Nancy Cott uses the term *bonds* to discuss how their womanhood held women down as well as held them together. Carroll Smith-Rosenberg argues in her chapter, "The Female World of Love and Ritual" (pp. 53–76 in *Disorderly Conduct*) that within their separate world women "valued one another. Women, who had little status or power in the larger world of male concerns, possessed status and power in the lives and worlds of other women" (64). These studies accept the antagonism of the separate spheres and argue further that strict social and familial gender roles left women and men emotionally estranged. (I have, of course, overstated the unanimity of this picture.)

See especially Welter, "Cult of True Womanhood"; Cott, *Bonds of Womanhood;* Motz, *True Sisterhood;* and Smith-Rosenberg, "Female World of Love."

Carol Gilligan's work has been important in further developing the concept and the psychological basis of women's separate values and ethical systems; see her *In a Different Voice.* For a provocative essay on some of the implications of this work, see Hewitt, "Beyond the Search for Sisterhood."

Much of the work on white middle-class women and men has focused on the separation of spheres that dominated nineteenth-century American life. This separation connoted not just differences but superiority and inferiority. Looking at husbands and wives, employers and employees, doctors and patients for examples, historians have documented multiple ways that women were systematically denied equal treatment, respect, pay, and opportunities and that in their relationships with men women were generally oppressed and victimized. These studies show deep legal, economic, and social inequalities and located the sexes in separate, often antagonistic, spheres.

See Lebsock, *Free Women of Petersburg;* Ryan, *Cradle of the Middle Class;* May, *Great Expectations;* Barker-Benfield, *The Horrors of the Half-Known Life;* Faragher, *Women and Men on the Overland Trail;* and Morantz, "Lady and Her Physician."

They also left some distortions in their wake, of course. Some distortions that various historians have been and are addressing include the real connection and love between courting and married couples, the necessity of shared spheres among farm families, and the quite different dynamics among African-American and working-class families where separation was not possible, whether or not it was desirable.

See Lystra, *Searching the Heart;* E. Rothman, *Hands and Hearts;* Mintz, *Prison of Expectations;* Stowe, *Intimacy and Power;* Rotundo, *American Manhood;* Frank, *Life with Father;* Tosh, *Man's Place.*

An especially thoughtful statement of the sharing of spheres that happened in rural life in the nineteenth century is Osterud, *Bonds of Community.* See also Jensen, *Loosening the Bonds.*

What these and other studies have made clear is that gender definitions varied—nor surprisingly—by race, by class, by occupation. I'm arguing here that gender definitions vary, as well, depending on the family itself. In addition, I'm making the larger point that brothers and sisters shared a sphere from birth and that the shared nature of their family experiences continued into and through their adulthoods.

# TWO

# The Putnams: The Family Circle

The Putnams may be the best known of "my" families. Anyone who has heard of Amelia Earhart has touched the Putnam family—it's like shaking the hand of the man who shook the hand of the man who heard the Gettysburg Address (as George Putnam might well have). George Palmer Putnam—the father of the siblings in this story—founded *Putnam's* magazine and Putnam Publishing Co.; his sons, Haven, Irving, and Bishop, became Putnam's Sons Publishing. Their sister Mary was one of the first professionally trained women doctors in the United States. Another sister was an eminent historian. Another brother was the librarian of Congress for more than thirty years. A son of Bishop's and a son of Haven's became the grandsons in the publishing company; the latter helped found the New School for Social Research at New York University; the former married Amelia Earhart.[1]

Clearly, the Putnams' is a story of achievement, of individuals who were striving and excelling. It was a value that they knew and articulated to themselves, to each other, to outsiders. As the seventy-eight-year old Irving said of his eighty-five-year-old brother, Haven, who went to work every day until his last days: "One of the traditions of our family is never to give up."[2]

The Putnams—I will introduce all thirteen of them momentarily—demonstrate two lessons about sibling relationships. First: within every family the parents and siblings together create and propagate what I am calling a "family culture"—a set of rules, values, expectations, and standards by which they measure themselves and each other. Second: family culture is powerful enough to offset the values, rules, and expectations

---

*The Putnams*

George Palmer Putnam (1814–72)
m. 1841    Victorine Haven (1825–91)
        Mary (1842–1906)
           m. 1873    Abraham Jacobi
               three children
        George Haven (1844–1930)
           m. 1889    Rebecca Kettell Shepard
               four children
           m. 1899    Emily James Smith
               one child
        Edith (1846–1930)
        John Bishop (1848–1915)
           m. 1882    Frances Faulkner
               three children
        Irving (1852–1931)
           m. 1878    Emma Brock
               five children
        Bayard (1855–86)
           m. 1882    Grace Thatcher
               two children
        Ruth (1856–1931)
        Amy (1858–1931)
           m. 1886    Robert Pinhey
        George Herbert (1861–1955)
           m. 1886    Charlotte Monroe
               two children
        Kingman (b. 1867)
        Sidney (1870–71)

---

in the larger culture, especially about gender. The Putnams' family culture encouraged achievement by both girls and boys and, in that, defied the larger social conventions about women's roles.

The Putnams also offer us an interesting story—which would have pleased them enormously—about a big, prominent, well-connected (intellectually and politically) middle-class, white, urban family living mostly in and around New York City from 1842 when the first sibling was born to 1955 when the last one died.

The parents of this Putnam clan were George Palmer Putnam and Victorine Haven. Born in 1814, George was raised and educated by his widowed mother, who ran a school to support her family. Even across the years her strength and determination are evident, as are that of her son. After being educated in her school and then on his own, he found work in publishing, eventually forming half of Wiley and Putnam Publishers. His family connections must have helped. A cousin married Nathaniel Hawthorne, one of the most important American novelists of the nineteenth century; another cousin married Horace Mann, one of the most important educators and educational philosophers of the nineteenth century.[3]

Victorine Haven, born in 1825, had lost her mother when she was four and was then taken care of by her mother's sister for eight years. Then, Victorine's older sister married and took over her care. Victorine was enrolled at Mrs. Putnam's school, where she met her teacher's son in 1840. A year later, when she was sixteen and he was twenty-seven, she married George Putnam, and they started their extraordinary family. Between 1842 and 1870 they had eleven children: four girls and seven boys. Their youngest boy died at seventeen months, another in his midthirties. The remaining nine lived well into old age and well into the twentieth century.

Here is the rundown of the siblings. The oldest, Mary Putnam Jacobi—called Minnie—was born in 1842 in London, where her parents lived for the first six years of their marriage and of George's publishing work. Minnie studied first with her mother, then hired tutors, then at a boarding school, then a day school. She studied a curriculum not of sewing and the ladylike arts but of Latin and Greek and science.

Minnie had medical ambitions that found an early outlet among her siblings. In 1863 her next younger brother, George, a Union soldier stationed in New Orleans, contracted malaria. She prevailed upon her parents to let her travel across contested war territory to nurse him (given the speed of midnineteenth-century mail-train service, her brother would either be dead or on his way to recovery by the time she could arrive, but that did not deter her). She went, found him on the mend, and spent several undemanding months living with a New Orleans family from the North and teaching their son. In the public biographies Minnie selflessly nursed her brother through his illness. Not entirely false but not compellingly true, either.

In the next year, 1864, Minnie again traveled from New York to the South, again in family service. Her eighteen-year-old sister, Edith, had taken work teaching freed slaves at Port Royal, South Carolina, and almost immediately had come down with typhoid. Minnie raced to her assistance. Minnie, as the oldest daughter, always felt responsibilities for her younger siblings, and her expeditions to the South certainly fell into that category. Nonetheless, Minnie probably could not have made such adventurous trips except under the mantle of familial duties.

In 1863 Minnie had completed a course of study at the New York College of Pharmacy and the next year earned her medical degree from the Women's Medical College of Pennsylvania. Not satisfied with the education and the clinical opportunities available to her as a woman in the United States, she spent 1866 to 1871 studying medicine at the Sorbonne. She earned another medical degree, as well as honors for her thesis (in French, of course). When she returned to New York, she focused on treating women patients and lectured at the New York Infirmary for Women and Children. In 1873 she married Abraham Jacobi, a German-born and -trained pediatrician and, her sister Ruth reported, "a citizen of the world of liberal ideas."[4] He was twelve years Minnie's senior, a Prussian who had fled first to England, then to the United States in the mid-1850s. He was neither too strong for her nor too weak. He was cosmopolitan and European but was content to live in her family circle—a perfect match for her. They had three children. One died in infancy, a son died at the age of ten—a pain from which Minnie never quite recovered—and a third child, a daughter, was the only one who lived into adulthood. Dr. Mary Putnam Jacobi published more than one hundred papers on medical subjects and a defense of woman suffrage called "Common Sense." She died in 1906, fourteen years before American women won the right to vote.

Throughout all her adult years she lived in New York City and stayed in constant contact with her siblings and her mother (her father died in 1872). She set up her first office in her parents' basement. When her brother Bayard died, Minnie invited his pregnant widow, and child, into her household. Ruth pronounced that Minnie "remained the sympathetic elder of her own clan throughout her life."[5]

George Haven Putnam—called Haven—was born two years after Minnie and a little bit in her shadow, as Minnie was "always *the* great interest" in their father's family life, as he recalled. Haven shared Minnie's schoolroom at home, where their mother set them to learning Latin together—and Minnie excelled. Minnie and Haven spent much of their time together during both their London and U.S. years of childhood. They played together and, as they got older, turned to more serious pursuits. They formed a teenage debating society; she was "the moving spirit among the girls" and he among the boys. The day they were finally sent to separate schools was traumatic for both.[6]

He had some early interest in forestry and was studying in Germany when the Civil War began. He came back to the United States and joined the 176th New York Regiment. He served with honor and spent the better part of his war service in Confederate prisons in Richmond, Virginia. The high point of his life seems to have been his war years. He preferred to be called Major throughout his life and, a nephew reported, World War I "was never 'the war' to The Major. That phrase to him meant only the war of 'sixty-one, the war of his youth, his war."[7]

In 1871 Haven became the first son to join his father in the publishing company of Putnam and Son. He handled accounts and finances and took over when his father died the next year. He worked there for fifty more years. His father had died at his desk, and Haven hoped for such a fate for himself. He wrote and published several volumes of autobiography—one about his Civil War experience, another specifically about his prisoner-of-war time in Virginia (the frontispiece was a photo of him by the premier nineteenth-century American photographer, Matthew Brady), one book of memoirs of his early years, another of his years in publishing. In addition, he wrote biographies of his father and of Abraham Lincoln, plus several novels. In addition, he wrote and Putnam's published his books *Censorship of the Church of Rome* (1906) and *Books and Their Makers During the Middle Ages* (1896), as well as several editions of *International Copyright* (1879, 1891, 1896), about his father's passion.

Haven lived in the family home with his parents, then his widowed mother and several other siblings even after he married in 1889 at the age of forty-five. He and his wife, Rebecca Shepard, had four daughters. He was widowed at fifty-one. At least one of his daughters was raised by her uncle Bishop and his family. Haven remarried at fifty-five to Emily James Smith, who was dean of Barnard College. Their son, Palmer Cosslett Putnam, helped found the New School for Social Research and, so his cousin reported, helped lose the publishing company.[8]

"It was only at the beginning," their sister Ruth wrote, "that Minnie found the little brother an encroachment on her privileges." As they grew older, Minnie and Haven formed a solid twosome. They became a family subset—not unusual in large families. Minnie wrote about Haven as "my twin and part of me." She announced to her mother that she would marry only if she felt as she felt for Haven.

Haven also reported a special relationship with Minnie. In his memoirs he occasionally referred to "we children," or to one or another of his siblings, but none so often or as prominently as "my eldest sister and myself," "Minnie and myself," "my elder sister," "my sister Minnie." The absence of the other siblings is as notable as the vibrant presence of the one.[9]

The third-born Edith was four years younger than Minnie and two years younger than Haven. It must have been a tough spot to occupy. She was not "first" anything but was second everything. No one wrote her biography, nor she her own, so much of her life is not visible. She demonstrated a fair bit of spunk, even courage, when in 1864 at eighteen she went South to teach freed slaves (and it was amazing that her parents allowed the teenager to take such an adventure). Haven characterized her as "the second sister, the permanent daughter at home." Edith lived with her mother until Victorine died in 1891, then with two of her sisters until her own death in 1930. She worked for a time in the publishing company but never became one of the "sons." We do not have any evidence that she minded, but she must have bristled some days at being the "permanent daughter at home" in a family of such powerful engagement with the outside world. She did report once that money worries had "limited her life." Minnie's French education and Haven's German education must have strained the family's resources.

As I encounter the successively younger siblings, I know less and less about them. It is rather like going through my family's photo albums. The lives of my older sisters are documented extensively—formal photographers' portraits, baby books, snapshots of their first birthday parties. By the time my fourth sister came along, the pictures trail off; the baby book has almost no entries and her birthdays are no longer recorded for posterity. With the Putnams too the documentation diminishes. A fact of big family life?

The next two Putnams formed another pair of pseudo-twins. John Bishop and Irving, born in 1848 and 1852, respectively, became the other "sons" of the publishing company. Both lived and worked close to the family circle around New York City. Both also demonstrated the Putnam passion and dedication to whatever they did. Bishop's son reported that his father "suffered from photography." It was not that the Putnams did not enjoy life, for they certainly seemed to have, but that they did not do much in small measure. Bishop added to the family library with his book, *Norwegian Rambles Among the Fjords, Mountains, and Glaciers* (1905), and describes rambles that would for the rest of us constitute strenuous and dangerous expeditions.

That same son described his uncle Irving as "erect, nervous, muscular and full of conviction." Some Putnams even considered Irving opinionated. In the context of the family this is an amusing characterization. One suspects that every one of them could be accurately described as opinionated. Both Bishop and Irving married and had children. Bishop's oldest son, the presumed heir to the family business, died in the 1918 influenza epidemic and was succeeded by the next son, another George Palmer Putnam, who stayed for a few years, then de camped for Hollywood. He met and married Amelia Earhart after promising her that he would never limit her freedom. After her disappearance he moved to Bend, Oregon, where he served as mayor, then secretary to the governor. In the Putnam tradition he also wrote books, his own memoir and an account of his life with Earhart.[10]

Ruth, the seventh-born child and the third female, graduated from Cornell University and became an historian, focusing especially on Dutch history. She specialized in biographies of important European monarchs: *Queen Louise of Prussia, Charles the Bold,* and *William the Silent*—all books published by G. P. Putnam's Sons, the latter two in the "Heroes of the Nations" series. In addition, she edited her sister Minnie's letters, added commentary, and created a biography of her sister that was published as *The Life and Letters of Mary Putnam Jacobi.* Like her sister Edith, Ruth did not marry. She and Edith lived in New York with their mother, then alone together after Victorine's death. Ruth lived with a brother for a time, then she and Edith moved to Geneva, Switzerland, to live with their widowed younger sister, Amy. The three sisters and Herbert and Irving all died within thirteen months of each other.

Amy was the fourth Putnam daughter. She and Ruth died within ten days of each other. As the *New York Times* reported, "In the course of [Amy's] recent fatal attack of grip Miss Ruth cared for her continuously, with the result that she came down with a severe case of grip that caused her death within a few days." Amy was born in 1858, the seventh child in the family. She lived the farthest outside the family circle. Early in her adulthood she moved to Europe, where she attended school and in 1886 married Robert Spottiswoode Pinhey, an English barrister at law who became a judge of small cause court in Karachi, in the Bombay Judicial Department in Indian Civil Service. After his death within five years, Amy made her home in Europe. When her family members wanted her company, they went to her.[11]

Eighth-born Amy and ninth-born George Herbert Putnam were the only two Putnams who lived outside the New York orbit. Herbert, as he was called—to distinguish him from his father, George, and his brother George Haven—was born in 1861, nineteen years after Minnie. He shared his family's professional interest in books but not as a publisher. Instead, he became a librarian. He did it on a grand scale too. He was director of the Minneapolis Public Library, president of the American Library Association, and from 1899 to 1939 served as the librarian of Congress. He married, had two daughters, and outlasted all his siblings, surviving until 1955.[12]

I know the least about sixth-born Bayard and tenth-born Kingman. Both avoided the publishing work and the Putnam interest in writing. Kingman went into the insurance business, and while his name appears from time to time in the family correspondence—never with rancor or any hint of discord—he never emerges with any strong definition. In the *New York Times* obituaries for his sisters and brothers, Kingman was mentioned only once among the survivors.

Bayard too took a path other than publishing, and in 1886 he and his wife, Grace—never a favorite of the Putnams—were in the midst of a move to Rhode Island when he committed suicide in 1886 at the age of thirty-one. He was considered one of the most promising geologists in the United States. The newspaper account explained the causes and circumstances of his suicide only as "temporary insanity," which was more of an explanation than can be gleaned from the family correspondence. From reading the letters I had detected nothing about how Bayard died. His wife referred only to "my own trouble." His pregnant widow and son went to live with Minnie.[13]

Finally, the youngest, Sidney, was born in 1870 and died in 1871 at seventeen months, an event that seems to have caused special and deep pain within the family. Forty-six years later, Irving still remembered and noted Sidney's death in a letter to Ruth: "It is strange to think that it is nearly 50 years. . . . I had forgotten the exact day of Sidney's birth."[14]

Surprisingly, this remarkable family is in various ways typical of nineteenth-century white middle-class American families. Although there is no such thing as a typical family, when we categorize families—especially by race, class, and place—we can identify common patterns and see changes over time.[15]

First the changes over time: white families in the northern colonies of North America in the seventeenth century functioned as an economic and an emotional unit. Every member of the family contributed to the family's economy and as early as possible. Emotion was restrained and controlled. The internal hierarchy of patriarchal father who "ruled" over his wife and children paralleled and continued the hierarchy of the larger society: a natural order that followed in a stepped way from God to minister to congregation. The family—not the individual—was the basic unit of society, so all members of the society needed to be attached to some family. This meant that the poor, the aged, the orphaned, the insane, the single, and the widowed all found a place in the society by being connected to some family or another, their own or someone else's. Families that take in outsiders cannot keep many secrets, so inevitably these families were relatively public and had relatively permeable boundaries.[16]

By the nineteenth century, the family had become a much more private institution. Local or state government had taken over many of the family's societal functions: education, poor relief, care of the mentally sick and feeble. Moreover, as families became more urbanized and industrialized, the father increasingly took over the family's economic responsibilities, whereas the emotional responsibilities of family life became women's work. He went to work; she stayed at home. He earned the money; she got her money from him. She became his connection to the family— and often the emotional negotiator between father and children. He became her connection to the world outside. They expected to develop what historians have called a "companionate marriage," a marriage of companionship rather than economic partnership. The husband's sole responsibility for the family's economic well-being elevated his role. His control of the family's resources reinforced his authority. His work took him out of the household and distanced him from the family's emotional life.

In this nineteenth-century family, moreover, the children's emotional needs took precedence over their contribution to the family's economy. Children stayed children longer; adolescence emerged as a separate developmental stage; children who in an earlier period would have been considered capable of beginning their own families instead lived to a later age in their parents' home. The presence of children, a greater regard for emotions, the increasing desires to protect children from adult responsibilities for a longer period of time and to relieve them of economic responsibilities created a household more and more separate from the outside world. Ideally, it served to protect all its members from the harshness of the world outside. It became what Christopher Lasch has called "a haven in a heartless world," fostering closeness, dependence, and privacy.[17]

In many ways the Putnams fit centrally into this picture. The father of the family—George Palmer—was clearly the pater familias, the patriarch of his clan. He was the man in charge. He was also the breadwinner—an enthusiastic, energetic breadwinner. He traveled widely and often, leaving most of the child rearing to his wife. Victorine was at home full time and devoted her energies largely—if not entirely—to her husband and children. She paid close attention to the schooling of every child and to their individual development. She sheltered her children for as long as possible. She created the haven while George attended to the heartless world.

Moreover, the Putnam children stayed at home, lived at home, and returned home throughout much of their lives. They constituted a very large, extended family that revolved around their parents and their parents' home. Haven, the oldest, lived with his parents until he married at forty-five and again after his wife died six years later. When Minnie finished her medical training abroad, she moved back in with her parents as a matter of course. Their father's death gathered the children—many of them adults by 1872—even closer in. Haven and Bishop were running the family business, and Irving was called home from Amherst College to help out; Minnie and Edith, who were living at home as adults, no doubt assisted with Ruth, Amy, George Herbert, Bayard, and King, all of whom were younger than seventeen when their father died.[18]

In these various ways the Putnams demonstrate in particular what historians report in general about such families of their time. The Putnams, however, were also dramatically atypical.[19]

The Putnams were a large family, even by nineteenth-century standards. While we might have expected that large families were the norm 150 years ago, in fact the trend was toward fewer and fewer children, especially among middle-class, native-born whites such as the Putnams. George Palmer had been an only child and Victorine had had only one sibling.

In the nineteenth century, rural families tended to be larger than urban families, but the size of the Putnam family cannot be ascribed to the need for farm labor. Catholic families have also tended to be larger than Protestant families, but the Putnams were not Catholic. Victorine did marry younger than many women of her generation—she was sixteen—and this put her "at risk," as the demographers say, for a larger number of children.

The Putnams were clearly atypical, additionally, in the size of the geographic circle they occupied. Most of the family lived in and around New York City. Bishop, the adventurous one, moved out to Rye, New York, today—and then—about a half-hour train ride from Manhattan. (Given traffic in the New York metropolitan area today, it probably took less time to get from the train station in Rye to their mother's home then than it would now.) The family lived a remarkably cosmopolitan and international life. The publishing business, and especially the family's interest in international copyright law, took father and sons to Europe often and on at least one occasion took Bishop to Japan to discuss Western school books. When American educational opportunities proved insufficient, Minnie headed off to France. Ruth traveled abroad for her historical research; ill health sent Amy to England, then marriage took her to India. In writing to congratulate her on her marriage, her various siblings included promises to visit her in India—a promise that certainly most of them had a reasonable hope of honoring and probably would have, had Amy's husband had not taken sick and forced the couple to return to Europe after only a few years. Amy never did return to New York to live, and two of her sisters lived out their lives with her in Geneva. Few other American families of the Putnams' generations traveled as much or as widely as the Putnams did.[20]

The family is also atypical in its achievement. The elder George Palmer Putnam, Minnie, Haven, Ruth, and Herbert each merited a separate entry in the *Dictionary of American Biography* (along with an ancestor, Israel Putnam, a Revolutionary War general). Certainly the proximity of the family to the publishing circles of the day made the Putnams especially visible to those who compile such compendia. Nonetheless, all five certainly achieved at a level that entitled them to inclusion.

In some ways this atypicality is the most interesting feature of the Putnam family, especially because of the stellar achievement of two of the sisters and the unconventionality of the others.

Success meant quite a different thing for women and for men in the nineteenth century, especially among people like the Putnams. In that time white middle-class society encouraged and rewarded the kinds of success achieved by the Putnam brothers. That same society, however, actively discouraged the kinds of successes achieved by the Putnam sisters. In that world a successful man was one who was married and had children (the wife devoted and the children agreeable). More important was that he be economically successful through a job at which he worked diligently and faithfully. He lived long and well, in comfort and surrounded by his loving family.

In most ways, then, the Putnam brothers were quite normal white, middle-class, native-born American men. They married and had children. Several went to work in their father's business, and a couple rebelled and went off on their own. If they did not live in an extended household that included their parents—not all could have done that, anyway—they did generally live close to their parents and near to each other. Only Haven's marriage was unusual in that he married late and married a woman also older than usual for women for first marriage—Rebecca Shepard was thirty-five. Generally, the Putnams' lives were out of the ordinary only in the success of their endeavors and the public prominence of several family members.

By contrast, the Putnam women were quite unusual. They faced the conflicting expectations of their family and their society. In their time a successful woman was defined as one who was married to an economically successful man who supported her and to whom she was devoted. She had children, to whom she dedicated the part of her life left after her husband had taken his share. In historian Barbara Welter's words, she was to be pious, pure, domestic, and submissive. None of the Putnam sisters fit this definition.[21]

Professional medicine was virtually closed to women when Minnie was growing up. The era of midwives had given way to (was grabbed by) medical doctors, which women could not become. Elizabeth Blackwell, the first woman medical doctor in the United States, finished medical school in 1849, when Minnie was seven. When Minnie applied for medical training, most schools remained closed to her and she attended the Women's Medical College of Pennsylvania, a school she judged as not up to the standards of the men's schools but the best then available. Thus her venture to the Sorbonne where she was the first woman admitted to its École de Médecine and the first to graduate. She had not yet been admitted when she left New York, but she nonetheless took herself to Paris to secure her admission and to learn the French that would be the exclusive language of instruction. That she felt some bitterness about her treatment there is indicated by her decision to dedicate her thesis to the one anonymous member of the medical faculty who had voted to admit her (and whose decision apparently was crucial).[22]

She knew just what she was doing. After a year in Paris, she wrote, "An Englishman would say that it was indelicate to admit women to study medicine, a Frenchman, that it was dangerous." She continues, "It was upon my appreciation of this kind of prejudice that I based my calculations in coming to Paris instead of to London. . . . Of course I have met with opposition to going to some places—the lectures, and certain clinics at the largest hospitals."[23]

When she finished her French training, she returned to New York and joined the New York Infirmary for Women and Children (founded by

Blackwell). Minnie spent most of her life treating women and children and educating women in medicine. Most of her publications concerned women's health.

Another sister became a professional historian when women did not. Medicine was exceptionally open by comparison with the field of history. The study and teaching of history was undergoing a revolution at the end of the nineteenth century, as Ruth was developing her own ambitions. She finished Cornell University in 1878. In 1878 virtually no women were writing history in the United States. Mary Beard, considered by many to be the first woman historian, was born in 1876, twenty years after Ruth. Beard published her pathbreaking books *On Understanding Women* in 1931 (the year of Ruth's death) and *Women as Force in History* in 1946, whereas Ruth published her first book in 1894. Ruth took no teaching job, and I have no record that she applied for any such job. She could do and did her work outside a university setting. She seems to have worked in a research vacuum, without an academic position and with no formal academic community in evidence. Her first book was a two-volume biography of the Dutch king William. She published again in 1897, 1904, 1908, 1911, 1915, 1916, 1918, and 1925 (her biography of Minnie). Nine books in less than thirty years. Which of us would not consider our lives spectacularly successful if we had written and published so many books?[24]

Of the four sisters in the family, only two married, and we could not call those conventional marriages. Minnie married her professional partner, a man who shared her medical passion and respected her liberty. Amy married an English judge; they had no children. She was widowed less than five years later. She did not remarry, nor did she return home or even to the United States. She stayed on her own and apart.

Minnie had three children, but only one survived to adulthood. That was the sole child of the four Putnam sisters to survive. Insofar as women's success in the nineteenth-century required marriage and motherhood, three of the sisters did not succeed. Insofar as women's success required women to be at home with children, none of the sisters succeeded.

For the Putnam women their family's ideas about achievement mattered enormously. They lived them out in a society—and in a family— that also cared about gender roles. It would be wrong to suggest that the Putnams were completely divorced from the gender definitions of their generations. They certainly were not. Victorine and George were both quite conventional, as were all the Putnam children. Let me give a few examples. George Palmer Putnam created a family business in which he included only his sons—despite the obvious intelligence and interest in books of at least two of his younger daughters. When Minnie decided she wanted to attend medical school, he pressured her into waiting for two years:

> I really and deliberately think that you owe more to your mother and the younger children than you do to any one else or to any other plans or enterprise, however worthy and important. I think you may be of *immense* use in relieving and cheering your mother and that she will *need* your aid at home—and that you may benefit the young children and aid generally in *systematizing* home and rendering it cheerful and happy—and that for the next two years, this is quite as important, and *more* obligatory than any other claims.

When the two years had passed and Minnie still persisted, her father issued several admonitions: "*Don't* let yourself be absorbed and gobbled up in that branch of the animal kingdom ordinarily called strong minded women! *Don't* let them intensify your self-will and independence for they are strong enough already." He concluded by urging her to "preserve your feminine character" and along the way "study a little the proprieties and elegancies of life. Be a lady from the dotting of your i's to the color of your ribbons—and if you must be a doctor and a philosopher, be an attractive and agreeable one."[25]

Victorine herself was in many ways a conventional woman for her times—she married young, stayed home, had lots of children, organized her life around husband and children, had few ambitions to venture beyond. She also seemed to need people to take care of her, her children if not her husband. Victorine suffered from migraine headaches, but it was more than that. Minnie addressed her father as "Dear Father." She called Victorine "my dear little mother." In his *Memories* Haven recalled that "the care came to be given from them to her rather than from her to them." All the older children played parent to their younger siblings and to their mother.

Minnie once referred to herself as her mother's "boy-girl" and wrote with a note of complaint: "I believe, with feminine perversity, you care more about me, precisely because I am of so little account to you as a daughter, but am more like a son." Thus both parents had strong gender definitions.[26]

So did the Putnam brothers and sisters. Minnie worried about her first fiancé and admitted that she did not respect him because his intellect and character were not "as strong as mine" and because "his desire for my approbation sometimes strikes me as childish, and unbecoming in a man who should be my master and superior." Others of the Putnams expressed various concerns about manliness. Was Amy's fiancé "manly" enough? Herbert wondered. He made several references to his brother-in-law's manliness. "From the little you told me of 'Rob' . . . I knew he must be a thoroughly manly fellow." By *manly* the Putnams seemed usually to mean a man doing his duty.[27]

Edith too voiced conventional notions of manhood, in this case about a certain Mr. Gold who was courting her—unsuccessfully. "I like Mr. Gold better the more I see of him," she wrote. "He is so upright simple and manly. If he were only a strong man he would be lovable." She sounds here so like Minnie. Edith continued: "It is curious how fragility, bearable, even attractive at times in a woman is so distasteful in a man." Minnie wanted a superior man; Edith wanted a strong and manly one.

The brothers also voiced various other gender conventions. Haven wrote Minnie that he was "fully convinced that marriage is to be thoroughly a good thing for you and your man, especially if he does not let you have your own way too much." Here he sounds very like a brother teasing his sister, particularly an older and no doubt slightly bossy older sister. In a more sentimentalizing mode, Haven told Amy he considered American women "certainly the most satisfactory specimens of womankind in the world." Bishop thought women "a queer kind of institution" and men the "inferior sex." Following an illness Irving raved about the care he had received and wrote, "I have become quite convinced that it is the intention of Providence to have the ills of mankind looked after by the spindle side of the race. The best of them have qualities that cannot be found in the male of the species."[28]

Even with these strong gender conventions, the Putnam women came to be atypical. How? Why were gender roles so powerful—even seemingly determinative for so many women—and how did the Putnam women avoid or circumvent them? The answer lies in what I call family culture, that world that each family creates inside itself, among its members, a world that is affected and shaped by the outside but is also separate. In this world the Putnam women learned to be something other than pure, pious, domestic, and submissive.

A family's culture is located in a particular time, place, and socioeconomic category; it shares commonalities with its neighbors, but it is always itself. We only have to make a friend, visit someone else's house, or get married to know that every family has its own ways, customs, rituals, even language. What seems completely normal in one household can seem bizarre or at least peculiar or rude in another. In short, every family creates a set of rules and norms that govern the household. Each family has its own way of understanding, of making sense of, and of living out its definitions of family, appropriate behavior, and rules. Many young (and old) married couples clash most sharply at just those places where in their families of origin they learned particular ways of doing, being, living, making the bed, squeezing the toothpaste tube, being married, acting out gender roles, being successful.

Some differences are inconsequential (though even the decision about which things fall into this category can ignite controversy and conflict). Others of the differences figure more largely in how individuals live out their adult lives: how they understand and judge themselves, what they hope for, and what they will settle for. The Putnams cared about the pursuit and achievement of success in the public eye. Success to the Putnams did not mean being happy, finding inner peace, having many friends, even having a good marriage. It meant, instead (to use what might have been a family imperative), "making use of opportunities."

It is remarkable, given the family opinions about gender, that the Putnam women did turn out to be atypical. But they did. They got more encouragement—and training—in achievement, finally, than they did in gender. Their family's emphasis on success proved the stronger imperative.

Both parents urged and encouraged their children. They provided education for sons and daughters. Minnie and Haven both studied Latin; when Minnie preferred science, no one insisted that she abandon it for sewing. When Minnie became engaged, her mother expressed her disappointment at "the unsettling of all the further plans in life." The syntax suggests that these were Minnie's plans but also the plans of others for Minnie. George and Victorine made sacrifices so that Minnie and Haven could go to Europe for school.

Although George tried to dissuade his daughter from the study of medicine, when she completed her training he was the one who presented her with her first set of professional cards. When she set up her practice in her parents' house—with their blessings—her father hung out her shingle. Victorine too proved a strong ally and taskmaster. Victorine was "seriously anxious" to see Minnie "at something," and when she doubted Minnie's "constancy of purpose" she demanded—and got—an accounting. "Have I satisfactorily explained myself?" Minnie asked.[29]

Among the Putnams the parents alone did not create this family culture. It was not simply "parental" but familial. The siblings encouraged, helped, and supported each other. The siblings helped create the world in which they developed and grew and then continued to encourage, help, and support each other throughout their lives.

When I remember my own childhood, I certainly remember lessons my parents taught me, but I also remember my siblings' lessons, the ones they taught through teasing, through admonition, through praise. I also know that all that continues in my and our adulthood. Minnie's experience was similar. Toward the end of her medical training she wrote to her mother: "If you and Edith and Haven are satisfied with me when I come home, that is all I want." She did not mention her father, but she did care about how she would be judged by her mother *and* her brother *and* her sister.[30]

In the Putnam correspondence we can even see the siblings enculturate each other—especially Amy. She was not the only one to get such training, but because she saved more of her letters, more of the training is visible to us. Twenty-four-year-old Edith, for example, lectured twelve-year-old Amy that "life is worth nothing unless one is pursuing some system of study." Thirty-two-year-old Haven wrote to eighteen-year-old Amy that he was "delighted to hear that you had the pluck and persistency to take hold at once of your lecture-work." He continued with an even more eloquent statement of the family philosophy, even naming it as the family characteristic: "I have the fullest confidence that the family 'staying power' and your own individual persistency (the extent of which impresses me . . . with fresh admiration) will enable you to get from your European residence the full profit, and to show at the end a fair balance sheet."

How could the eighteen-year-old Amy have resisted this combination of praise and admonition? Or this from Irving: "I think you are capable of getting much more satisfaction alone than most people I know. I guess you exaggerate the time you waste." Or this from Bishop: "I am exceedingly glad to hear that you are not neglecting your opportunities in [painting]. You certainly should make the most of them." From Haven again: "It is refreshing to hear of your independence and enjoyment in your work, and the general gumption you show by making use of your opportunities." We might suspect that she went to Europe and stayed there to escape so much encouragement. Family culture cannot mandate that all members act in the same way, but it does guide which actions are praised. The family norms and expectations become the ones that family members either attain or rebel against, but they are not avoidable. Amy did not achieve in a Putnam way. She also kept herself out of the

New York circle. I suspect that the two are related. She never returned to America for more than brief visits.[31]

In advice or encouragement we see one statement of family values. In praise we see another. The Putnams encouraged Amy, but they praised Minnie. In his autobiography Haven made passing reference to Ruth and to Irving, Bishop, and Herbert. He said nothing about Amy, Bayard, or Kingman and mentioned Edith only once, to identify her as the stay-at-home sister. But he wrote many times about Minnie: they went to school together, they rode ponies together, they attended teas together, they went swimming, they visited their father's friend, the writer Washington Irving. Haven shows that they bonded early and solidly—and exclusively. If he felt jealousy as well as admiration, he hid it in his memoir. Instead, he reported her "such a *big* portion of the family circle" and highlighted his sister's "brightness and originality."[32]

Ruth too found Minnie a big portion of the family circle and deserving of her own biography. Ruth did not write a biography of her other siblings and even explicitly excluded them from much mention.

The Putnams also gave and got praise for hard work and success. Their father complimented Edith for having "proved her pluck" and said "she needn't fear being suspected of shirking." Herbert, while a law student, praised himself for being "always discontented without an ostensible . . . task in hand." Irving called Haven a "remarkable man!" And he wrote to Herbert that "I always have had the greatest admiration for you," especially for his persistence: "It is this quality which has made your work so successful." Irving wrote his congratulations when the new *Dictionary of Similes* included two entries from Plato but three from Ruth. Edith, at eighty-one, gloried in Herbert's successes. "To have developed the provincial library [of Congress] which it was when you took the helm into the not only National, but world wide institution is something to be justly proud of as I am for my brother." Again, the absence of praise for other kinds of successes makes these remarks stand out starkly. Clearly these siblings were proud of each other—especially for their public successes.[33]

Historians of women have written a compelling picture of the forces that shaped women's lives. What has been harder is to show how and why the forces of gender worked differently—particularly among women who shared race, class, and regional characteristics. This notion of family culture, however, offers a useful way to account for some differences. In the case of the Putnams one of their most strongly held family values—public achievement—was so strongly held that it offset the force of conventional gender roles for the Putnam women.

One other aspect of the Putnam family culture seems relevant here. Almost as much as they valued achievement, the Putnams valued closeness to each other. This closeness solidified the family culture and made it less susceptible to outside pressures. It offered protection for those on the inside and safety as well. Minnie, for example, met up with discrimination and opposition to her ambitions outside her family, but inside her family she got cheered on and applauded, eventually even by her father.

The Putnams' closeness vibrates across the years (and feels cloying or reassuring, depending on the reader's family culture). Throughout their lives most of the Putnams looked to each other for support, help, companionship, community. When George Sr. created his publishing business, he looked to his sons. Haven studied forestry, but when called—first to service in the Civil War and then to Putnam Publishing—he did his duty. When their father died and the brothers needed help in the family business, they called Irving home from college. He came. The "Sons" turned to their own sons for more help in the company. Their closeness meant that they knew they could rely on each other to answer these duty calls.

They also did for each other. Haven remembered—and reported—that as a child he traded his carpenter's rule for a sled so that Edith could be "one of the coasting party." Minnie presumed that it was up to her to help when Haven and then Edith needed nursing in the 1860s. When Bayard died in 1886, Minnie took his wife and child into her home. When Haven's wife died in 1895, his brother raised his daughter. When Amy's husband died in 1891, Herbert invited her to live with his family. Minnie paid for one sister's education and left money in her will to her other two sisters (apparently none to the brothers). Similarly, Edith gave money to Ruth because "Ruth has worked so hard during her life and received so little return."

They also expressed their closeness in their response to being apart. Of course, while she was in Paris Minnie told her mother, her father, her sisters, and her brothers how much she missed them and wanted to see them. That could be expected. Herbert's sadness that he would miss Amy's wedding in 1887 seems more poignant. He found their separation a "sore trial" and more. "It seems pitiful indeed that you & I who have been so close in sympathy in what concerned us most nearly should be so far away from each other at the time that means most to our lives." He felt her absence from his 1886 wedding even more sharply. "It will seem like treason to those old days . . . and to the companionship that came out of them, for you not to be at my wedding. It is the time when a man wants to feel his proudest & is apt to feel his littlest. Unless he bolsters his own undeserving with the unusual deserving of his family."[34]

Outsiders too commented on the family's closeness. Amy's sister-in-law noted that "your mother & brothers & sisters do love you more than most," and, she added, "I have often envied the love of your family for you."[35]

Marriage into such a family (or out of such a family) could present difficulties. When Minnie announced her engagement (the one she subsequently broke), the family first ignored it, then responded as if some catastrophe had occurred. According to Victorine's report, Minnie's father was dumb-founded. Haven pouted. Bishop played dirges on the piano, and Irving refused to come to dinner. Ruth sulked—refusing to pass something to the unfortunate fiancé (though King, showing either brotherly bullying or a dot of male solidarity, "soon pommeled her into reason"). Perhaps most tellingly, their mother worried, about the "broken circle, the foreigner intruding." He was not a foreigner, as Minnie's eventual husband actually was, only a foreigner to their family. Even if Victorine was exaggerating, the depiction is revealing.[36]

Minnie, for her part, took the family's reaction seriously. "I was extremely disappointed that none of the family liked him better, and both astonished and angry at myself that their opinion seemed to have such a subtle influence over my feelings." It hardly seems subtle from the outside.[37]

Victorine was not the only Putnam to express her concern in the family language of breaking the family circle. The term's very ubiquity in the family writings highlights its importance. Haven used the term repeatedly in his *Memories,* as did Ruth in her *Life and Letters.* When Minnie did break off her engagement, her father wrote consolingly, "Now we shall claim you and it will go hard but you can find ample scope for your mind and your acquirements without cutting loose from the family circle."[38]

The absence within that circle of criticism of each other, even made indirectly to a third person, seems noteworthy. It was simply not tolerated, it seems. The in-laws, however, were another story. Irving wished that Minnie's husband, "that wretched man" Abraham Jacobi, "would manage to break his neck in Europe. It would be a blessing to all parties. They can never live together five years longer." It is a statement both critical of him and protective of her. Irving was not much more enthusiastic about Bayard's fiancée, Grace, whom he considered "very nice, but too square & devoid of sentiment." He extended his criticism to her family, decrying "their utter lack of grace, especially in dress." Bishop too did not care much for Grace, but after Bayard's death she won him over in perhaps the only way that could have persuaded a Putnam, by her "great pluck and determination." In short, she demonstrated that other value central to the Putnam family culture. She earned her way in.[39]

The two facets of the Putnam family culture served to reinforce each other. The family members' closeness to each other reinforced the family lessons and buffered them from the outside world. The larger society was saying that women should do this and not do that. The Putnams were not immune to these gender imperatives, but they did offer an even more insistent imperative to achieve. The family circle kept in and kept out.

So the Putnams offer several lessons. First, families create their own worlds, which are both connected to and separate from the larger world, and individuals live in both. Second, a family culture can create a space in which family members can escape some of the larger social conventions by conforming to competing family conventions. Third, sisters and brothers are crucially important in both the creation and the continuation of that culture.

The Putnams lived in a society that had strong notions about proper behavior for women and men, and the Putnams shared some of these ideas. Nonetheless, they also had a family culture that valued achievement—despite gender. The Putnam family culture was not immune from larger social notions, but the family's emphasis on "making use of opportunities" and the family's creation of such a tight "family circle" provided an alternative context for the Putnams' lives.

Fortunately, it did not keep irony out. "The sober, stay-at-home, conventional Putnams!" Bishop called them. Hardly.[40]

### Notes

1. The sources for this chapter are rich and varied. I'm drawing especially from the correspondence among the Putnam siblings that Amy Putnam Pinhey collected and that are held in the Herbert Putnam Papers at the Library of Congress. This correspondence makes up a small part of Herbert Putnam's papers but are especially rich for my purposes because all the siblings are represented in the correspondence. In addition, Ruth Putnam edited a collection of family letters, mostly but not exclusively from Mary Putnam, added a commentary, and published *The Life and Letters of Mary Putnam Jacobi*. In addition, various family members wrote about themselves, and these books were, of course, published by G. P. Putnam's Sons. George Haven Putnam was especially prolific, publishing a biography of his father, *George Palmer Putnam: A Memoir* (1912), his own *Memories of My Youth, 1844–65* (1914), and *Memories of a Publisher* (1915), in addition to two versions of his Civil War experiences: *Some Memories of the Civil War* (1924) and *A Prisoner of War in Virginia, 1864–65* (1912).

In addition, various of the Putnams show up, helpfully, in biographical dictionaries. See, especially, the entry for Mary Corinna Putnam Jacobi in James, James, and Boyer, *Notable American Women,* vol. 2, 263–65, and the entry for Mary Corinna (Putnam) Jacobi in Kaufman, Galishoff, and Savitt, *Dictionary of American Medical Biography,* vol. 1, 389–90. Entries for George Palmer, Mary Putnam Jacobi, Ruth Putnam, and George Haven Putnam appear in *Dictionary of American Biography,* vol. 15, 278–79, 279–80, and 285, and in vol. 9, 222; and for George Herbert Putnam in *Dictionary of American Biography,* suppl. 5, 554–55. Obituaries also provide some useful information, and the *New York Times* published obituaries for George (Dec. 21, 1872), Mary (June 12, 1906), John Bishop (Oct. 9, 1915), Haven (Feb. 28, 1930), Ruth (Feb. 14, 1931), Irving (March 13, 1931), and Herbert (Aug. 16, 1955).

2. *New York Times,* Feb. 28, 1930.

3. See the entry for George Palmer Putnam, *Dictionary of American Biography,* vol. 15, 279–80; Ruth Putnam, *Life and Letters;* and George Haven Putnam, *George Palmer Putnam.*

4. Ruth Putnam, *Life and Letters,* 311.

5. Ibid., 316.

6. George Haven Putnam, *Memories of My Youth,* 51.

7. George Palmer Putnam, *Wide Margins,* 14–15.

8. Entry for George Haven Putnam, *Dictionary of American Biography,* vol. 15, 278–79. Emily James Smith Putnam, Haven's wife, appears in *Notable American Women,* vol. 3, 106–8. See also George Palmer Putnam, *Wide Margins,* 24.

9. Ruth Putnam, *Life and Letters,* 16, 251, 141; George Haven Putnam, *Memories of My Youth,* 43ff.

10. George Palmer Putnam, *Wide Margins,* 9, 12–22, 282–98.

11. *New York Times,* Feb. 14, 1931.

12. A member of a large family might feel that having anything of one's own is difficult. How must Herbert have felt about sharing even his brother's name?

13. *New York Times,* Oct. 16, 1886; Grace Putnam to Amy Pinhey, Dec. 12, 1886. While I was looking for something else in the 1886 editions of the *New York Times,* I came upon the story by lucky chance. The newspaper had reported Bayard's death as a news story, not as an obituary, so his name had not shown up in the obituary index to the *New York Times.* The vagaries of research.

14. Irving Putnam to Ruth Putnam, May 15, 1917, George Herbert Putnam Papers, Library of Congress, Washington, D.C.

15. There is no such thing as a typical American family even in one historical period, and it is possible and especially important to identify differences that are the result of economic circumstances, of ethnicity (obviously Ojibway families, Chinese-American, African-American, and the Putnam families had different opportunities and options and different family dynamics because of the power of race in American society). When I explore the Putnam family, I am carefully circumscribing the population of which they are representative. Initially, that circle includes only white, middle-class, northern urbanites, from a northern European background.

16. As Steven Mintz and Susan Kellogg also point out, the society allocated voting rights based on that household unit (which partially explains why only propertied men could actually cast ballots—one per household, a proper household

defined as one that was attached to property, and the proper spokesman for that unit was the man at the top). See Mintz and Kellogg, *Domestic Revolutions*.

17. Lasch, *Haven in a Heartless World*.

18. Ruth Putnam, *Life and Letters*, 310.

19. In fact, the Putnams even demonstrate something about the difficulty of locating a family precisely in a particular period. The parents' marriage spanned the years 1841 to 1872; the children's lives, however, locate the family from 1842, when the first child was born, to 1955, when the last sibling died. So is this a mid-nineteenth-century family or late nineteenth- or even twentieth-century family?

20. This suggests some speculation about the family's economic circumstances. The family was certainly among the literary elite of the United States. Book publishing put the Putnams into contact with many of the most important literary and political people of their time. An advertising blurb for Haven's biography of his father lists among the people "with whom Mr. Putnam had personal relations" such prominent writers and public figures as Abraham Lincoln, James Fenimore Cooper, Nathaniel Hawthorne, Henry Wadsworth Longfellow, Oliver Wendell Holmes, and Ralph Waldo Emerson. The claim to *close* personal relations may have been something of an exaggeration but not much. Irving Putnam was named after Washington Irving, one of George Putnam's best authors and close friends. The family was not, however, among the very wealthy families of its times. The Putnams' 1857 bankruptcy ensured that. The family's fortunes were coming back when George Putnam died in 1872, but his death precipitated another setback for the family. In her later years Edith set aside money for Ruth so that "she should not have the money worries which have limited my life" (Edith Putnam to Herbert Putnam, Jan. 19, 1927). Clearly, these were not the worries of a working-class immigrant family, but they do suggest that the family was not immune to economic worries. See George Haven Putnam, *George Palmer Putnam*, endpapers.

21. Welter's "Cult of True Womanhood" has been one of the most influential studies of the ideology of nineteenth-century womanhood. The article is more than thirty years old and cannot carry quite as much weight as other historians have perhaps asked it to carry. It says nothing about how women actually behaved; it is not careful to specify which women this "cult" would have influenced. Nonetheless, as the statement of a particular ideology that was directed at a particular subset of American women, it is enormously helpful in articulating some key ideas about women in the nineteenth century.

22. Walsh, *"Doctors Wanted, No Women Need Apply"*; Morantz-Sanchez, *Sympathy and Science*. See also Blackwell, *Pioneer Work for Women*.

23. Ruth Putnam, *Life and Letters*, 120–21.

24. See Cott, "Mary Beard Ritter," 71–73, and *Woman Making History*.

25. Ruth Putnam, *Life and Letters*, 61, 67.

26. Ibid., 141; George Haven Putnam, *Memories of My Youth*, 24, 25, 47; Ruth Putnam, *Life and Letters*, 124.

27. Ruth Putnam, *Life and Letters*, 80; Herbert to Amy Putnam, Aug. 1, 1886; Herbert to Amy Pinhey, Jan. 1, 1891.

28. Edith Putnam to Amy Putnam, May 20, 1876; Ruth Putnam, *Life and Letters*, 313; Haven Putnam to Amy Putnam, Nov. 11, 1876; Bishop Putnam to

Amy Pinhey, Nov. 12, 1887, and Jan. 9, 1887; Irving Putnam to Ruth Putnam, Dec. 23, 1892.

29. Ruth Putnam, *Life and Letters*, 76, 103–5.

30. Ibid., 298.

31. Edith Putnam to Amy Putnam, Dec. 18 [1870]; Haven Putnam to Amy Putnam, June 9 and Nov. 11, 1876; Irving to Amy Putnam, July 22, 1876; Bishop to Amy Pinhey, Jan. 9, 1887.

32. George Haven Putnam, *Memories of My Youth*, 42; Haven Putnam to Amy Putnam, July 10, 1876.

33. Irving Putnam to Ruth Putnam, Dec. 9, 1918.

34. Ruth Putnam, *Life and Letters*, 75; Herbert Putnam to Amy Putnam, April 27, 1884; Irving Putnam to Ruth Putnam, Dec. 9, 1918; Irving Putnam to Herbert Putnam, Feb. 20, 1924; Irving Putnam to Ruth Putnam, Oct. 31, 1916; Edith Putnam to Herbert Putnam, Jan. 19, 1927.

35. George Haven Putnam, *Memories of My Youth*, 57–58; Edith Putnam to Herbert Putnam, Jan. 19, 1927; Herbert Putnam to Amy Putnam, April 4 and Aug. 1, 1886; Emily Langhorne to Amy Pinhey, March 8, 1891.

36. Ruth Putnam, *Life and Letters*, 75–76.

37. Ibid., 80. This quotation from Minnie appears in a letter she wrote to her father seeking his advice about whether she should break her engagement. It is a long, careful, deeply revealing letter. She admits to being able to manage the man and to his being narrow. She finds herself too often feeling "vexed, annoyed, tied down. . . . Do not most self-reliant women marry men a little weaker than themselves?" It's interesting that she's written this letter to her father and not her mother, except that the central question she asks is whether it is acceptable to break a contract. He answers unequivocally that while contracts are important, she must break off immediately and irrevocably. See pp. 80–83.

38. Ruth Putnam, *Life and Letters*, 83.

39. Irving Putnam to Amy Putnam, July 22, 1876; Bishop Putnam to Amy Pinhey, Jan. 9, 1887.

40. Bishop Putnam to Amy Pinhey, Jan. 9, 1887; Bishop Putnam to Amy Putnam, Aug. 4, 1886.

# THREE

# The Arthurs: Playing Catch

The best evidence of family culture lies in the contrast in the cultures of the Putnams and the Arthurs. The Arthurs—a brother-and-sister pair who were contemporaries of the younger Putnams—were white, upper-middle-class New Yorkers. They had an even more prominent father (vice president and then president of the United States) and a loving, graceful, and domestic mother. In several other ways the Arthur family was quite different from the Putnam family.[1]

The first difference simply has to do with size. There were two Arthurs, eleven Putnams. Being in the one is like playing baseball and in the other like playing catch. In baseball you can do a little standing around, part of the game but not every play. In catch, though, both players have to be present and attentive. A person standing around will get bopped in the head or drop the ball.

As a member of a big family, I feel more at home with the Putnams. I find hubbub comforting and reassuring. I know how to make a private space in a crowd. Certainly, as the conventional wisdom holds, in a big family the older ones look out for the younger ones. Nevertheless, a big family also requires a kind of independence. There's also freedom. As a middle child, I felt that my older sibs had broken lots of trails. They had already crashed the car, gone out with "inappropriate" boys, brought home a bad grade or two, gotten into some trouble or other. They'd also already gotten married and given my parents grandchildren. By the time I came along, I could rather go about my own business. In all these ways the Putnams feel familiar to me.

The Arthurs are a whole different matter. There were only two of

*The Arthurs*

Chester Alan Arthur (1829–86)
m. 1859     Ellen Lewis Herndon (1837–80)
            William (1860–63)
            Chester Alan II (1864–1937)
                m. 1900     Myra Fithian Andrews
                            two children
                div. 1929
                m. 1934     Rowena Graves
            Ellen Herndon (1871–1915)
                m. 1907     Charles Pinkerton

them. To me that feels a little close, actually. What happens when you want to rest and there is no one to fill in? Alan and Nell Arthur's relationship had the exclusive and intense quality that this metaphor suggests. Of course, I would not say that the Putnams (or my sibs) were not connected to each other. Of course they were. But I would say that the Arthurs' experience of family was different from that of the Putnams' and their dependence on each other more intense.

A second big difference between the Arthurs and the Putnams is that they held different values. In these we see the powerful statement of the Arthurs' family culture. Most important, the Arthurs cared little for achievement and cared enormously about expressing emotion.

Nell often scolded herself or her brother for not writing more often and occasionally and even desperately urged him to be more responsible—but never urged on him hard work or achievement. And neither "succeeded" on Putnam terms—male or female. Neither Alan nor Nell did any work that they mentioned in their correspondence.

The obituaries for Haven Putnam and Alan Arthur in the *New York Times* are instructive in their differences. Both men were the sons of famous and prominent men. Haven's obituary mentions his father but focuses on Haven's accomplishments under the headline "Major G. H. Putnam, Publisher, Is Dead." The story ran to nearly two full columns, with one story the day before about his illness, one the day after the obit with funeral details, a third two days later about the private burial. Of course, that he had lived in New York certainly made the story more noteworthy. It was Haven's life story, though, that the newspaper noted.

Alan Arthur's obituary ran to about three inches and was headlined

"Chester A. Arthur, Ex-President's Son." The story identified him as a "Sportsman and Connoisseur of Art." It listed the clubs he belonged to, some of his more prominent friends (John Singer Sargent and James McNeill Whistler), and some of the people with whom he played polo. If Haven had friends, they were not listed. If Alan ever held a job, it was not mentioned. It is impossible to imagine a Putnam man without a job. It is also not entirely easy to imagine a Putnam man with a close friend— apart from his wife—outside the family circle.[2]

The *New York Times* also ran prominent stories about the deaths of Mary Putnam Jacobi and Ruth Putnam. It did not note Nell Arthur Pinkerton's death. She lived quietly in Mt. Kisco, New York, on good terms with her husband and brother and various nieces and nephews and cousins and friends. She had what she wanted, but the *New York Times* did not notice. She would not have minded.

Looking inside the Arthur family, we can see several factors that explain why Alan and Nell would not care about "making use of opportunities." Their parents, Chester and Ellen, were both ambitious. Chester was a minister's son, their fifth child and their first son. Four more children followed. He rejected his parents' religion, left rural Vermont, went to law school, and became a New York lawyer, then an important public figure in New York City, then vice president and president. That rise took drive. He married Ellen Lewis Herndon, a Virginia-born woman who had grown up in Washington, D.C., in a comfortable household served by at least one slave. When she married in 1859, she was ambitious to reproduce that comfortable life. Both Chester and Ellen had expensive habits and, according to Arthur's biographer, "a strong desire for money."[3]

At the same time, both were sensitive, loving, and emotional and capable of strong and deep friendships—with each other, with their siblings, with friends and colleagues. And, we might presume, their children.[4] Losing their first child must have struck them especially hard.

Chester and Ellen Arthur had their first child, William, in 1860. By 1863 he was dead of what was called a swelling of the brain. Some say that the death of a child is the worst tragedy for a parent to endure. The Arthurs felt that. Worse, they blamed themselves (perhaps each other a bit too) in the belief that they had caused his brain fever by "overtax[ing] the infant's brain with intellectual demands." They must have felt the death as a rebuke to their ambitions. So when their second son was born in 1864, they resolved that they would not make that same mistake. They kept their word. Alan's father taught him to ride and to sail. They taught him vanity and charm; they certainly lavished on him attention (and nice clothes). They did not push him too hard academically.[5]

Nell was not encouraged academically either—for reasons of William's death but more surely because she was a girl. Her mother had had little education, and Nell's education seemed generally immaterial. Like Alan, she learned social skills and graces and appears to have been a charming young woman. Neither Alan nor Nell developed any of the drive that characterized the Putnams.[6]

Other internal family dynamics also inclined the Arthur children not to work too hard. The Arthur parents, like the Putnam parents, divided their responsibilities by gender. Ellen took care of the house. Chester took care of the finances. Because they both had expensive tastes and because Chester enjoyed the work, he spent long hours away from home. Alan and Nell grew up mostly in the company of their mother and witnessed her attitudes and feelings, even if they did not entirely absorb them. Ellen came to resent the time that Chester spent away from her and the family. How could her world revolve around someone who was never there? Nearly ninety years after the fact, Alan's son, Chester Alan Arthur III, reported that when Ellen died in 1880, she and her husband were on the verge of separation because of his absences. Whether the story is actually true or not, that the grandson had learned it (passed on by Alan, certainly) testifies to the power of the issue in the family. Both Nell and Alan, so much in their mother's emotional field, could well have sided with her and agreed that working so hard was not such a good thing.[7]

Their mother's sudden and premature death clearly added to these lessons. Ellen Arthur caught cold on January 10, 1880, and was buried on January 15. She died of pneumonia and heart failure at the age of forty-two. Sudden deaths often encourage relatives to live more immediately, to gather rosebuds, to dismiss delayed gratifications. We do not have direct evidence that this was the case with Alan and Nell, who at fifteen and eight would have been too young in any case to articulate it, but Alan at least made a life's work of rosebud gathering.

One last family event certainly reinforced the lesson. Not long after President James Garfield was assassinated and the Arthurs moved into the White House, Chester Arthur was diagnosed as having Bright's disease, or nephritis, a kidney ailment. He was slow to acknowledge the diagnosis and slower to announce it. He simply slowed down without explaining why. He did not much like being president and rarely had a lot of energy for the work. He did, however, enjoy giving parties and came to be known for the vitality of the White House social life. He had the building redecorated and refurbished and then invited his sister Molly McElroy to be in Washington for four months each year to serve as his hostess (and friend, surely). They entertained graciously and often. She made the White House a "center of generous & stately hospitality." Entertainment was the focal point of this administration. From their mother Alan and Nell would have learned to resent their father's work; when they presumably spent more time with him after her death and he was in the White House, they would have seen him dragging around, resenting his work, enjoying only his parties.[8]

So the Arthurs did not turn into international publishers or break down gender barriers. Instead, these various events left them fragile and vulnerable. The Putnams invite my admiration, the Arthurs my sympathy. Their mother's death, the circumstances of their father's political career, and then their father's death left both of them lost, disconnected, and a little desperate.

Moreover, Alan and Nell had lived in the shadow of their brother's death, but it was their parents' shadow, not their own grief. In fact, they may have been more precious to their parents because of the earlier loss, and their parents might have loved them with even greater intensity. When their mother died, they must have felt as if a powerful beam of warm light had been turned off. Her death was a terrible fact they had to deal with. Of great significance too were the effects of their mother's death.

Their mother had been the "haven" maker in the family; when she died, the haven was broken up. It may have been less hard for Alan, for he was already at school. The circumstances of his daily life did not change much. Nell's life, however, changed dramatically. In the nineteenth century, men who were widowed did not presume to take care of their children themselves but found help. Help sometimes meant remarrying quickly and sometimes meant giving the children over to someone else's care, especially a relative's (parents or siblings). Chester Arthur turned to the household servants, the governess, and his sisters. He had the capacity for strong emotion. What he did not have was the ability to take care of his children.[9]

He was crushed by his own loss and, it seems, not entirely attentive to theirs. His sister Regina described one telling incident. Soon after his wife's death he "called little Nell to him to kiss her [and] he completely broke down and said 'there is nothing worth having now.'"[10] Poor Nell, did that "nothing" include her or did she think so? Did Alan?

His sisters and the New York City servants and governess assumed

the care of Nell; that certainly helped him, but it meant that his children—
especially Nell—faced the almost simultaneous loss of their mother and
their father.

Even if Chester had had the emotional resources to take care of his
children, his career took such a momentous turn that he could not possibly have had the time to tend both to his children and to his career. Within months of his wife's death Chester Arthur was rather surprisingly nominated by the Republican Party to be its vice presidential candidate.

Chester's personal life brought him grief and disrupted his family. His
professional life also brought him grief. He was publicly removed from
one position. His election to the vice presidency was not entirely trium-
phal, nor was his subsequent elevation to the presidency following Garfield's death.

From 1871 to 1877 Chester Arthur had held one of the most important and lucrative political appointments in the United States. He was
the collector of customs for the port of New York. He had earned a good
income as a prominent New York City lawyer in the years before that,
but he accrued most of his wealth during these seven years. He was a
man of good reputation in a period of American politics not known for
incorruptibility. He was a political appointee in a time when such appointments fueled local and national debates. Controversy about such patronage appointments—and who controlled them, as well as whether they
were a good thing—served as one of the most important and volatile
issues of the politics of the 1870s and 1880s in the United States. Arthur
was investigated and ultimately removed from his customs position for
political reasons, not especially because of allegations of corruption.[11]

When in the summer of 1880 the Republican Party was tearing itself
into factions over the issue of patronage, some party people decided that
a balanced ticket should include someone in favor of reforming the system and someone opposed to reform. Garfield, an opponent of political
appointments and proponent of a fairer, less corruptible form of civil
service, was nominated for the presidency. Much to his own and other
people's surprise, Arthur was nominated to maintain the status quo, that
system in which political loyalty earned the favor of a job. He had no
previous experience in elective office. In the language of late nineteenth-
century politics, Garfield and his backers were Half-Breeds and Arthur
and his branch of the party were Stalwarts.

Even given the shorter duration as well as the lesser intensity of political campaigns in 1880, we can safely presume that Chester Arthur was
preoccupied by the campaign during the months that immediately fol-

lowed his wife's death. The Garfield-Arthur ticket was elected in 1880 and took office in March 1881. Just weeks after the election the issue of patronage/civil service took a violent and cruel turn when a failed office seeker shot Garfield, shouting, "I am a Stalwart and Arthur is president now!" Garfield did not die immediately but lingered for three months, leaving the country in political limbo and leaving Arthur in agony. Arthur destroyed most of his papers the night before he died, so we do not have a written chronicle of these months, but by the time he was sworn in as president in mid-1881, he had changed his mind about political patronage. In 1883 he signed into law the Pendleton Act, the first comprehensive reform and standardization of the civil service in the United States.[12]

He did not campaign for the Republican presidential nomination in 1884, and no groundswell of support rose up to encourage him. He did not stand much chance of being elected, but more important, he knew before the convention in 1884 that he was ill, deathly ill. He also must have suffered enormously regarding Garfield's death. He had blamed himself for his son's death, and although he was not in any way involved in Garfield's death—despite the allegations of some of his enemies—the assassin's cry must have echoed painfully in his memory.

After Chester left political office, he went home to New York, ostensibly to resume his private life but more truly to die. He had been very sick in the last weeks before leaving the White House. Once in New York City he had one especially bad spell in February 1886. Two of his sisters left their families to tend to him, and Alan and Nell kept constant watch at his bedside during the worst days. He recovered but only slightly and only temporarily. He lived only six more months and died in November 1886. He was fifty-seven. Alan was twenty-two, Nell just fifteen.

Alan had entered Princeton University at seventeen in 1881, at just about the time that his father became president. Like his father, he was tall and good looking. He did not make inordinate intellectual demands on himself, but he did excel at social life. He earned a reputation for knowing how to have a good time, how to charm women, and how to drink large quantities of alcohol.

When he heard the news of Garfield's death, Alan raced home from school to be with his father and watched him being sworn into office. He often spent holidays and vacations at the White House. He took part in some official occasions and organized some unofficial ones of his own. According to one story, he and the crown prince of Siam were once arrested for swimming nude in a pool on the White House grounds.[13]

In 1885, the same year his father finished his term as president, Alan entered Columbia Law School. In 1886, the year his father died, Alan dropped out of school and went to Europe, where he stayed for the better part of the next thirteen years. He had friends or made them in every major European city and enjoyed their company. His inheritance allowed him to travel and to enjoy a European gentleman's life.[14]

In 1900, when he was thirty-six, he finally returned from Europe and settled in Colorado Springs, Colorado, with his new wife, Myra Fithian Andrews. *Settled* is not perhaps the right word for Alan Arthur. He was still a playboy and still liked to party, to drink, and, unfortunately for Myra, to womanize. He and Myra had one son, Chester Alan Arthur III, then lost a second child, a daughter named Ellen after his mother (and sister).

In 1909 Myra discovered that her husband was having an affair. "I still can hardly realize, Alan dear," she wrote in a heartbreakingly pathetic (and melodramatic) letter, "that those pink letters were written to you." She released him to follow his heart but would not countenance losing her son. "Don't try to get Chester, for then I will fight." They did reconcile and their marriage—always tempestuous—lasted another twenty years but ended in divorce in 1929. Alan remarried in 1934 at the age of seventy to a woman thirty-one years his junior. Alan died in Colorado Springs in 1937. His widow, Rowena, survived him by thirty-two years.[15]

Nell's life took a different path. In 1881, when her father went to Washington, she stayed in New York—away from publicity. Her father was an extraordinarily private man and, as a general rule, even as president refused to answer questions from the press about either personal or professional issues. So she was part of his private life at home for his first year in office. She visited, usually in the company of her father's sister Molly McElroy. In late 1882 Nell joined him at the White House, where they stayed until March 1885.

When her father died in 1886 she was only fifteen and still needed parenting. She spent time with various aunts. She attended a girls' school in Farmington, Connecticut, with a cousin. "We have neither of us been homesick once although at first we felt very strange indeed. So dreadfully like new girls you know," she reported to Alan shortly after arriving there. She did not go to Princeton as Alan had, nor to college at all. She spent much of her time with cousins and aunts and uncles. She had many friends and a lively social life in New York and Albany. Like her brother, she did not have money worries and took several "western" tours, visiting Idaho and the World's Columbian Exhibition in Chicago in 1893: "It really is like a most beautiful white city and at night when it is all lighted up with the most wonderful electric light effects, it is like Fairyland." In 1895–1896 she took her first trip to Europe, celebrating her twenty-fourth birthday there. She visited Alan several times in Europe and saw him more frequently when he and Myra were in Colorado Springs. Nell lived the leisured social life of most women of her class and background. In 1907 she married a Mr. Charles Pinkerton. They lived mostly in Mt. Kisco. They had no children, but she took a lively interest in Alan's son and in her cousins' children. She seemed often to be in frail health and died in 1915 when she was only forty-six. Her husband survived her by more than fifty years.[16]

The letters between Nell and Alan span their adulthoods. And what letters they are too. They are the letters of two people desperate to keep some kind of connection with each other who expressed their emotions in a direct and raw way. They cared deeply about keeping their game of catch going and did until Nell died.

This is the other most significant difference between the feel of the Arthur family and the feel of the Putnam family. Certainly, the Putnams felt strong emotions, but they did not express them in their letters. Theirs was a different emotional diction.

The fact and the tone of Alan and Nell's lifetime correspondence and closeness show how they sustained each other in powerfully emotional ways through their lives. Their relationship also had a particular sweetness about it. They cherished each other, sometimes close-up, more often from a distance. Both their closeness and their distance are instructive.[17]

Nell and Alan demonstrate how the family connection holds despite time and distance, a characteristic common in sibling relationships. Siblings can be in irregular or intermittent contact, but when they are in touch the time between contact melts away, and they return quickly to the former state of connection. Some people are lucky enough to have such connections with friends, but it is more fully a characteristic of siblings. They can be apart and then come together with only a minimum of disruption.

We have a few letters from Nell to Alan when he was away at Princeton, but we finally get a fuller view when, within a few months of his father's death, Alan decamped to Europe. We might have expected Alan, as older brother, to become a surrogate father to his younger sister. He might even have moved back home with her. None of the above. More truly, he did nearly the opposite: he dropped out of law school and took off for Europe—a tour that kept him away from the United States for thirteen years.[18]

Alan's trip to Europe, so quick on the heels of his father's death, looks like running away, but from what he fled we cannot tell—perhaps his grief, public life, responsibilities, a life of duty. He did not say. Whatever his motivation, he found himself lost and lonely. "I feel the need of a home most confoundedly," he told Nell. The truth of this admission is touching. But what home would he have come to? That was his problem. "I am getting awfully sick of this wandering," he told her. He yearned for a home that he did not have, for a life he did not have—as if someone else were in charge of his life—and he yearned for Nell, the only family he had left. "Have you missed me a little, if you have I will tell you that I have missed you very much." It was to her that he confessed all these yearnings, to her that he reported and accounted for himself, to her that he entrusted his longings.[19]

He also missed her but could not bear the prospect of returning to the United States for most of those thirteen years. Whether it was the United States or the end of drifting that he could not bear, I cannot tell. It was not because he did not want to be with Nell. He did, and couldn't she come live with him in Europe? "We might build ourselves a very cozy nest somewhere for after all we have together as much money as the dear governor had the last years." "Can't you get anybody to bring you abroad this summer? I should so love to see you again!" "Don't you think you could find a nice chaperone to bring you over this winter?" He considered short visits "home," warning Nell that "I am afraid I cant promise to stay." And he would tell her that, in any case, his only purpose would be "to see you."[20]

If Alan yearned for Nell, she pined for him too. She needed him and wanted him closer by. First her mother, then her father, then her only brother—all three had left her in such a short time and she was so young. What was her home? No wonder her letters are replete with expressions of missing Alan and requests for him to come home—to visit, to stay, just come. "I miss you dreadfully dear."[21] This was decidedly not Putnam language. But more than that, she seemed to need him in a way that the Putnams never needed each other.

When Nell and Alan were together, she had a hard time parting from him. She had an extended stay with Alan in the mid-1890s, when she was in her twenties. Their time together connected them even more securely. On the day of her departure, she penned this sad note to him: "Last night I was so afraid of breaking down & disgracing myself that I couldn't trust myself to say half I wanted to. But you understand I am sure dear without being told how much I love you & how it hurts me to say goodbye even for two months. I should like to hold on to your coat tails all the time. . . . When you want me just cable 'come' & the date & I'll be there."[22]

A short time later she wrote him again, lamenting their separation: "Not a day goes by without my longing for my dear Boy for I never can be perfectly happy without you there is always a big hole when you are away." She reminded him to send for her when he wanted her: "I love America dearly but you better always." After a long visit by Alan to the United States the next year, Nell again had trouble watching him go: "If you felt half as badly as I did when I saw that horrid ship starting out I'm sorry for you for my heart just ached and the way you looked standing alone on that deck haunts me yet."[23] Oh, so sad and her pain so evident.

She worried about holding on to him too tightly, that he would resent it. Pleading with him to come for a visit, she promised that she would not "tie an iron rope around you" and would let him leave "without a murmur whenever you want to." Or, if they lived together in Europe, they could live in an apartment and "you could go off when the spirit moved you." The fierceness of her loneliness might well have frightened even Nell. "I really feel that we must see each other some way soon."[24]

One characteristic of siblingship is its tendency toward egalitarianism. In any family one child will likely be favored over another with various kinds of resources—education, love, property—but the relationship itself tends to balance the members through affection or age or birth order or gender. This does not, however, keep family members from advising each other. The Arthurs are interesting because Nell gave the advice. We might expect that Alan, because he was older and male, would be the advice giver, but he rarely assumed the role. He did advise her once on a subject he presumably knew well: "There is one thing I want you *not* to do, get engaged; don't dream of any such stupid thing as matrimony until you have had all the good time you want." This was also the only subject on which she explicitly asked him for advice too. In her letter announcing her engagement, she did encourage him to come home soon, "as I want your advice about lots of things."[25]

She both advised him and spoke to him as she might have imagined/remembered that her mother had spoken to him. She liked, for example, to call him "my dear boy" or "my dearest boy" and thanked him for writing as soon as he reached Europe, for it relieved "the old woman's mind." She was sixteen. She knew what she was doing and complained about it once. At twenty-five Nell wrote to her thirty-two-year-old brother that she always felt "as if you were a little boy and as if I ought to take Mamma's place and bring you up in the way you should go."[26]

She may have felt like the mother, but she advised him about things of the world, much as their father might have. Throughout their correspondence Nell's was the voice of responsibility, reason, and maturity, even wisdom. She knew better than he how old he was—he was one year older than he seemed to think. He asked if she were sure. "I don't want to be 30 any sooner than necessary." She was sure. She was not eligible to vote herself, but she told him how he needed to register and even how to vote (against William Jennings Bryan in the 1896 presidential election). In 1897, when Alan was looking for a political appointment from President William McKinley, Nell advised him, and quite astutely, to talk directly to the president: do what you can to counter stories about him in the newspapers; take a less important job if it's offered. "You can't expect to walk in at the last moment and be given something near the top of the tree." Finally, she advised him, do not return to Europe because "in the eyes of people it looks very indifferent & you cannot expect people to work for you—if as they think you are gallivanting off to Paris enjoying yourself instead of doing your best here." And in another letter she wrote, "I don't want to preach a sermon" and of course proceeded to preach a sermon. This one was that "people who are really happy are those who have responsibilities and accept them." In another she wrote, "You know it is only because I love you so much that I want you to have the best of everything for your happiness & I'm so proud of you that I want you to be somebody—as Papa's son ought to be."[27] This is the closest Nell ever came to a Putnam "encouragement" and, even at that, note that her goal was his happiness.

When speaking of these things, she wrote with authority and confidence; then, as if she were not really entitled to advise him, she quickly apologized or took it back somehow (as if she had overstepped her boundaries). "Forgive me dear if I have bored you." Sometimes with self-criticism: "As usual I seem to be a nuisance but I simply can't help it." Sometimes with a plea: "Don't hate me for being a bore please." She gets caught in conflicting roles. As a parent substitute she must give the sermon; as the younger and the sister, she shrinks from the audacity of having expressed herself so forcefully, so she apologizes.[28]

Alan did not seem to mind the advice and admitted even to feeling unable to deny anything to Nell, "I *owe her so much.*" He even took on the role of little boy to her parent from time to time. Shortly after arriving in Europe in 1887, for example, Alan reported to Nell that he had been feeling well and leading a disciplined life: in bed by twelve, only a little claret from time to time, reasonable eating, minimal smoking. In response she wrote: "I want to tell you dear Alan that I think you are the best boy in the world and I am so glad you have taken good care of yourself. I knew you would be good while you were away." A few days later he signed off with "I am very good & in consequence reasonably happy."[29]

She often called him a "good boy" or a "bad boy" (or referred to herself as a good girl or bad girl) but used these phrases mostly in relation to their obligations to write to each other—either fulfilled or neglected. When she was most angry at him about not writing to her, she pronounced him a "very, very bad man." In her estimation good and bad had to do primarily with doing their duty, and the primary form of badness was not staying in close touch with each other.[30]

In their family roles Alan and Nell both embodied and defied conventional gender roles. He was older and male; she was younger and female; the contours of their lives were certainly shaped by their gender—he took off for Europe when he wanted, whereas she had to find a chaperone, for example. "I am a girl," she wrote to him, "and can't go romping over the world after you but you are a man and could come and go often even if you do want to live over there. For that I don't blame you in the least."[31] Even so, they did not relate to each other in ways that are easily identifiable as male and female. Alan lived mostly outside the family circle and in the "public" world. Nell lived closer to relatives and in closer contact with kin and not in the public world, but she was the more responsible and mature, even worldly. Nell gave advice to her older brother about how to get a job; Alan advised Nell about her love life. They configured themselves as partners to each other.

Alan's marriage in 1900 to Myra occurred off the stage of the letters, as did Nell's to Charles Pinkerton in 1907. Their marriages did distract them from their sibling relationship—as would be expected. They turned their attention to their spouses and got more of their needs satisfied closer to home and separate from each other. This is common among siblings. The intensity of childhood turns sometimes into the junior marriage of early adulthood. When the real marriages come along, however, the siblings reinvest their energy—though not all of it. Alan and Nell's relationship moved into a more quiescent period, but quiescent does not mean less affectionate or less meaningful.[32]

In any case, Nell would not tolerate too much quiescence. She sent her most angry letter to her brother several years after his marriage. "Do you realize you have been gone four months and have written me one note and one letter in that time. . . . Ever since you've been married you lean back and let Myra do the whole thing. . . . I don't think it fair. Besides which dearly as I love Myra she isn't you and I don't want to get all out of touch with you and if you never write me how can I keep it."[33] In one letter before Nell became seriously involved with anyone, Alan wrote of his fear that "when you marry I shall feel that my last tie to any family is broken."[34] She may not have remembered, but she was careful to treat him tenderly when she did become engaged: "Of one thing you may be sure that my love for Charlie hasn't interfered one wit with my love for 'my dear boy.' . . . That's one nice thing about hearts they seem to have such a nice big roomy faculty of enlarging. Just as I am sure you love me perhaps even more for loving Myra and Chester too." She also gave him the news before she told anyone else, "for you must be the very first to know about it."[35] When Alan and Myra were traveling just after their wedding, Alan wrote reassuringly too. "I am as happy as a man can be," he wrote, "but I do miss your soft fingers stroking my head." In another note: "You two are my bestest loves." When Alan's wife became pregnant, Alan told Nell before anyone else.[36]

Nell's husband, Charlie, also respected his wife's connection to her brother. When Nell got sick—deathly sick, her husband thought—he contacted Alan immediately, for sympathy and for help. "I am going through 'deep waters' and you do not know the grief that fills my heart to write you such grave news." Come quickly, Charlie urged: "Nell loves you dearly and you are the only close soul to her besides myself."[37] After Nell's death some years later, Charlie tried to keep in contact with Alan. When Charlie eventually remarried, he sent Alan a note: "Sarah [his bride-to-be] said to me 'I never want you to stop talking of Nell to me and I always want her picture around as I know I owe much to her for what you are.' That is her spirit and she means all of it and I want you to love her too."[38] Alan did not reply.

For nearly forty years Nell and Alan wrote to each other and stayed in touch. Perhaps not as close touch as Nell would ideally have liked— in her last letter to him she was still asking for a closer connection—but close enough that neither ever seemed to doubt the affection of the other. As Nell wrote in one letter, having given many details about her health: "This is all very egotistical and selfish but I know you will want to know all about it & be interested."[39] He was interested and cared a lot about her well-being and happiness.

Alan and Nell provided important sustenance and continuity for each other. There were other relatives—but they were family and that meant something special and intense to each of them. When Nell died, their game of catch was over. Alan must then have felt very, very alone.

## Notes

1. This chapter is based largely on the letters between Chester Alan Arthur II (Alan) and Ellen Herndon Arthur Pinkerton (Nell) in the Arthur Family Papers, Library of Congress, Washington, D.C. For general family information I have used Reeves, *Gentleman Boss*. See also Howe, *Chester A. Arthur*.

On family dynamics see esp. Bank and Kahn, *Sibling Bond;* Lamb and Sutton-Smith, *Sibling Relationships;* Cicirelli, *Sibling Relationships Across the Life Span;* and Skolnick and Skolnick, *Family in Transition*.

2. For Haven Putnam's obit see the *New York Times*, Feb. 28, 1930; for Alan Arthur's, see the *New York Times*, July 19, 1937.

3. Reeves, *Gentleman Boss*, 13, 33, 51. On the Herndons' slaves, see p. 20.

4. In his biography of Chester A. Arthur Sr., Reeves quotes from his letters to a friend. Like the nineteenth-century letters between women quoted by Carroll Smith-Rosenberg that sound too intimate by twentieth-century standards for heterosexuals of the same sex, these letters between Chester Arthur and his friend Campbell Allen are expressive in a way we would not expect from midnineteenth-century American males. Arthur, for example, wrote: "What a life we did lead last winter! you and I particularly . . . laying bare to each other our mutual plans, hopes & fears, adventures, and *experiences* & so cosily chatting & smoking—& then tumbling into bed in the 'wee sma hours' & falling soundly asleep in each others arms." Or, from a letter some time later: "But I would so much like to see you. . . . I look back to some of those hours which I have spent with you, in the open-hearted, confiding sympathizing fellowship which has always existed between us as among the happiest of my life." Or: "How I desire to be with you!"

That his friend had been diagnosed with tuberculosis may have intensified their friendship (and their language), but these letters nonetheless suggest that the language of emotions had not become the exclusive property of women by mid-century. They also suggest the intensity of Arthur's homosocial world, one he may also have fostered in the many late nights he spent with his friends after his marriage. Reeves uses the letters to demonstrate Arthur's sensitive side, which they certainly do (Reeves, *Gentleman Boss*, 12–13). See also Smith-Rosenberg, "Female World of Love and Ritual," 53–76.

5. In the 1870s Chester Arthur dropped a year from his age and consistently reported that he'd been born in 1830, rather than the correct 1829. Even the *Dictionary of American Biography*'s entry for President Arthur lists his birth as 1830. Perhaps coincidentally, Alan also dropped a year off his age—only to be reminded by Nell that, unfortunately, he was a year older.

6. Many women of Nell's social position and class—including her mother—did not concentrate too closely on education. See Herbert, *Dearest Beloved*.

7. Reeves reports this story from an interview he did with Charles Alan Arthur III in 1970 (Reeves, *Gentleman Boss*, 72 n).

8. Ibid., 273.

9. On roles of fathers see Rotundo, *American Manhood;* Griswold, *Fatherhood in America;* and Frank, *Life with Father.*

10. Regina Caw to Alice Arthur, June 11, 1880, Arthur Family Papers.

11. Here and following, I'm drawing on Reeves, *Gentleman Boss.*

12. Reeves's biography focuses especially on the issues of political patronage in the 1870s and 1880s. I have here summarized the story of Arthur's political life, with an eye only to imagining his feelings during these years and to how his children might have experienced their father's life. Arthur really did hate publicity—having found it mostly hostile and hurtful during these same years. He therefore orchestrated the burning of most of his personal papers in the last days before he died. What remains in the Arthur Family Papers are collected mostly from other members of the family.

13. Reeves, *Gentleman Boss,* 275, 475 n. There's plenty of evidence in the letters themselves of Alan's immaturity—throughout his life—and Reeves certainly found much there. It's also clear that Alan's son, a man with whom Reeves conducted oral interviews, highlighted that aspect of his father. Alan's son made enough margin comments on the letters of his father's that he collected and gave to the Library of Congress that his ambivalent attitude toward his father is evident there too.

14. While in Europe he contracted a venereal disease. He talked only about being sick, without naming his malady; years later his son added a note to the margin of one of his father's letters: "he had vd." See Alan Arthur to Nell Arthur, Dec. 11, 1887.

15. Myra Arthur to Alan Arthur, May 17, 1909. For their obituaries see the *New York Times,* and November 13, 1965, and July 19, 1937.

16. Nell Arthur to Alan Arthur, May 6, 1887, and Sept. 13, 1893.

17. Much of the literature on family history emphasizes questions about the extent to which families have been nuclear or extended. This question has to do with intergenerational habitation—do parents and children live together and when? This research, then, concentrates on the relationship between parent and child and how that relationship changes over time. My research suggests that the relationships with siblings may be less fraught than that with parents, and for all that can be especially sustaining when any disruption occurs in the parent-child bond. Moreover, the thrust of the research on family history seems to be that a person belongs to the birth family and then to the adult intentional family, rather than that the adult family meshes in some way with the family of origin. Most people for most of their lives are part of at least two families—the one they were born into and the ones that they create in their adult lives.

Both Alan and Nell married, but both Alan and Nell valued each other throughout their lives in a meaningful way. This is the important point that so much family literature misses.

18. Birth-order studies are problematic for many methodological reasons, but they are provocative and interesting nonetheless. Among the problems are those suggested by Alan Arthur's situation. He was second born, and we can see that the birth and death of his older brother significantly affected the nature of his upbringing. He was, in the birth-order language, not a biological firstborn, nor

was he really a "functional" firstborn. For seven years he was raised as an only child and, I would argue, an especially cherished only child, until Nell was born. Only then did he become a "functional" firstborn, certainly an elder to Nell. She often called on him to behave as an elder would, but he instead acted as an only child or even a younger child by not taking responsibility, by not helping, by not taking care of Nell. For an especially interesting recent account of the effects of birth order by a nonpsychologist, see Sulloway, *Born to Rebel*.

19. Alan Arthur to Nell Arthur, Jan. 3, 1893.
20. Alan Arthur to Nell Arthur, Jan. 3, June 1, and Nov. 11, 1893.
21. Nell Arthur to Alan Arthur, August 3, 1887.
22. Nell Arthur to Alan Arthur, Feb. 16, 1896.
23. Nell Arthur to Alan Arthur, Feb. 28, 1896, and May 4, 1897.
24. Nell Arthur to Alan Arthur, August 5 and July 17, 1893.
25. Alan Arthur to Nell Arthur, Feb. 12, 1891; Nell Arthur to Alan Arthur, Aug. 4, 1903.
26. Nell Arthur to Alan Arthur, Aug. 3, Dec. 3, and July 25, 1887, and June 10, 1897.
27. Alan Arthur to Nell Arthur, Nov. 11, 1893, and March 27, 1897; Nell Arthur to Alan Arthur, May 5 and June 10, 1897; Alan Arthur to Nell Arthur, March 27, 1897.
28. Nell Arthur to Alan Arthur, May 5 and June 10, 1897.
29. Alan Arthur to Myra Arthur, April 8, 1892; Alan to Nell, Nov. 12, 1887; Nell Arthur to Alan Arthur, Dec. 3, 1887; Alan Arthur to Nell Arthur, Dec. 11, 1887.
30. Nell Arthur to Alan Arthur, July 14 [1903].
31. Nell Arthur to Alan Arthur, July 17, 1893.
32. See esp. Cicirelli, "Sibling Influence Throughout the Lifespan," and Connidis and Campbell, "Closeness, Confiding, and Contact."
33. Nell Pinkerton to Alan Arthur, July 14 [1903]. Someone has penciled "1900" in as the date, but that can't be correct because in the same letter Nell sent thirty-nine kisses for Alan's birthday and he turned thirty-nine in 1903, not 1900.
34. Alan Arthur to Nell Arthur, Feb. 12, 1891.
35. Nell Arthur to Alan Arthur, Dec. 27, 1902.
36. Alan Arthur to Nell Arthur, May 10, Sept. 5, and July 27, 1900. These cluster around the time of Alan's marriage—and long before Nell was involved with Charlie Pinkerton. Perhaps Alan knew that Nell needed even more reminders of his loyalty and love just then.
37. Charlie Pinkerton to Alan Arthur, Oct. 21, 1912.
38. Charlie Pinkerton to Alan Arthur, Jan. 17, 1918.
39. Nell Pinkerton to Alan Arthur, March 11, 1914.

FOUR

# The Janins:
# Albert, His Brothers, and His Wife

Violet Blair and Albert Janin had a remarkable marriage. In any time it would have been unconventional, but for their time it was downright odd. They did not make a common household, they did not live out of a common economy. They had different friends and social circles. Yet they married in 1874 and stayed married for fifty-four years until Albert's death in 1928. In her portrait of their marriage Virginia Jeans Laas shows how this particular marriage suited Violet's temperament and class aspirations and was a response as well to the limitations imposed on women of her circumstances. Albert's part gets less play and cannot be explained so easily in light of his historical times. But his marriage does make sense.[1]

Violet Blair was born to a prominent Washington, D.C., family in 1849. Her father, the rebel in his family, did not become a lawyer (as his brothers had); he did not like Washington life, so he moved to California; and he did not live a long life—he died when he was only thirty-three, leaving a pregnant wife and two small children. His widow, Mary Serena Jessup Blair, returned to Washington and settled back into life near her own sisters and her widowed father, as well as her in-laws, to raise Violet, Jessup, and Jimmie (a girl, named after her dead father).[2]

Violet's mother outlived her husband by more than sixty years. She never remarried. From 1853 until 1914 she made Violet the center of her life and attention. Grieving, sympathetic, and loving grandfathers and a grandmother, as well as uncles and aunts, all doted on her as well. Critics might have called her "spoiled" as a result; she more likely felt her-

*The Janins*

Louis Janin (1812–74)
m. 1835    Juliet Covington (1815–89)
    Louis Jr. (1837–1914)
     m. 1865    Elizabeth Marshall
         three children
    Henry (1838–1911)
     m. [?]    Mabel [Mendell?]
         two children
    Alexis (1840–97)
    Eugene (1841–62)
    Edward (b. 1843)
    Albert (1844–1928)
     m. 1874    Violet Blair
         one child

self special. She certainly warmed to the part, to the annoyance, apparently, only of her younger brother and sister.

Violet was educated as other young ladies of her set and day, in various private schools and in various ladylike arts. She had an intellect that would have felt confined by such a dainty education. Later in her life she demonstrated her linguistic acuity by learning French, German, Italian, and Spanish, plus Danish, Russian, and Swedish. For the intellectual fun of it she studied, in addition, Anglo-Saxon, Flemish, Hebrew, Icelandic, Volapük, Walachian, and Chinook. Her father had been a good businessman in California and the uncle in charge of the estate made wise investments for Violet's family. Violet, however, demonstrated her financial acumen by assuming control and managing her family's money as well as her uncle had, and the family lived comfortably for the remainder of their lives.[3]

By Laas's account, Violet Blair at twenty was the belle of Washington, D.C., society in the late 1860s. She beckoned and dismissed suitors as it pleased her. She was flattered by their attentions but developed few feelings for any of them. She did, however, develop a strong sense of herself. Laas quotes from Violet's travel journal in 1868: "Am I not the belle of Nice, the queen? Some people say the Beauty. . . . Here I am without a rival." Even if she does say so herself.[4]

Albert and Violet met in 1867. He courted her and she tested him for the next seven years. To say that she had ambivalent feelings about marriage dramatically understates their magnitude. No doubt, she felt herself in a painful bind. Violet knew that in order to fit into her society—a society that she cared about deeply—she had to be married. But marriage held for her the end of independence, of autonomy, and of the Washington social life that had given her so many pleasures. Other women of her generation must have shared her dilemma. She could not settle happily into a life organized around husband and children, yet she saw few other palatable choices.

Making every effort both to warn Albert, though she would not have called it that, and to control the shape of her future, she set terms and conditions for her future husband. She demanded that following marriage she would control her own property without any interference from Albert. He agreed. He could live in New Orleans, but she would live in Washington, D.C. He agreed. Most dramatically, she insisted, "Nothing but *absolute obedience* can satisfy me." Albert agreed even to this. They married in 1874. She feared marriage to anyone and could only tolerate the prospect of marriage to Albert because she trusted that he would make few demands on her. She was right.[5]

Violet and Albert spent most of their first year apart. He was trying to make something of himself in Louisiana, and she continued to live with her mother in Washington. When he suggested, after that first year, that it would be useful for his floundering political career for her to spend more time in New Orleans, she let loose one of her "thunderbolts," as Laas calls them. Furiously, she reminded him that she had never agreed to such a living arrangement, so he was not to start pestering her now. Violet had not set any conditions about motherhood, though she did fear childbirth and death from childbirth. She came to want a child and was deeply disappointed when her only child was born two months prematurely and did not survive.

In the course of their lives they spent many years apart. Violet had a brief but intense affair with perhaps the only man she ever let herself love, an Austro-Hungarian count. Albert knew at least the general contours of her relationship, but even when he visited her, he did little to restrain her (as if he could have).

Violet had her own money and was financially secure—a prerequisite for her independence. Albert was less secure. The difference did not concern her because she believed that when they were not living together, she should pay her own way. She was also an astute manager of her money and investments. While Albert speculated and spent himself into financial chaos, Violet was consolidating her family's financial security. She gave and loaned money to Albert until it seemed foolhardy to do so anymore.

Albert tried one scheme after another to support himself, including a doomed canal project and an ice-storage project. In the last quarter of his life he finally settled into the control and management of Mammoth Cave in Kentucky and finally did quite well.

As Albert's financial situation worsened in the 1880s and he borrowed more and more money from Violet and her mother (and lost that too), he confided less and less in Violet. Their openness and frankness with each other, according to Laas, had been one of the strengths of their relationship. As that diminished, so did Violet's sense of her marriage's success. A period of even greater emotional distance between them reinforced their physical separation until their later years.

In her sixties Violet found herself lonesome for Albert. After her mother died in 1914 and then her brother, Jessup—her contentious sister, Jimmie, had died more than a decade earlier—Violet more frequently urged Albert to come to her, and she more often went to him. For their last ten years Violet was quite solicitous of Albert's welfare, and when he really needed her care physically, she moved him to Washington, D.C., where, Laas reports, Violet "loyally and tenderly cared for him until his death" eight months later.[6]

This marriage suited Violet. It suited her vanity and allayed her fears to have a husband who yielded so fully to her will. Her marriage gave her the respectability of the married state in a stratum of society that cared about appearances. It also allowed her to choose where, how, and with whom she wanted to live, which usually meant in Washington with her mother. Why Violet wanted this kind of marriage is apparent.

But what about Albert? Why did he accede to Violet's conditions? Why did he agree to live on his own, two thousand miles away, with at best only intermittent sexual companionship? He accepted—with apparent equanimity—a position of subservience. He countered her often sharp tongue with soothing words and protestations of his love. He did not seem to object to her involvement with other men. We might presume that he was simply a weak man, but that only moves the question back another step. Why, then, was he a weak man and why was he weak in that way?[7]

Understanding a marriage is a daunting task—whether looking at one's own or another's. As my father says, no one ever really knows what the inside of another person's marriage feels like. How often are we surprised when one couple that had seemed so happy announces its divorce, or another couple that cannot possibly stay together somehow does? The impermeability of relationships to outsiders has long hidden domestic abuse, affairs, passions, varieties of intimate peculiarities, and mysteries. I don't pretend to understand all the dynamics of Violet and Albert's marriage, but Albert's choice of this partner makes sense when we look at him in the context of his birth family.

Albert and his five brothers were born to a French father and his Kentucky-born wife and raised in New Orleans. The three oldest boys, Louis, Henry, and Alexis, all became mining engineers at their father's urging. The three youngest, Eugene, Edward, and Albert, became lawyers like their father. The oldest was born in 1837, Albert, the youngest, in 1844.[8]

Albert grew up, then, surrounded by boys. His world was governed by a particular definition of what it meant to be "manly." The gender role definitions of Albert and Violet's day idealized women as pure, pious, domestic, and submissive (whether they were or not) and, identifying men as the "opposite" sex, cast men into the opposite roles: experienced, secular, worldly, and dominant. The woman's responsibility was to find a way to cede control and power to others, except within the home; the man's responsibility was to control himself and others—including his wife. Whatever we think about the nature of power relations in marriage—and however complicated they actually are—the expectation in white middle-class society in the nineteenth-century was that the man would be in charge and the woman would organize her life around his.[9]

In his marriage Albert violated the gender role definitions of his time, but he strictly acted out the role that he had learned as the youngest of six brothers.

Louis, born in 1837, was the oldest of the Janin brothers; he was named after his father, a Frenchman who was sixteen when he emigrated to the United States in 1828. The father trained in the law, became an American citizen, and settled for his lifetime in New Orleans. Louis and Henry, born in 1838, attended grammar school together in New Orleans, then went to Yale. At their father's insistence both went to Germany for training in engineering from 1856 to 1861. When they returned to the States at the ages of twenty-four and twenty-three, respectively, they did not return to New Orleans—this was during the Civil War—but to Colorado to work in the western mines, then to the Comstock Lode in Nevada, and next to California. Like most educated men of their generation, Louis and Henry passed their entire educational lives in the company of other men. Mining engineering as a profession was—and still is—overwhelmingly male. The two brothers settled themselves in mining towns that were also overwhelmingly male. Their next younger brother, Alexis, followed in their footsteps a few years later, after spending a few extra years in Paris. In 1865 he joined Louis and Henry, who had by then moved to San Francisco.[10]

The next three boys—Edward, Eugene, and Albert—all eventually followed their older brothers to Europe for their schooling. At thirteen he was too young for university, so Albert went to boarding school. With all her sons in Europe, their mother moved to the Continent to be near them. They one by one returned to the United States, but she stayed on for at least five years after all her sons had left. Her husband spent all those years in New Orleans. Eugene had returned to serve in the Confederate Army and was killed at Bull Run in 1862; he was twenty-one. When Albert left Europe in 1863, he did not join the army but joined his surviving brothers in the West. He and Edward both studied law, and for a time Albert clerked for his older brother. After the Civil War, Albert made his way back to New Orleans, then to Washington, D.C., where he met and married Violet Blair.[11]

His brothers spent their lives in the West mostly, but Albert felt most at home in New Orleans. He had some fanciful desire to run for Congress from Louisiana—he was neither well enough known nor connected nor politically astute enough—and he seems to have practiced law only intermittently and in a rather desultory manner. He really was a dreamer. He liked more than anything to speculate. While his mining brothers were doing the practical work of mineral assaying and surveying, Albert was borrowing money and hoping that this investment this time would pan out.

In the authority structure of the Janin family Albert was at the bottom. Laas writes of Violet that "there was . . . no man to whom Violet felt subordinate." By contrast, there seem to have been few men to whom Albert did *not* feel subordinate. If Albert learned anything from his brothers, it was subordination. When he met up with Violet, he was used to obeying, to letting other people set the rules, to letting someone else be in charge.[12]

His brothers found him alternately charming and frustrating. Mining historian Clark Spence reports that "the very nature of mining gave engineers a reputation for being pessimists"; if that was true of the Janin engineers, they may have found Albert's dreamy optimism especially annoying (as Violet did).[13]

Among these six brothers the emotional temperature was generally cool and their emotional expression restrained (except Henry—more on him later). They were not particularly demonstrative. In comparison with the Putnams, the Arthurs, and other families in this book, the Janin brothers maintained what we might identify as "masculine detachment," which to me, having been brought up in a family of mostly girls, feels positively chilly.[14]

Louis, the oldest brother, offers us the best example. Responsible, reliable, and dutiful, Louis advised his brothers about money and jobs; they sought his advice too. Louis, his biographer reports, "was recognized as a man of brilliant and worldly wisdom" who was known for his "courage and coolness." Louis often showed himself to be unflappable and in control of his emotions (or not feeling them? This is one of the ambiguities of coolness to an outsider—not having the feeling and not expressing the feeling can look remarkably alike.) He generally expressed himself in a flat, businesslike tone, whatever the topic.[15]

Upon hearing of their mother's death in 1889, for example, Louis wrote to Albert:

Dear Albert

I am just in receipt of [your] telegram announcing our mother's death. A few hours before, I received your letter of 27th inst from which I felt sure that she could last but a few days at most, and that death would be a relief from a lingering illness. I am glad to learn that Henry is with you. I feel sure that everything possible was done for her comfort and am grateful to Dr Suching and Miss Urquhart for their attention.

I shall inform our relatives immediately. Affectly Louis Janin[16]

This is Louis's response to his mother's death, and it is his response to his brother's experience of witnessing her death. The closest he came to comforting Albert was expressing his gladness that Henry was close by. No grief made its way into this or a later letter.

Another letter written in another family about another death highlights the detached tone of Louis's letter. Myra Arthur, Alan's first wife, wrote to her younger sister upon hearing of the death of their father. The situation, then, is quite similar: oldest sibling writes to younger one in response to a parent's death. The two letters, however, differ in style, tone, emotional transparency and intensity, and in length. Louis's letter was brief, whereas Myra's ran to several pages. It included these excerpts:

My darling sister;

When we were supping so gaily at Cartier's new years' eve we never thought that in 3 months our dear noble good father would be dead! It is *so so* awful that I am for one stunned & beaten. . . . He died of pneumonia but it was caused by his weak heart and general debility. He worried so, poor dear! We all were nothing but a burden to him, although he did not mind all that, and we were *so* happy when all together.

She continued: "Brace up then dear little sister, I am the eldest & the head of the family now and I shall do everything in my power to keep the family together & so keep us all up." She finished with, "Pray for him, Fannie dear, and I say now that *he* is not to be pitied, he is at rest at all; but *we*, how can we stand it!!" Finally, she closed with "Your sister who loves you."[17]

These two letters convey much of the same information. Louis acknowledges his mother's death and Myra acknowledges her father's. Louis notes that death was a blessing for his mother; Myra similarly declares her father to be at rest and not needing pity. Myra announces her assumption of the role of family elder; Louis implies his in taking responsibility for contacting relatives. Louis's statement of his gladness that Henry was with Albert could reasonably be read as an expression of sympathy and comfort—albeit implied—much like Myra's more explicit "but we, how can we stand it." So the two letters parallel each other in very large part. But how different the tone. How readers respond to the tone depends on the contours of our own emotional landscape, but the differences are apparent; if Albert had grown up with Myra, his adult relationships would likely have been different. But he grew up in the same household with Louis. He understood detachment and distance.

He also understood what it was like to have people telling him what to do and how to do it. Louis, Henry, Alexis, and Edward all took their turns. Albert should do this job or that, spend his money this way or that, get his life organized in this way or that. After some particularly disastrous turn in Albert's finances, Alexis told him to "pull yourself together, charge the past to experience account, and make a fresh start before it is too late." Alexis also was not above speaking quite patronizingly to his younger brother (younger only by four years, but that is enough in a family to establish age-based authority). After their mother's death, Albert had the job of sending some of her belongings to each of his brothers. Alexis wrote him a quite sharp note telling him to "pack the things *securely*" (his emphasis); Albert was then forty-five. In a further scolding tone Alexis told Albert to "send us Mamma's legacies without fail and without delay." This was how Violet talked to him too. Violet's commandments must have felt familiar to Albert, and he knew how to deal with them. Agree, do not contest, but ignore them.[18]

Albert's brother Henry, especially, but also Edward, prepared Albert for Violet in yet another way. Like his brother Louis, Henry was an engineer, and he and Louis spent much time together from childhood on. But Henry did not share Louis's cool demeanor. No one would have called Henry restrained, especially Louis. Henry drank, smoked, and ate to excess, about which he was alternately embarrassed and aggressively defensive. He had not had, he wrote petulantly, "a single drop" for nearly a year, nor had he smoked. But, he asserted argumentatively, "I shall resume & drink & smoke whenever I please, & stop again whenever I please & stop again." He did start and stop repeatedly. He lost seventy pounds one year, twenty-five another, gaining it back in between. So we would hardly think of him as a man of self-control. He died in 1911, of cirrhosis of the liver; while cirrhosis is not always caused by too much alcohol, it probably was the case with Henry. Louis once described him as quixotic.[19]

If not actually more expressive than Louis, Henry was more intense. He did use the word *love* from time to time, usually in the form of "give love to." His grief also showed itself in the starkness of his announcement of his son's death: "We have had an unexpected and severe blow at our home. Our boy has died!" He reported that "it is a blessing for Mabel that it lived one day and that she saw & fondled it," while not saying whether it was a blessing for Henry himself. Nonetheless, his plea to Albert to "come and see me to-morrow" feels plaintive even one hundred years later.

Henry conveyed to Albert his pain (and perhaps his annoyance) even more explicitly a week later when he declared himself completely occupied with his own affairs and "resolved not to open my mind or ears to any [other] subject." What a peculiarly formal little note: the language is stilted and the distance carefully fortified—"Therefore do not be offended that I do not take cognizance of and respond to your latest communications." This is a man paralyzed by his grief and we can feel it. He does not put it entirely into words, but he has communicated his feelings quite successfully.[20]

On at least one occasion Henry lashed out at Albert for a cause not evident in the letters. Even Louis called it a "fierce attack" and passed on Henry's explanation that he was "very harsh when he did not drink and thought only on such occasions of his rights and not the other fellow's"—even when that other fellow was his brother.[21]

Edward, according to Laas, caused something of a crisis between Albert and Violet. Apparently driven by a furious anger at Albert, Edward in 1880 told Violet—in an act that feels oddly like tattling—of the size of Albert's debts and financial losses. Edward accused Albert of lying, cheating, of misusing his clients' as well as Violet's mother's money. What moves a man to tell his sister-in-law such information, particularly in light of Albert and Violet's agreement that their business affairs were not to be the concern of each other? Edward surely must have told himself that he was protecting Violet, and he did counsel her not to give Albert any more money. However, my own sense of Edward's impropriety probably stems from my different view of privacy and my sense that it's right to mind your own business; these ideas that I share with many at the end of the twentieth century did not hold sway at its beginning. Nonetheless, it does seem that Edward was meddling in his brother's affairs.[22]

Albert denied his brother's accusations and suggested that the charges revealed more about Edward's alcoholism than Albert's financial dealings. He further disclosed that Edward gambled compulsively and often needed to be bailed out and had been by Albert himself. The validity of Albert's charges are as unverifiable as are Edward's. They are telling here because they hint at a layer of turmoil in these men's lives that may have left Albert both accustomed to tumult and with a preference for keeping it at a distance if at all possible. He married a passionate woman but generally kept out of her way.

Edward's and Henry's criticisms sound a lot like one of Violet's own thunderbolts. Albert could be hurt by both his wife and his brothers. Yet he seemed somehow ultimately unruffled by these encounters. He simply created a space around himself.

All the brothers were quite capable of being on their own and living independently. Brother number three, Alexis, traveled to Japan in 1874 and faced with calm the prospect of having "no one to speak to or to exchange ideas with," though he did ask Henry to send him some books and magazines and to write to him occasionally. In his times away Alexis seemed quite content on his own and was confident that he could get the Japanese operation running smoothly "if I am let alone." He was also willing to bear what he called the pigheadedness of the workers because his pay would make him independent. What he never sounds is homesick.[23]

Like his brothers, Albert contained his feelings. He only occasionally lashed back at Violet when she threatened him, insulted him, badgered him. Her words simply bounced off him. He did not retaliate, though when he got into financial troubles, he simply did not tell Violet very much—much to her consternation—and it caused a rift between them.

She had set a lot of stock in their honest dealings with each other, but in this case he withheld from her.

Interestingly, Albert's may have been the most successful of the marriages among the Janin brothers. When Louis was in his seventies, his marriage fell apart. Louis made only cryptic references to troubles and then to living alone. He reported, for example, that he visited his family "but lived elsewhere." Everyone was friendly, he wrote but enigmatically added, "There are wheels within wheels." When he did note his marriage's breakdown, he added: "What I say is merely a statement of fact, calling for no particular condolence or sympathy." He did, however, ask Albert to intervene and to "act amicus curiae" with Louis's estranged spouse. Maybe to the brothers Albert was the best at feelings and relationships?[24]

Henry's marriage also ended in divorce. The details are vague—who initiated what around what issues—but he ended up bitter and angry. So angry, Louis feared, and told Albert, that "Henry is going to make a fool of himself if not careful with his ex wife." Henry died in a hotel in London in the company of his (male) personal attendant of twenty years (another kind of marriage?) who was also the only one close to Henry present at the cremation of Henry's body.[25]

The brothers' different reactions to their divorces discourage hasty conclusions, either about men or even about Janin men. Louis wanted no sympathy, Henry wanted and needed a lot. Henry involved his brothers in his troubles, reporting regularly to Louis and even offering to send the whole husband-wife correspondence. (It does not survive in the family collection.) He also asked Louis to help with his divorce settlement, although Louis was an engineer and Albert the lawyer.

At the same time, in the midst of their foundering marriages, they found common cause in their sense of the peculiar and alien nature of women. Both Henry and Louis talked about "woman"; as Henry told Louis: "I have been occupied with burning matters of my own the outcome of which proves the truth of your true and rather sad lines re woman." We do not know, of course, what Henry had written, but note that he wrote not about women but about woman, a category, an alien force to be reckoned with.[26]

Henry most explicitly viewed women with suspicion, fear, worry. The wife of one friend "feels her oats" and her husband ended up "gently submerged by a perfumed tide." Of his own wife he reported that she "has plenty of money & that makes her defiant." His divorce sharpened his sense of women as powerful and untrustworthy. His estranged wife's financial proposal, he wrote to Louis, "reads innocently" but was not, he knew. He reported that he had retorted "with appropriate and indignant words which showed that I saw through the attempted trick." Suspicion of trickery and deception is not uncommon between divorcing spouses, yet I wonder how much of this "mystery" of the "woman" resulted from having no at-home contact with sisters. Did the Janins have a particular kind of trouble relating to women that had to do with their not having sisters?[27]

Growing up in this world of brothers and no sisters left all the Janin brothers without familial and informal dealings—fighting and loving—with females who were their rough equals in the family (though not, of course, in their society). We can imagine how the dynamics of the Janin family—as well as the Janin brothers' relationships with women—would have been different if they had had a sister like Mary Putnam or Nell Arthur.[28] The Janin brothers' lack of familial interaction in their growing-up years may have created a sense of women as alien and unfamiliar. They had no significant experience with women other than their mother, and then they were sent away to school—men's schools.

Albert found in Violet a woman who was in many ways like a mother to him and he liked it. She was affectionate, distant, without too many emotional—or even sexual—demands. More than that, with Violet he did not ever have to grow up. He could remain a child. It was a position with which he was familiar and apparently comfortable.

He was used to having people help him out, take care of him. All his brothers—like Violet—loaned him money. Repeatedly, frustratingly, finally with annoyance—but they did nonetheless. His brother Louis at one point gave him $3,000 and was not loathe to remind him. When Alexis died in 1897 at the age of fifty-seven, he was unmarried and divided his estate differently among his brothers. He left an extra $1,500 to Albert. The other brothers did not seem to mind, and Louis, as the apparent executor of the will, gratuitously added his two cents' worth: "This sum, as you are economical, may bide you over until you get started again. Keep it strictly for that." Louis even offered to hold the money and parcel it out to Albert as he needed it. Louis concludes with, "I will venture to say that with this $1,500 you will have far more cash than any of us and it would be amply sufficient to keep you going while working up a business." Albert was fifty-three.[29]

Alexis had died in California—where Louis was—but his ashes were to be interred in New Orleans—where Albert was. "I leave to you the drive out to cemetery, etc.," Louis wrote, but he asked Albert for some certification that the remains had been deposited and offered $50 "to pay you for your trouble as part of the expenses, not out of your share." What trouble? Burying his brother? Why was this Louis's responsibility and not Albert's? Does Louis not trust Albert to do this work, or is Louis being sensitive to Albert's constrained circumstances and trying to find a way to slip him a little extra?

Louis cannot stop himself from reminding Albert that this is not the first time that his brothers have bailed him out: "You must not again forget that you had about $3000 in cash from me aside from any portion of our parents estates."[30]

If Albert resented any of this, he did not say. If there were a family in which one might reasonably expect to find sibling rivalry, the Janins are it. Three brothers were in one occupation; three others in another. They were variously successful. Louis was the only one of the three engineers who merited an entry in the *Dictionary of American Biography*. Perhaps like other of their emotions the rivalry was just under the surface; perhaps Edward's and Henry's criticisms were little explosions of it. Perhaps, though, it did not dominate the brothers' interactions because the brothers accepted their places. Most significant here is that Louis and Alexis gave advice and Albert took it. He did not fight them. There is no evidence of Albert fighting back, retaliating, or even especially defying his brothers. He was, however, the only one of the brothers who spent little time in the West and most of his time—apart from them as well as from Violet—in New Orleans.

His "payoff" for accepting his position in the family was that he was also the affectionate center of the family. When Louis needed advice on affairs of the heart, "purely family matters," he turned to Albert, cautioning, "This *must* be private." On business matters Albert did not do so well, but on family matters he offered the wisest counsel and perhaps the warmest reception. Was this because he was the last born, the baby of the family, the baby who did less to impress but more to connect? Because he collected and saved the letters, it is fair to judge that he was the the one who kept the family members connected with each other. Albert wrote to Louis about his divorce. Albert paid attention to Henry's happiness and to Louis's "worry and anxiety." He took the family's temperature and responded.

When Louis—not unlike Violet in later years—wrote, "I shall be glad to see you at any time," or told Albert that he would be "most happy to welcome you" and "I mean what I say," it is easy to believe that he meant it.[31]

It was Albert with whom Louis discussed Henry's divorce. "In regard to his happiness of which you speak, I suppose he naturally feels mortified even incensed over the divorce, but it has given him the gratification of acting 'En Prince' of being generous to her and kind to her children to an extraordinary degree. It brought out all of his better qualities which had been for some years almost entirely submerged. The divorce absolutely unnerved him." There was not anything for either brother to do, but they did keep track and talk together about Henry's life and actions. If there was advice to be given, however, it was Louis who issued it.[32]

Albert's marriage did not fail, however peculiarly it was forged (perhaps because it was peculiarly forged). Albert and Violet never seemed to consider divorce. Laas argues that Violet felt increasingly lonely as the years passed, though Albert did not. Particularly once he settled in Kentucky, he seemed quite content and unwilling to consider setting up household with Violet.

By the standards of his day he could certainly have been considered odd and by some even to be unmanly. But he knew what he wanted and needed and sought that out. Moreover, Violet needed a husband for the sake of respectability, and Albert may have wanted the same respectability. Conforming to some of the rules and norms of society often frees one to violate others.

Certainly the reasons a man marries one woman and not another are many, and in Albert's case many of his reasons seem related to his experiences and the understanding of himself that grew out of his family life. He found a woman who suited him and who offered him a form of marriage that fit him quite well—perhaps even better than they ultimately suited her. He had his brothers to thank?

## Notes

1. I had written several drafts of a chapter about the Janin brothers before I was finally struck by the lightning bolt that Violet Janin was a Blair of the Blair families that are the subject of chapters 8 and 9 of this book. I hadn't figured this out, in part because Violet's father, James Blair, had left his family circle early and then died relatively young. His subplot then receded from prominence in the family story in the sibling letters. Similarly, because, as this chapter will explain, Violet and Albert lived so much of their married lives apart, Albert and his brothers did not write much about Violet. From the Blair family letters I did not know who Violet had married or even when. I also missed the connection because I read the Blair letters at the Library of Congress and the Janin letters at the Huntington Library—and most of Violet's papers are in Philadelphia.

The focus—and most of the research—for this chapter is on the Janin brothers; nonetheless, Violet is such a vivid character that her story keeps threatening to dominate, giving a tiny hint of what her real presence might have been like. Virginia Jeans Laas tells Violet's story, and here I'm drawing mostly on her work in *Love and Power in the Nineteenth Century.*

2. Ibid., 1–25, 91.

3. Ibid., 15.

4. Ibid., 37.

5. Ibid., 91.

6. Ibid., 119.

7. In her review of Laas's *Love and Power* Jeanette Keith draws this conclusion about Albert: "Alas, Violet's power within her marriage derived from Albert's weakness. Constantly broke, sponging on Violet's family and his own, continually involved in foolish get-rich schemes, Albert barely escaped disgrace." See H-Net Reviews in the Humanities and Social Sciences at <http://www.h-net.msu/reviews>.

8. Some information about the family appears in the Louis Janin entry in the *Dictionary of American Biography,* vol. 9, 608–9. The engineer brothers make appearances as well in Spence, *Mining Engineers.* The Janin family letters are located at the Huntington Library, San Marino, Calif.

9. After a generation of studies about gender role definitions for women and of many excellent studies about women's lives and relationships, books have begun to appear about men as men, as people who inhabit a prescribed, socially defined space. Presaging this work was Peter Filene's *Him/Her/Self* and Joe L. Dubbert, *A Man's Place.* The best of the more recent work is Rotundo, *American Manhood.* See also Carnes and Griffen, *Meanings for Manhood,* and Carnes, *Secret Ritual and Manhood,* as well as Tosh, *Man's Place.*

10. Spence, *Mining Engineers,* 14, 60–61.

11. Why the other Janin brothers did not enter the Confederate Army—or how they escaped it—is a puzzle. See the entry for Louis Janin, *Dictionary of American Biography,* vol. 9, 608–9, and Laas, *Love and Power,* 28, 29, 39.

12. Laas, *Love and Power,* 18.

13. Spence, *Mining Engineers,* 104.

14. Peter Stearns argues that a Victorian emotional style was replaced in the twentieth century by one more "consistently cautious where emotion was concerned." "Victorians," he goes on, "valued emotions as motivators, as the sources of energy in work and politics and as a crucial cement for family life." The style that replaced it "urged overall restraint as part of the need to present a pleasing, unobtrusive front to others. Emotions were recognized as inevitable but were seen as more risky than useful. . . . The departure from Victorian fervor was considerable." This shift may have occurred, but the Janins' cool style was contemporary with the more heated family dynamics of the Putnams and Blairs. This suggests that in this case the coolness is not best explained by chronology. See Stearns, *American Cool,* 300–1.

15. Entry for Louis Janin, *Dictionary of American Biography,* vol. 9, 609.

16. Louis Janin to Albert Janin, Dec. 4, 1889. For another example of a "cool" letter see Louis Janin to Albert Janin, Dec. 24, 1889, in which Louis asks for details of their mother's funeral and "other facts of interest."

17. Myra Arthur to "Fannie," March 29, 1898, Arthur Family Papers, Library of Congress.

18. Alexis Janin to Albert Janin, Dec. 16, 1895.

19. Henry Janin to Albert Janin, Nov. 13 [1900]; Louis Janin to Albert Janin, Jan. 19, 1905.

20. Henry Janin to Albert Janin, Jan. 28 and Feb. 3, 1892.

21. Louis Janin to Albert Janin, March 13, 1900.

22. Laas, *Love and Power*, 71–75.

23. Alexis Janin to Henry Janin, Nov. 5, 1873, and March 12, 1874.

24. Louis Janin to Albert Janin, Nov. 27, 1907, Jan. 19, 1905, and an undated letter in Box 21 that appears to have been written in 1912.

25. Louis Janin to Albert Janin, Sept. 21 [1906], and Jan. 29, 1911.

26. Henry Janin to Louis Janin, May 23, 1902.

27. Henry Janin to Albert Janin, Aug. 24, 1910, and July 2, 1902; Henry Janin to Louis Janin, May 23, 1902.

28. Mary's brothers picked strong women for their partners; Nell's brother picked Myra, who was certainly a quite warm and emotionally expressive woman.

29. Louis Janin to Albert Janin, Jan 10, 1897.

30. Louis Janin to Albert Janin, Feb. 15, 1897.

31. Louis Janin to Albert Janin, Sept. 21 [1906 or 1907], and March 13, 1900.

32. Louis Janin to Albert Janin, Jan. 19, 1905.

# FIVE

# The Channings: A Warm Family

In 1893 Hal Channing wrote to his older sister Grace: "What a novel our family history could furnish first and last? Why don't you do as C. Bronte did and base your novels on different parts of the family history. Theres plenty of material." Hal had a point. His family weathered lots of dramas—both before and after he he wrote this letter.[1]

Relationships between adult siblings come in various types. Psychologists have identified five major ones: intimate, congenial, loyal, apathetic, and hostile. On this scale the Putnams, Arthurs, and Janins all fall somewhere between loyal and congenial (with a little apathy around the edges). The Channings, however, show us a more intimate family, what I call a warm family.[2]

*Warm* does not mean more loving, nor does it mean without conflict. I do mean more expressive and interactive and, with that, more expressively conflictual as well. Getting along in some families means never exchanging any strong emotions; getting along among the Channings meant often expressing strong emotions. Among themselves they developed strong bonds that helped them weather the storms of their adulthood. In their times of trouble they turned to each other, not away. The Channings were that kind of intimate family.

In addition, the Channings were a family of many divorces. Divorce is not a particular sibling issue, but so many of them in one family is remarkable. Their father had divorced his first wife, one sister was divorced, another married a divorced man (and sheltered his divorcing wife), and a daughter also divorced. It was a fact of their family life, part of their

*The Channings*
William Francis Channing (1820–1901)
m. [?]        Susan Burdick
div. 1859
m. 1859    Mary Tarr
                Mary (Molly) (1860–1934)
                        m. [1880]   Charles Saunders
                                            two children
                        div. 1899
                        m. 1900        Clarence Wood
                Grace (Gay) (1862–1938)
                        m. 1894      Walter Stetson
                                            one stepchild
                Harold (Hal) (1869–1946)

family culture, and important in their family story. Divorce certainly would have been a theme in the novel that Hal proposed.

This is especially striking because in the popular imagination today divorce is a disease of the late twentieth century. We look at the current divorce rate against an idea of the past where people simply did not get divorced. We wonder what is wrong with us that we can't stay married—people in the past did. But people around and including the Channings certainly did divorce, and when they did they found support and understanding among the Channings—whatever the attitudes about divorce outside their family. Either they were modern or the traditional family was different than we imagine. I think it was the latter.[3]

Mary Channing—nicknamed Molly—was the oldest child, born in 1860. She married Charles Saunders when she was twenty, and they had two children, Dorothy and Ellery. Molly's marriage to Charles ended in divorce after nine years. It was a bitter divorce, including especially battles over the care of the children. Soon after her divorce Molly married Clarence Wood, a long-time family friend. He helped raise her children, and they took his last name. Molly, who had grown up in the East, lived most of her life in California and was the first of the siblings to die (1934).

Grace, the middle sibling—nicknamed Gay—was born in 1862. She lived a more public life than her sister and her brother. She wrote essays, short stories, and poetry that appeared in such magazines as *Harper's*, the *Atlantic Monthly,* and the *Saturday Evening Post*. She published two collections of short stories and one of poetry and coauthored several plays with Charlotte Stetson (later Perkins Gilman), who would become a leading theorist of the women's movement. For a time Grace Channing served as a European war correspondent. When she was thirty-two she married artist Walter Stetson, who was recently divorced from her friend Charlotte. Grace continued to write and publish throughout her life. After living on the East Coast and then in Pasadena, Grace and Walter spent many years in Italy (it was less expensive, they said, than the United States). Grace and Walter raised Katherine, his and Charlotte's daughter. Katherine considered Grace her co-mother. Grace and Walter had no other children.

Hal, formally Harold, was the only brother and the youngest sibling, born in 1869. He never married, nor did he commit himself to a career or even to a place until relatively late in his life. He was institutionalized several times—alcoholism and mental illness—and simply dropped out of sight at other times. From his earliest years he showed an interest in and affection for flowers and settled eventually into work as a gardener in Pasadena, California. He lived for long periods of time with his parents and his sisters.

Their father, William Francis Channing, was trained as a doctor but never practiced medicine, preferring instead to invent things and to write about his inventions. His speciality was electricity and his publications included articles such as "On the Municipal Electric Telegraph." By the time the children were born, he and his wife were living in Rhode Island—though they had come from Boston—and as the children grew up, the family lived variously in Rhode Island, New York, Washington, D.C., Seattle, Pasadena, and Europe. They did not number themselves among the well-to-do in the United States; they were, however, better off than many as well as better educated and better connected than most. Only Molly had money to speak of—enough at least to make loans to Grace and Hal, both of whom lived for long stretches on the edge of financial chaos. At the end of her life Grace was selling off Walter's paintings simply to pay for storage, though the market in Stetson paintings had virtually disappeared.[4]

In intimate families members know each other's struggles, their interior lives. Each of the Channings faced at least one significant struggle, and they played out these difficulties in part in their letters to each other. Their letters tell their secrets—to each other then and to us now.

The first of the Channing struggles centered on Grace and lasted at a high pitch for at least four years. In 1885 Charlotte Perkins Stetson, a childhood friend of the Channings from Rhode Island, visited the Channings in California. Charlotte, then twenty-five, and Grace, twenty-three, had much in common. They each had ambitions to write, to make their mark on the world, to change it if they could. Over the next several years Charlotte and Grace wrote two plays together, coproduced two others, and read and encouraged each other in their separate writings and their social critiques. In 1887 twenty-four-year-old Grace went East to visit Charlotte, to write with her, and to offer her friendship as Charlotte struggled with her marriage.

Charlotte had married the artist Walter Stetson in 1884, had her only child, Katherine, in 1885, and almost immediately had found herself miserable. She felt "her whole usefulness & real life was crushed out of her" and came to feel that she was a "useless and a wasted soul." It was not that she had found the wrong husband but that the institution itself was impossible for her. As Charlotte Perkins Gilman, she published *The Yellow Wallpaper*, a chilling novella about a wife and mother imprisoned in her roles and slowly, certainly, going mad. Her account mirrored her feelings about her marriage but did not match her actual experiences because she—unlike her central character—had a friend, Grace Channing, who offered solace, support, and a new life.[5]

When Charlotte decided in 1888 to leave her marriage, she accepted an invitation from Grace to settle in the Channing household in Pasadena, California. Because Charlotte identified the institution of marriage—not her husband—as the enemy, they remained friendly through the separation and subsequent divorce, though Walter resisted. He followed her to California to be near to their daughter and to attempt a reconciliation. By this time Charlotte and Katherine had moved into their own little house, and Grace invited Walter to move into the Channing household. He did, for a year.

When Charlotte arrived in California feeling that she could not stay married, she found a comforting nest among the Channings. Divorce was not new to Grace or her family. Her father, William Francis Channing, was married for a time to a Susan Burdick. They divorced in 1859 and he married Mary Tarr—the mother of Molly, Gay, and Hal—four months later.

Moreover, the Channings' religious beliefs fostered an openness to Charlotte's social critique of marriage. William Ellery Channing, the Channings' grandfather, had founded the American branch of Unitarianism, a theology that advocated free thought and that stressed the au-

thority of the individual conscience, the reliability of reason as a basis
for making a decision, and the obligation to reform social injustice. According to one biographer, he "committed what, in the eyes of his critics, was the unpardonable sin of doing his own thinking"—a tradition
the Channings carried on and from which they could offer support to
Charlotte. By the family standards Charlotte was behaving both moral-
ly and responsibly.[6]

As Charlotte and Walter moved toward divorce within the protective circle of the Channings, Grace and Walter moved toward each other, perhaps within a protective circle created by Charlotte. Charlotte
approved, even encouraged, the relationship. What better solution she
might have thought: to leave her husband in her friend's hands—thus
diminishing his pain and her own guilt. In fact, she had more concern
about losing Grace than about losing Walter. In 1890 the couple agreed
to a "no blame" divorce, and by 1893 Grace and Walter had agreed that
their "best life meant living together." In 1894, when she was thirty-two
years old, Grace married Walter Stetson. Walter and Charlotte's daughter, Katherine, came to think of Grace as her second mother, and Grace
and Charlotte remained lifelong friends.[7]

One aspect of divorce that has changed dramatically is the legal one.
Walter and Charlotte may have agreed to "no blame," but in the nineteenth century, the law made no provision for what we have come to call
"no fault" divorce. Divorcing partners had to show cause, provide
grounds. Adultery, insanity, and desertion were almost the only grounds
considered legitimate. For six years Walter and Charlotte tried to obtain
a divorce in different courts, in different states, claiming different
grounds. If these years proved difficult for Walter and Charlotte, they
were excruciating for Grace. For six years Grace waited. She cooperated
where she could—including going to Europe for a time to deflect accusations of adultery. The divorce laws drew her into emotional and moral
contortions. At one point, decrying the "three year falsehood" that the
law had forced on them (lying about desertions and making claims about
Walter's marital rights' being violated), Grace wrote that she should simply "have taken up the beautiful title of his Mistress and done my utmost
to bear it beautifully."[8]

Her family's main reaction was support, sympathy, and encouragement. "You can always depend on me to uphold you as long as you do
what your conscience dictates," Hal wrote. On another occasion he
urged: "Never be ashamed or act ashamed of what you believe in." Molly

wrote similarly, "You need never doubt that I believe in you" and reassured her that "the same blood flows in our veins." In these sentiments they echoed their father, who reminded Grace of "the fullness of my love and sympathy. I will try to help you in all possible ways & to sustain you to the utmost."[9]

Grace sent them in return "boundless love." She missed them "more than there are words in my English and Italian languages to say!" She wrote too that "it would be impossible to say how my heart yearns for you all at times." Grace told Hal: "Were we together there is nothing we would not talk of nothing we would not be to one another. Be sure of *that* and some day we shall be together again."

Grace's family included Walter in their expressions of support and affection as well. Hal wrote to Walter: "You may always consider me as a friend to come to for support." Grace's father reassured Walter of "the sincerity of my sympathy with you."[10]

They did not, however, want her to cause scandal. Within the family circle and to her individually they could be and were deeply supportive. When her behavior threatened the family, they did not withdraw their support, but they did not hold their tongues, either. When the divorce and therefore a legal marriage looked impossible because of the legal hurdles, Grace and Walter thought simply to live together. Molly reacted most quickly and strongly—and lived to rue her response. "For however willing any one of us—or any two of us—may be—to suffer martyrdom for what we conceive to be right," Molly wrote to Grace, "it is impossible to forget that we cannot suffer alone . . . and that others who have not any of the sustaining happiness must suffer also." She was not concerned for herself, she protested, but for her children. Couldn't you, Molly wrote, "spare us what suffering you can?"

As Molly explained her position to Walter, she feared that Grace's "exaltation & enthusiasm for the principle" would lead her to forget about others and that as a man who has "practical knowledge of life— you realize far better than Grace (who does not realize it at all) that the future would be harder for her than for you if the legal barrier is not removed & that that is a hard fact for us to consider."[11]

Hal too reminded Grace that she did not act in isolation from the rest of them. Do what you will, he wrote, "And it wont be without some hardship to me, as I think right to tell you, not because I care a fig for that where principle is concerned, but because I believe it right that one should know and realize the effect of his (or her) actions upon others, so that one can weigh the compensations against the losses and judge of the worth of the results."[12]

Grace must have felt that she was being abandoned by her family. Molly's and Hal's letters said essentially the same thing. Molly's was longer and more vehement and perhaps stung more, so both Grace and Walter reacted to it strongly and angrily. Walter felt that Molly was urging them to abandon their principles, and Grace felt a violation of their family bonds. Molly responded to them in separate letters. To Walter she wrote that he had "cruelly misjudged" her and was "wholly wrong" in his understanding of her motives. "I too . . . am my father's daughter," she continued, "and am not as poorly supplied with the principles and conscience as you may suppose." She also reminded him of the Channing family philosophy: "I am sure that Grace knows—tho' you do not—that it would be impossible for me to do anything *but* stand by her."

The impossibility of doing anything other than standing by her came through even more strongly in Molly's letter to Grace on the same day. That letter is an outpouring of apology, explanation, love, ragged emotion. Molly called herself a fool and her letter "ill judged." "Dear girl," she wrote, "I want to show my real heart to you," and it was full of turmoil, not all of which she could put on paper. Their mother had urged Molly not to write, but "we shall know each other better if we are frank & honest. We are not obliged to agree—but we will be true." Molly did open her heart. "You even do not know how entirely I sympathize with you." That construction of "you even" presumes that if Grace did not know, no one did, so Molly was showing herself to the person closest to her—closer even than her own husband. "I fairly starve for congenial and sympathetic intercourse," Molly concluded. Interestingly, she did not, however, apologize for anything she had said, only tried to say it in a way that would elicit Grace's understanding.[13]

Because Molly and Hal agreed and because Grace had not taken offense with Hal, Molly also wrote to Hal and asked him to intercede on her behalf with their sister. He did. He reassured Grace not only that he would stand by her no matter but that Molly would also not abandon her. He tried to mediate by pointing out the error on each side. "Molly wrote in her bungling and intense way & made the letter express . . . what she didn't intend it should." He also tried to calm Grace by pointing out that "your taking it in such a way shows how high-strung your nerves are and how unwell you really are."[14]

The divorce did finally come through. Grace and Walter were married, and the family never needed to cope with a scandal. Would she have brought it down on them? We do not know. We do know that as she struggled through the matter of Charlotte and Walter's divorce, her ties to her family were strained but not broken, and certainly they sustained her through several very difficult years.[15]

Molly and Hal were right—Grace's actions did have an effect beyond herself. "Private rumors," Grace's father reported to Walter—but not to Grace—"have done something to isolate [Grace's] mother socially," an acknowledgment that just outside the Channing fortress, ideas and attitudes were different. The historian Glenda Riley is right that divorce is an American tradition but not one approved of generally and certainly not in 1893. The Channings, however, held their own in the midst of that disapproval and never once disapproved of Grace's marrying a divorced man or, next, of Molly's getting a divorce.[16]

Grace's struggle may have given Molly the courage to act on her own marriage. In the course of their exchanges about Grace's life Molly had confided her own unhappiness. "You cannot abhor conventional marriage more than I," she wrote, "I doubt if you can as much!" Talking about "sexual harmony," she declared "I very keenly comprehend all that is lost to life where that is not present." She concluded with, "Dear I think the most terrible thing is to live with one you have loved & can no longer respect!" This is a woman speaking from experience, as she adds toward the end of her letter: "I also assure you that you can not have arrived at much broader convictions than I. . . . You have the advantage of having Walter so wholly in rapport—& I hope you can & do properly appreciate your blessing in this respect."

Molly's marriage had been in trouble and, though Grace might have been preoccupied with her own affairs, at least Hal knew. "I have known of the critical state of affairs for a long time," he wrote to Grace. Both Hal and Grace helped Molly as best as they could. Hal helped her find a place to live. Grace took in Molly's daughter Dorothy (Dot), who was then about eight, for a period of several months. It had taken Charlotte and Walter six years to divorce; it also took Molly that long. Molly's divorce elicited little of the familial agony that Grace's had, however, because Molly was not involved with another person and because the only scandal that could attach to it was the kind that the Channings could countenance and did. It was only a divorce, after all. They knew about divorces.[17]

Grace's struggle passed and then Molly's settled. Hal's was of longer duration and more pathetic. Unlike Grace and Molly, Hal, the baby of the family, had difficulty finding his path and making his way. In his twenties and thirties he lived with his parents, then with Molly and her husband—no wonder he knew about the troubles in their marriage—and was often unemployed and slow to settle down. He did not marry at all. While he was in his twenties, Grace urged him to make a move: "The time has come when I feel that I must tell you that to stay one day longer . . . is to lay a very heavy burden upon Mama, to expose you to the just criticism of the Woods and the Saunders etc. and to hurt very much my pride in you. You can't afford it beloved!" But what was he to do? He did not know. So he wandered.

From 1905 to 1910 he was in only occasional contact with either of his sisters until he was institutionalized. During this time he asked Grace to "make allowances for my poor nerves" and asked Molly, "Don't judge too harshly til you know all."

During those five years we see his life as his sisters must have: only in fragments. He sent one note "just to tell you I am alive." He was sick and "in desperate trouble" but asked Grace not to look for him: "I shall either make good by Jan. 1908 or be out of all trouble." Six months later he sent another note "just to let you know I'm alive & kicking." By way of explanation he could only say that he was "working out my salvation." Or, more poignantly, "It has been no use to write as I was so blue & discouraged."[18]

Unlike the Janins, Hal grew up with two sisters and he spoke much as they did. He wrote of his sadness, grief, loneliness, and pain. About Grace and Walter's struggles of some years before, he wrote that he sorrowed for them "as if it were myself" but admitted he envied their relationship, for "I have nothing." He could also tell them of his continuing grief at the death of their father in 1901. "My greatest pleasure was in the pleasure our father took in all I did & it was to me a blow of lasting power when he died & took much out of my life. He and I had come closer together in the last few years." This litany of sorrows betrays Hal's depression, his sense of isolation, and his self-pity, and his life got more desperate before he got better.[19]

He was also the youngest sibling. His sisters took seriously their responsibilities to help and advise him. He felt always that he had to prove himself, especially to Molly, and that he never quite succeeded. When he had trouble with Molly, he turned to Grace for sympathy, intervention, understanding.

In 1905 he and Molly, he confided to Grace, "misunderstand each other," and while he tried to "read her letters aright," he treated her silence as abandonment and declared "so be it—it is only one more disaster." Three years later Hal and Molly had an especially pointed difference to which Hal responded angrily, telling Grace: "I got a line from Molly which has fairly made me ill." After some fracas with a creditor that was reported to Molly, he declared, "I finally wrote M. that as she had believed it in its entirety she would have to retract by May 18th or never write me again and I absolutely mean it." Here we get a sense of the history of Hal's problem: "I will not be judged without a hearing as I neither use tobacco or drink anything stronger than coffee nor have for quite a number of weeks." "Weeks" might not have been long enough to prove anything if drink really was his problem. Whatever their family relations, he declared, "No one shall be given the privilege to write me as she has."[20]

His silence and his roaming worried his sisters enormously. Molly wrote to Grace that she was troubled about Hal's confusion and his memory as well as about what she thought were unrealistic expectations and beliefs. She wondered in mid-1910 if "the psychologic moment is at hand when Harold can be induced to go to some institution for treatment." Her concern seems to have been well founded. Six months later she received word of his "'serious mental state,'" which she did not know how to interpret (did it mean "violence, hallucinations or what"?), and the time clearly had come for institutionalization. The only question was where. Hal was in Seattle when he had his breakdown, or "episode," and it was Molly's ex-husband, Charles, who sent news of Hal's trouble. After Hal was institutionalized, Charles continued to be closely involved. He took him his mail, supplies, and clothing. He reported to Molly about Hal.[21]

Molly made temporary arrangements but wanted to hear from Grace before she did anything final. She wanted Grace's advice. They also wanted to involve Hal in decisions about his care. "Yes, I think it will be well that he should know what the doctors think the result of another attack would be," Molly wrote to Grace. The yes at the beginning suggests that Molly is answering and agreeing with an opinion expressed by Grace. Molly continued: "A frank & free discussion of his case with him is *far* the best plan, enlisting his cooperation & assuming his power to assist himself." This plan did not seem to work entirely, or at least Hal resented Molly's attitude: "Molly's whole attitude has been that I'm no more able to take care of myself than a child which is maddening."

By contrast, Hal credited Grace with supporting him: "If you had failed me, I should have given out entirely I think, but now there's new life in me."[22]

The sense of shared responsibility for each other characterized these three throughout their lives. Money was one way that they helped each other—with mixed results. Grace seemed chronically short of money, during Walter Stetson's lifetime and after. She turned to Molly and Clarence for loans, which they gave her in 1899 and 1903—neither of which was repaid by 1906 when Clarence wrote to ask Grace to sign a note for each one. "I have been left so often by members of my immediate family," he wrote, "that you will pardon my skepticism as to good intentions unless in writing and legally drawn." He apologized for the "very hard business sound" of the letter but nonetheless did not soften it. Twenty years later Clarence was still after Grace to pay up, and the tone of his entreaties had changed considerably. He wrote, "We are unwilling to be your bankers any longer" unless she would go to California "and stay with your people." He complained that "you never have been frank with us. You never have told us what your business was. . . . We know nothing of your life." Then, in almost exact repetition of himself on page 2, he wrote, "We never have known anything of your activities" and "I have never had any information, I know nothing of your business." He offers, then, to pay her way to California and then one year's support. Note that it was not her failure to repay the loans so much as her not confiding in him that rankled and that provoked his ire in this case.[23]

Clarence's letter brought a swift near-apology from Molly. Molly clearly resented Clarence's treatment of her sister. "I had a talk with him about the letters," Molly wrote Grace, "and he swears he totally forgot he had promised me never to write business letters to you or any of my family without letting me know, for he gets things all mixed & is very inaccurate &c. And now he cannot understand why you or *I* should feel that his letters were so wholly unpardonable." The loans, Molly attested, were hers, in any case. "He seems *temporarily*—at least—to have grasped the fact that it is I [underlined three times] & not *he* who has been trying to help you for many years." Molly did not ask for or expect this kind of accounting from her sister. Grace needed money. Molly loaned it. Clarence had no business getting involved. But he apparently stayed involved, even though Grace rejected his offer of support for a year (and the implicit threat of a cut-off thereafter). In 1931—when she was nearly seventy—Grace asked Hal for a loan: "Would you feel able, without causing yourself *any* anxiety, to lend me even up to five hundred dollars, if I should want so much." She hoped, in fact, to repay something to Clarence out of this money: "Just at present C. is extremely friendly. I want to give him every reason to stay so."[24]

Grace and Hal also helped Clarence and Molly. When their son, Ellery, in 1916 wanted to "contribute his services in this epochal struggle" (a reference to World War I), they asked Grace, who was then living in Italy, to find him a position in France. "We would wish that he could come while you were over there and that you might be together." He did. Hal also took an interest in Clarence's family, particularly his brother John, who seems also to have lived in Pasadena. When John was failing in 1933, Hal wrote to inform Clarence and to give him the particulars. Clearly, although Clarence is handling John's finances (as he had earlier complained about), Hal is in closer touch with John than is his brother.[25]

Enough help and love passed among all three siblings that their commitment to each other is apparent. Grace and Hal, however, demonstrate a kind of closeness with each other that is different from what they feel with Molly. When Hal threatened to break off relations with Molly, he wrote to Grace and told her. When Grace felt similarly, she wrote to Hal:

> I have just passed through a fresh experience of the kind of strain involved in dealing with them [Molly and Clarence] even at second hand, and I assure you—I feel *older*. Because it saddens one so. They don't mean the things they do and say—but they are just as deadly in effect, After awhile I feel like closing all correspondence. Which would be inhuman, One must just bear patiently, and wait till the mood passes. But it is not a thing to expose one's self to extensively: bad for both parties. And you know how kind they have been the past year or two, and how well they mean.[26]

This is the loving, resenting, going back and forth of intimate sibling relations. When Grace was sixty-seven and Hal sixty, Grace wrote to him again to complain about their sister, this time about Molly's crediting Hal with being the only one writing letters, a statement that Grace labels "about as grotesquely unfair a statement as our erratic and beloved sister has yet indulged in. If there is one thing I ha[v]e earned a heavenly crown in doing, it should be in writing he[r] letters. Millions of them— always two or three a week." This complaining/annoyed defense lasts nearly a full typed page and concludes: "None of this will you repeat: we'll never let her know, but really—it is to laugh! I bet I write her three letters to your one! But such is life. And it does not alter the fact that you are a splendid letter-writer and that we do all appreciate it. I am specially glad she does." On the envelope that contained this letter Hal noted the letter's contents: "about my good letter writing." (That's one way of identifying it, I suppose.)[27]

Throughout their lives there is evidence of their special closeness. When Walter Stetson died in 1911, Hal wrote Grace: "I shall not write more as you will know how my heart aches for you & Katharine," and "I can say nothing that will adequately express my feelings, but you will know." Grace wrote to Hal, "I have you always in mind." As she was preparing to return from Italy, Grace wrote to Hal to give him her plans, including having "a good talk with Molly . . . about one or two things I have in mind." Then, after spending Christmas on her own—still in grief and mourning Walter's death—she would meet him "soon to be near you and *with* you." Grace felt a similar oneness with Hal, as she demonstrated when she wrote: "Your sympathetic heart will need no explanation—and can understand."[28]

They each complained to the other—about Molly, about Clarence. Grace told Hal: "Now Molly, thoroughly disgusted with me, I gather,—though I don't know for what." And, about Clarence, "Clarence has to know and follow every detail: he would have suggestions for you and want information, and question every step,—not meaning to be anything but properly 'businesslike,' and it would wear you—or most people—to tatters." They worried together about their now-grown niece and nephew. She grieved with him for Molly's children—Ellery, "that boy of ours," as she called her nearly fifty-year-old nephew, was turning bad, and Dorothy, the older of the two, was "slipping away into a world of her own." Oh, what sadness, "but you and I have rather a tough spot, in seeing our family, the last of it, so far from all the standards it was our happy privilege to be reared in."[29]

Grace also intervened between Molly and Hal. When Hal had not heard from Molly for some time—numbered in days, not weeks or months—and had therefore not received from her money that he had come to depend upon, Grace gave excuses for Molly and sent him some money beside. In the same letter she reassured him: "Be sure I do not forget you,—and my tired brain and heart have still space to remember all I love." She also mediated between Molly and Hal by passing on Molly's compliments about Hal: "She writes that you have 'been a perfect jewel.' . . . That should please you."[30]

Hal and Grace bonded ever more deeply in their later years. "Memories are a large part of our lives—yours and min[e]—are they not? Even Molly's too, in spite of the fact that she is surrounded by the immediate stimuli of family. Oddly enough—she sometimes seems the hungriest of us three, constantly crying out for 'news', for letters, for all sorts of things that one would think she would have little need of, little time to miss in a family of her own. But so it is," Grace told Hal. About a play that she was going to see, she told him: "Wish you could see this with me. I often wish we could see things together." When she asked Hal for a loan, she wrote, "It is pleasant to be conspiring with you." And in 1931 Grace wrote explicitly to Hal: "I love you." This had been clear for years but not previously expressed on paper. For his part Hal sent, "As always a whole galactic world of love to you from your loving brother." At seventy-four Grace wrote to the sixty-seven-year-old Hal: "You are so very much in my mind" and "I beg[i]n to think you need your sister at hand to look after you."[31]

Throughout their lives the two sisters had stayed close to each other and as close to Hal as he would allow. Their love for each other is still powerful and powerfully evident in their later years. When Molly was sick in 1927, Grace wrote to Hal, "We should all be desolate without Molly." So, Grace declared, "I have made up my mind she *has* to live, and if only I had nothing to do but devote myself to her I feel as if I could *make* her live."

And Grace did take more and more care of Molly—physical and emotional—including explaining her and protecting her. Regarding some financial issues where Molly said she would do something but apparently did not, Grace wrote: "She has been, but *don't* speak of it to her, under some special strains, and it has taken a good deal out of her" and "Thus, you see, life is made more complicated than need be, but we mustn't let M. feel it, for she is bearing all she really can." One form of care Grace took—since financial was out of the question, of course—was writing letters to Molly. She reported to Hal that she wrote "everything I can think of to interest her, just because I know how starved her life is, and she so appreciates the letters." Oh, how Grace grieved not to have such letters to write after Molly died. Noting Molly's birthday, Grace wrote, "You don't know how I miss her. The habit of constant communication, which I had kept up so long,—the endless letters,—all the daily thoughts and fears about her—it is very hard to shake off quickly, or rather, to realize that all have come to an end"—which it did in 1934 when Molly died. Grace died four years later. Hal was on his own.[32]

What a family of passions, loves, connections, and so much so evident. Perhaps the Janins felt things as poignantly as did the Channings, but if they did, they did not show it to each other or to us in their letters. Where the Janins' letters generally ran not quite a page in length, the Channings' letters regularly covered front and back of page after page. Three to five was hardly unusual. They had much to talk about with each other, and the paper could hardly contain it.

When Hal spoke about the novelistic possibilities in his family's stories, he was not speaking as a public figure used to public scrutiny but as a man reflecting on the drama of his family's intimate life. It was a life lived in much close contact and one that generated and radiated warmth.

*Notes*

1. Harold Channing to Grace Channing Stetson, August 10, 1893, Grace Ellery (Channing) Stetson Papers, Schlesinger Library, Cambridge, Massachusetts. See the preliminary inventory (1985), prepared by Adelaide M. Kennedy, Jane S. Knowles, and Lucy Thomas, "Grace Ellery (Channing) Stetson, 1862–1937," with the Stetson papers.

2. The research on these five family types estimates percentages in each category: intimate, 14 percent; loyal, 30 percent; congenial, 34 percent; apathetic, 11 percent; hostile, 11 percent. As Victor Cicirelli himself points out, such typologies have many problems. They slot individuals by family without taking account of variations within one family. In my own large family our relationships with each other probably include all five—I'm intimate or loyal or congenial depending on which of my siblings I'm relating to. What's notable about the Channings, however, is that all three seem to have been intimate with each other, even though for a time Hal withdrew from much contact with his sisters. See Cicirelli, *Sibling Relationships Across the Lifespan*, 59–60.

3. In the current despair about the decline of the family, rising divorce rates figure centrally. There is not a simple straight line from no divorces then to many now. As the historian Glenda Riley has documented, divorce has been a part of the American experience, allowed in law and present in fact throughout the American past.

The rate of divorce has increased, but other changes must be factored in if we're to understand why. Changed expectations about marriage, happiness, and personal satisfaction have had a powerful effect. So too have changes in the law and the lowering of the legal hurdles to divorce. In addition, life expectancy has risen slightly faster even than the divorce rate. More people are living longer, so marriages can last longer. It may be that divorce is serving the function that death did in the nineteenth century when people died earlier.

The other change is a formalization of divorce in the present. Many a nineteenth-century marriage was ended with a divorce "by foot": desertion. How many of those nineteenth-century pioneers were husbands on the run? Some, for sure. In Minnesota at the time of World War I, the state registered all "aliens," foreign-born residents who had not been naturalized. Their registrations tell tales of marriages stretched pretty thin, of husbands long away. In 1917, for example, Andrew Anderson reported that he had arrived in the United States in 1911 while his wife, Hilda, remained in Sweden. Similarly, George Andreikuk had left his wife in Russia for the three years since he had come to America, and Juho Otto Hakkarainen had been in Minnesota for five years while his wife and their three children remained in Finland. Each reported that he planned to return to his home, but such a long separation might well have felt like divorce (or may have staved off a divorce).

See Riley, *Divorce,* and *Building and Breaking Families;* Griswold, *Family and Divorce in California;* May, *Great Expectations;* and Shorter, *Making of the Modern Family.*

See also Minnesota Commission, "Alien Registration and Declaration of Holdings," and Peavey and Smith, *Women in Waiting.*

4. See the entry for William Francis Channing in the *Dictionary of American Biography,* vol. 4, pp. 8–9. See also Hill, *Endure,* 279. Charlotte Perkins Gilman turned her pain into several remarkable books. In addition to *The Yellow Wallpaper,* she published *Herland,* a utopian novel about a society of women, and *Women and Economics.* The last was a study that, among other things, proposed joint kitchens so women could share the company and work of cooking meals. In her marriage and in her writings she chafed at conventional marriage, and she tried to invent alternative forms of marriage that would diminish women's subjugation.

Part of Grace's story is so interconnected with that of Charlotte Perkins (Stetson) Gilman that Grace shows up as a major character in Gilman biographies. The best of these is Lane, *To Herland and Beyond.* See also Buhle, "Charlotte Perkins Gilman," and Scarnhorst, *Charlotte Perkins Gilman.*

In his diaries Walter Stetson often quoted from and paraphrased Charlotte's letters. They also show us some of his own pain, in a collection aptly, if heartbreakingly, entitled *Endure* (Hill, *Endure*). See also Hill, *Journey from Within.*

Gilman herself gives Grace short shrift in her autobiography, mentioning her only twice—once as her good friend who married Walter and once as the stepmother of Gilman and Stetson's daughter, Katherine (Gilman, *Living of Charlotte Perkins Gilman,* 162, 167).

5. William Francis Channing entry, *Dictionary of American Biography.*

6. Lane, *To Herland and Beyond,* esp. 137–55 and 307–27.

7. Grace Channing to "My dear People [father and mother and Hal]," Jan. 1, 1893. See also Lane, *To Herland and Beyond,* esp. 137–55 and 307–27, and Gilman, *The Living of Charlotte Perkins Gilman,* 142, 167.

8. Hal Channing to Walter Stetson, Feb. 26, 1893, and Hal Channing to Grace Channing, Feb. 19, 1893; Molly Saunders to Grace Channing, March 28, 1893; William Channing to Grace Channing, March 2, 1893.

9. Grace Channing to "My dear People," Jan. 1, 1893; Grace Channing to Hal Channing, Dec. 29, 1890, and July 1 [1893]; Hal Channing to Walter Stetson, Feb. 26, 1893; William Channing to Walter Stetson, Feb. 18, 1893.

10. Molly Saunders to Walter Stetson, March 12, 1893.

11. Hal Channing to Grace Channing, Feb. 19, 1893.

12. Molly Saunders to Walter Stetson, March 28, 1893; Molly Saunders to Grace Channing, March 28, 1893.

13. Hal Channing to Grace Channing, April 18, 1893.

14. Grace's parents also had opinions about her course. William Channing had offered her boundless love and support in her decision to marry Walter. He did object, however, to her threat to live "in open disregard of the current marriage law," reminding her that adultery was punishable in most states by imprisonment. Moreover, both social and religious interests would "unite strenuously in resisting any invasion of the marriage system" and "the *animus* against public offenders in this direction is bitter & malignant." He had a fatherly duty to her to caution her, which he did. He also reminded Grace and Walter that it was "absurd that we should be even in appearance, at cross purposes." They were not.

Mama was a shadowy figure but a strong presence in this story. She was not, Hal reported to Walter, "as progressive in some ways as I used to think her [and] cannot see the wisdom of your & Grace's proposed course." After another of the attempts at divorce failed, Hal reported to Walter that "the consequences of the laws atrocity in refusing justice to you will come especially hard upon my mother." Nonetheless, when Grace and Walter finally married, Molly wrote: "I don't believe you can realize how glad Mamma was to hear of it." (William Channing to Grace Channing, Oct. 10, 1893; William Channing to Walter Stetson, Feb. 18, 1893; Hal Channing to Walter Stetson, Feb. 26, 1893; Molly Saunders to Grace Stetson, June 17, 1894).

15. William Channing to Walter Stetson, Feb. 18, 1893.

16. Molly Saunders to Grace Channing, March 28, 1893; Hal Channing to Grace Channing, Aug. 10, 1893.

Grace's care for Molly's daughter, Dorothy (Dot), occasioned a letter from Dot's father, who worried that he would lose his children. He feared that Dot—like her brother, Ellery—would be "completely weaned" away from him by their mother. He feared that "no effort will be spared" in trying to separate Dot from him. He was right to be concerned, apparently. Both children were eventually adopted by their stepfather and took his name. See Charles Saunders to Grace Stetson, April 29, 1900.

17. Grace Channing to Hal Channing, Aug. 12, 1891; Hal Channing to Grace Stetson, May 12, 1905, May 27 and Nov. 27, 1907, and March 5, 1910; Hal Channing to Molly Wood, Aug. 4, 1907.

18. Hal Channing to Grace Stetson, May 12, 1905.

19. Ibid.; Hal Channing to Grace Stetson, May 3, 1908.

20. Molly Wood to Grace Stetson, Sept. 29, 1910; Hal Channing to Grace Stetson, Nov. 11, 1910.

21. Molly Wood to Grace Stetson, Sept. 29 and Nov. 22, 1910; Hal Channing to Grace Stetson [Sept. 27, 1911].

22. Clarence Wood to Grace Stetson, March 4, 1906, and June 28, 1927.

23. Molly Wood to Grace Stetson, July 14, 1927; Grace Stetson to Hal Channing, March 24 [1931].

24. Clarence Wood to Grace Stetson, Oct. 6, 1916; Hal Channing to Clarence Wood, April 3, 1933.

25. Grace Stetson to Hal Channing, Feb. 7, 1923.

26. Grace Stetson to Hal Channing, Dec. 9, 1929.

27. Hal Channing to Grace Stetson, July 22 and Aug. 7, 1911; Grace Stetson to Hal Channing, Oct. 22, 1911.

28. Grace Stetson to Hal Channing, July 28 [1936].

29. Grace Stetson to Hal Channing, Nov. 3, 1911 and [Dec. 10, 1928].

30. Grace Stetson to Hal Channing, April 19 and 9, 1927, and March 24 and Jan. 30 [1931]; Hal Channing to Grace Stetson, Sept. 6, 1931; Grace Stetson to Hal Channing, July 28 [1936].

31. Grace Stetson to Hal Channing, April 9, 1927, Jan. 30 [1931], June 5, 1932, and Oct. 25, 1934.

# SIX

# The Norths and the Loomises:
# A Traditional Family on the
# American Frontier

Ann Loomis North and her husband, John Wesley North, had an amazing ability and proclivity to create family and community wherever they
went. It was their life's work as they settled successively in Minnesota,
Nevada, Tennessee, and California from 1849 to 1890. Ann and John
made one family out of their children, her brothers, and his sisters. Instead of looking at one set of siblings, then, this chapter looks at both
Ann and John and their making of a family together. The web of family
that they wove around themselves helped them, comforted them, and
supported them. In this way it is the family that best fits the definition
of a "traditional family."

Ann, born in 1828, was the oldest of the three children in her family.
Her brother Charlie was five years younger and George seven. They were
born to Mary Ann Lewis Loomis and Dr. George Loomis in De Witt,
New York, near Syracuse. Ann was twenty-one and had been married for
a year in 1849 when she left her parents, grandparents, two younger
brothers, other relatives, and a world that she knew and loved to settle
in the newly organized Minnesota Territory with her husband, John
Wesley North.

John was born in 1815, the youngest child in a family with five daughters. He had trained as a Methodist preacher (an "exhorter," he was
called—and no more prophetic name was ever conferred on a man) and
attended Wesleyan University in Connecticut, where he was president
of the student antislavery society. He had studied law, had been married

| *The Norths* | *The Loomises* |
|---|---|
| Minerva North Finch | |
| Polly North (d. 1827) | |
| Elizabeth North Harris | |
| Sarah North | |
| Clarissa North (1813–78) | |
| John Wesley North (1815–90) | |
| m. 1845    Emma Bacon (d. 1847) | |
| m. 1849    Ann Loomis (1828–95) | Ann Loomis |
| unnamed son (1850) | Charlie Loomis (1833–58) |
| Emma (b. 1852) | George Loomis (1835–?) |
| George (b. 1853) | m. 1856    Kate Ashley |
| John (b. 1855) | one child |
| Charles (b. 1857) | |
| Edward (b. 1858) | |
| Mary (b. 1860) | |

and widowed. He and Ann met when he was traveling through DeWitt, got sick with fever, and received medical help from Ann's father and hospital-like lodging in the North household. From the first Ann assumed the role of taking care of John. They married in 1848 and went west together the next year.[1]

In the 1830s and 1840s their part of New York State was alive with religious fervor and the reform impulse and produced hundreds of people who wanted to save the world. Among the most important causes were the abolition of slavery and the prohibition of alcohol. Both Ann and John cared deeply about these issues.

John was driven by a vision of a better world. He dreamed of a Christian, temperate, and civilized community in which holding slaves would be illegal and the citizens would be entertained by public lectures, educated at fine universities, and immersed in the vital political issues of the day. If he could not find such a community, he would found one. This vision led him to help found the Republican Party in Minnesota, to work for Abraham Lincoln's nomination and election, and to help establish the University of Minnesota. In Nevada, where he and Ann lived from 1861 to 1866, he tried again to build a godly community. They then moved to Tennessee, where he worked for free public education and racial equality in the early years of Reconstruction. In 1870 he founded Riverside, California, hoping still to create a better world, then tried for a better world yet in Oleander, California.

He earned his living doing legal work—much of it by filing land claims and buying and selling property ("Buy high and sell low" seemed to be his motto, however). He made and lost several fortunes. Mostly, however, he served as both informal and formal settlement bureau, bringing settlers west.

Ann shared this vision of a better world, though at twenty-one her own version of it may have been less developed than his was at thirty-four. She too opposed slavery and alcohol. She too wanted to create a better world, but she would do it with her family, as many of her relatives as possible. Her family was always at the center of her better world, and whatever her enthusiasm for a new world, I suspect she might have been happier if she had stayed in De Witt.

Ann grew up in an emotionally stable household among people who had stayed put for at least two generations, surrounded by family and supported by the love of many relations. She tried to recreate that life wherever she lived.

Ann lived apart from her two brothers from 1849 when she left for Minnesota until 1856 when they were in their early twenties and joined her in Minnesota. With the exception of these seven years, the siblings lived near each other for the rest of their lives. This was no easy matter, either, because Ann and John moved at least eight times. But each time their family—families—moved with them. Each move turned into a kind of tribal migration—dozens of people had to change their places and their lives to stay in the Norths' orbit. After 1856 Ann spent more time with her brother George than she did with her husband.

She might have known what she was getting into from the beginning. Even during their courtship, John felt torn between love for his wife and his duty to improve the world. Duty usually won. Even before they were engaged, he was away; she wrote and told him she missed him, and he sent her a warning: "But my *sweet girl*, if you cannot bear such a separation as *this now*, how will you endure the separations of more than a year to come?" If he had been able to read the future, he would have said "the separations of the years to come."[2]

Their first significant separation came shortly after their wedding. John left Ann with her parents for several months while he determined whether Minnesota would be a good spot for them. One wonders why he did not take her along. Certainly it was rough country in 1849. Newly admitted to the Union as an organized territory, Minnesota had a population of about six thousand white settlers—mostly men—and five thousand Native Americans.[3]

But the country was no tamer when, that November, he and Ann climbed out of the riverboat that landed them in St. Paul. And what a terrible time to arrive in Minnesota—at the beginning of winter, without a house ready, without a garden to provide food (and months ahead of the start of the growing season). They settled on an island in the middle of the Mississippi River—Nicollet Island today and in the center of Minneapolis—that was difficult to get to and from until the river froze and they could walk across the ice to the little settlement of St. Anthony on the east bank of the river. Most wrenching for Ann was that between November and May they could expect only the most intermittent mail delivery, at best once a month, when it came in by dogsled.

The mail was vitally important to both of them. It was by mail that John recruited settlers to join him in Minnesota. Wherever he went, he spent a good part of his time writing letters to get other people to join him. He wrote to friends, relatives, neighbors, almost anyone for whom he had an address. He encouraged, cajoled, urged, and pleaded with people to join him, and eventually they did—in the thousands. Ann shared in this work. She copied John's letters and added her own perspectives at the end. He addressed the men, she the women.

She was heartsick lonesome that first winter on Nicollet Island, and she decided that she never wanted to be that lonely again. She would do what she could to surround herself with family, friends, and friends of friends, and she did a good job. In addition to the letters she wrote with John, she wrote hundreds of letters of her own. They told of the weather, of ice in the winter and mosquitoes at dusk in the summer, and the doings in St. Anthony—the new school, the new church, the sight of the Red River wagons (trade caravans moving overland from the Mississippi River to the Red River of the North), and the growth of the town. She watched St. Anthony boom and described what she saw, week after week, month after month. She offered a wonderful chronicle of town building and her part in it. While John worked with land and timber, with such Minnesotans as Henry H. Sibley, Alexander Ramsey, Henry Rice, and Franklin Steele, Ann took in boarders, taught Sunday school, gave piano lessons, and formed the local sewing circle. Both Ann and John played a part in making and sustaining community. John was not seeking single male settlers. He wanted families. Ann too wanted families, and she worked to create the community into which families could and would come.

Especially her own. More than with the wonders of her new life, Ann filled her letters with her longing for family and friends. In every letter Ann asked someone to come or commented on an impending arrival or too-recent departure. She kept her loneliness in some check and tried generally to balance it with news of her happiness, but the salutations in one series of letters to her parents, written during her journey and shortly after her arrival, suggest her rising tide of longing for family and connections. October 18, 1849: "My dear parents"; Oct. 28: "My dear dear Parents"; Nov. 6, "My dear *dear* Parents"; Nov. 19: "My dear precious Parents." Oh, how she missed them all, parents, grandmother, friends, and brothers, her dear younger brothers.[4]

From her distant new home she took pains to sing Minnesota's attractions to Charlie and George. She was not explicitly recruiting them, but she did call attention to what they would like in her new place. You'd enjoy the hunting, she wrote to Charlie, and the skating. She noted too, "There are so many things to be seen that would make you laugh." She did not forget to worry about them, either. You're probably lonesome for Charlie, she wrote to George when Charlie went off to school.[5]

She also gave them advice, as she must have been accustomed to doing, but as a married woman embarked on a big adventure she offered it liberally. Cultivate patience, she advised the fifteen-year-old George. Study French, learn self-denial. "If you are sorely tried sometimes—never mind—try to think, it's all to improve you—'it's all for your good,' as Pa used to try to make us think when he whipped us." She advised Charlie to "cheer and encourage" George.[6]

She also offered to her brothers a sympathetic ear and a safe place to try out ideas and plans, without the consequences of asking parents. She encouraged them to tell her all and promised not to pass it on.[7] They were friends but better than friends because they had known each other all their lives. They might even have known each other better than they knew themselves.

Her biggest fear was that they would forget her. She prayed that their love for each other would not lessen, whatever the distance between them. "I'm afraid you wont miss me any more," she wrote more than once and certainly felt more than she wrote. She also expressed her love for them. To Charlie she nearly moaned: "How I *long* to see you." In 1851 she was so lonely she dreamed of being with George. "You don't know how much I have wanted to see you all."[8]

Two years after arriving in Minnesota, Ann wrote George about how alone she felt. Oh, how frightened and fragile she sounded, how little

ready she felt for the adulthood that marriage, the move, and motherhood had already presented to her at twenty-three:

> I do not think so much is required of woman as of men—and yet,
> although I am four years and a half older than you, I find it difficult
> to act my part as a woman—to perform well all the duties that de-
> volve upon me, as such—I grow to feel my own nothingness more
> and more. I have no great troubles, so I manage to let very small ones
> vex me exceedingly. In short I am only a little child, and fear, at times,
> that in spite of my earnest endeavors to the contrary, I shall always
> remain so.
>
> You may call this all "twaddle," but I know if you are ever thrown
> entirely upon your own resources, and so far from our best of par-
> ents, as to be unable to advise with them, whenever any little trou-
> ble may arise, you will feel it. You cannot imagine how much I have
> missed their precious counsel and comfort on some occasions.

Of course, she continued, she had a husband, her "good friend," who
would and could help her, but "our father and mother have known us
from our infancy, and know precisely what we need at some times better than anyone else can."

Oh, how Ann missed them and needed them all. She also betrayed
her inexperience with writing in this way: "I don't know what you'll think
of this way of writing, but my heart is full of love for you, and so, you
must read it, and perhaps you will not, if now, always think it foolish."[9]

She felt herself unable to confide in her grandmother, and though
she was "accustomed to say" to her parents "all I feel," she sometimes
feared that they might think her too enthusiastic in her emotions, so she
held back. She did confide in her brothers, to George and to Charlie both.
"I am more low spirited than usual of late," she wrote to Charlie. "I
hardly know why—but at times I have to make a desperate effort to throw
off the 'blues,' and even then, do not always succeed." There was no
chance that her parents would join them, but she had a good chance with
her brothers.[10]

Ann really struggled with loneliness, not just early in her married life
but beyond. John's activities often kept him away from home—in Chicago for the 1860 Republican convention, then campaigning with Lincoln in Illinois; in Washington, D.C., waiting for for months in early 1861
to be appointed surveyor general of the Nevada Territory; the year he
spent in Nevada getting settled before Ann joined him in 1862. Their
daughter Emma remembered that "since my earliest remembrance I had
been accustomed to my father's goings and comings." She knew, she said,

that "his interests extended over a larger field than was circumscribed by his saw-mill and his grist mill." During those months that turned into years Ann kept the household together and made a life for herself.[11]

She built an active life. Ann had seven babies—five of them during her Minnesota years. She made friends, arranged a household, earned what money she could, supported and encouraged her husband, involved herself in town building, school building, and church building. She entertained prospective settlers and local politicians and business leaders. In St. Anthony the Norths' house became the center of town life. When they moved to Northfield, Ann arranged another household and again became involved in school, church, and town building. And she tried to build her own community by birth and by accretion.[12]

During her early years in Minnesota, Ann successfully attracted company. Her aunt and uncle moved to St. Anthony. Her parents came for visits. In 1850 Ann's grandmother came and stayed for about a year (during which Ann had and lost her first child). At the end of that time Ann's parents visited for two months, and they and her grandmother then went home together. Charlie and George visited too. When she could, Ann went home to New York. Even today the distances are not easy to traverse, but they crossed them in both directions repeatedly. Her parents, though, had their lives in New York and so did her grandmother, so they only visited. Only after her mother died in the late 1860s did her father think about and then join his daughter's entourage in California.

In the mid-1850s George, the younger of the two brothers, finished his schooling and moved to Minnesota to join his sister. From his arrival George worked with John variously as a bookkeeper, accountant, and manager of timber or quartz mills. He married Kate Ashley in 1856. Where the Norths moved, George and Kate moved. It would be technically accurate to say that George and Kate "followed," to Nevada, Tennessee, and California, because John's career was their lodestar, but George was hardly a hanger-on. Although he started as a kind of apprentice, he quickly turned into the more responsible and, by far, the more astute businessman of the two. Moreover, Kate's sister and brother-in-law, the Feltons, joined the North tribe and provided a good deal of the financial backing for North's various schemes from the 1850s through the 1880s. Ann's father provided much of the rest of the funding and more than once dug John and Ann out of a financial hole. So various family members followed John's lead but before long took over taking care of John (much as Ann had).

Ann and her sister-in-law, Kate, did not get on entirely. Ann was discreet in her correspondence and did not give much vent to her feelings about Kate, so her irritation shows up only occasionally and only in passing, most strongly when Kate wanted to return to New York in 1858 to be closer to her family and Ann took a sharply critical tone: "I should rather deny myself *that* happiness, than feel that I could do it only at the expense of others, or even at the sacrifice of my husband's interests."[13] Perhaps Ann would not have gotten on perfectly with any woman married to her brother. Perhaps Kate's expressed wish to live near her parents so closely reflected Ann's own unexpressed desires that even the voicing of it threatened Ann.

When he was twenty-three Charlie joined the Norths in Minnesota but with much sadder results. He arrived in 1856 and moved in with George and Kate and spent time with Ann and John. He was welcome and at home in both places. When George and Kate had company, Charlie ate with the Norths. "He knows we are always glad to have him come, and you know we live more in the old home way, that I presume seems pleasant to him sometimes. I hope so, certainly." She fed him, she darned his socks when he let her, "but he does not tell me and you can appreciate that I do not like to go into Kate's house to hunt them up." She wanted to do more. "I do so much wish we had a good comfortable room for him." When they built a house, Ann planned a special room for Charlie, but that never happened.[14]

In 1858 Charlie was bitten by a rabid dog—owned by George and Kate—and died after several months of suffering. During these months Ann could not admit how gravely ill Charlie actually was. She did not inform or warn her parents, nor did she call for their help. Her letters to their parents revealed nothing amiss. She must have been frozen by fear, anguish, worry. George too. At Charlie's death Ann sent, finally, the full story to her parents, who raced to Minnesota to be with their children and to mourn their lost son.[15]

The loss must have been horrible and fraught with guilt and regret. Charlie was only twenty-five. George and Ann both blamed themselves. The dog belonged to George. Charlie had come west at Ann's pleading. Their mother reported: "Ann bears up better than I feared she would and for her sake we try to do so but *sometimes* it seems as though we could scarcely be reconciled and fail to say 'They will be done &c.'"[16] They tried to bear up for her, for Ann. They all suffered.

So as adults George and Ann became each other's only sibling and spent most of the rest of their lives together—or down the street, anyway. Perhaps just being together was a value in itself. John and Ann helped George by finding him work, offering him a place to stay, taking him along on their new life. For their lifetimes George played an active role in Ann's life, not as surrogate husband or father but, well, as a brother: available to help, responsible, full of love, devoted. When John left on another adventure, George stayed behind and helped Ann move. George's presence freed John from familial responsibilities—he did not have to worry about leaving Ann and the children because he knew that George would be there. Moreover, John was leaving his wife with one of the other people she most loved in the world.

Good sibling relations did not translate automatically into good in-law relations. The Loomises and Norths, however, worked at getting along. John—the only male in his family—and George—the only brother left after Charlie's death—made each other into brothers of a sort. They formed a close and lifelong relationship. George fostered it by living around the Norths, by helping them as much as he could. Ann paid attention to it from the beginning. Just after her wedding, perhaps while on her honeymoon, Ann signed her letter as usual, "With much love." Then, on second thought, she squeezed in "from both of us." Until she had made a habit of "our," she had to correct "Give my love" to include John's love too. In letter after letter she wrote some version of "Mr. North sends an abundance of love to each one of you."[17]

The language of family permeated the Norths' relations. John's sister Clara called Ann *sister.* George called John *brother.* Ann called John *"your* brother" when she wrote to George and Charlie. Ann even used *brother* to refer to her husband's first wife's brother. Many religious people in the nineteenth-century used the terms *brother* and *sister* to designate their religious brothers and sisters, but John and Ann saved these terms for their family and extended family. John also addressed Ann's father as "Dear Father" and signed himself "Your affectionate Son." He once even commented on his language: "It gives me great pleasure in this far off land to know though we are here in the midst of strangers, and *I* without parents on earth, or any friends, other than my *Dear good wife* within many hundred miles of me, we have a Father & Mother at the East that *I* am permitted to call such in the truest sense of these terms."[18]

Like Ann, John carried his relationship with his siblings into adulthood, and he drew them into his daily circle. His sister Minerva Finch and her husband, Cyrenius, joined up with the Norths in Minnesota in 1850 and stayed on. Another brother-in-law moved in with the Norths, and a nephew stayed for months at a time. John's sister Sarah joined them for a time. Clarissa (Clara), however, joined the Norths in 1851 and stayed with them for almost thirty years, until her death in 1878.

Clarissa was the youngest of the five sisters and just two years older than John. When Clara arrived, Ann was a little cool at the prospect of her new live-in guest. She lamented to her parents that Clara had come "*to live*"—her emphasis. When her parents visited not long after Clara arrived, Ann accepted a neighbor's offer and moved Clara out for a time. "We must be alone," she wrote to her parents, "a part of the time." Alone, without Clara. Ann at this point wanted to be surrounded by family but her own family, not John's sister.[19]

Clara overwhelmed Ann. Clara was fifteen years older than Ann and, like her brother, had a strong personality and strong views. When she arrived, she was quite unhappy, perhaps depressed. This matter of becoming "sisters" took some time. Clara occasionally washed or wiped a few dishes, Ann reported, and at the same time she "requires a good deal," both attention and care. Ann skipped Sunday meeting because Clara had the blues and wanted company. On Monday Clara required breakfast in bed. Ann complained that Clara "makes me a great many steps." But the complaints were only for her parents' eyes. Please, she penned into the margin, do not "refer to what I wrote of Clara's whims."[20]

But Clara and Ann made common cause before long. Clara had originally come to Minnesota with the dream of opening her own school, but she got caught up in the Norths' daily lives and became a loved comrade, ally, co-mother, and co-housekeeper. Eventually, even Ann's friend.

Clara took an active part in raising Ann and John's children—not just by tending them when John or Ann or both were away, but she took them as part of her responsibility all the time. While she and John lived in Nevada in the summer of 1861, Clara wrote home to her nephews and Ann back east about "Bad Ben," a murderer who had himself been gunned down in Carson City. "How do you suppose Sam Brown became so bad," she asked didactically. "He began by being ugly when he was a little boy: getting angry, and striking and kicking other boys. If his mother had taught him to govern his temper then he would never have been what he was. Be good when you are a boy and then you will be a good man." This was a story worthy of a diligent parent—but in decidedly auntlike language.

Ann came to appreciate and love Clara and Clara to love Ann. After Clara had lived with them for most of ten years, Ann made clear that "we should *none of us* be at all satisfied to have her separated from us *all*. She is too dear and good a sister to be allowed to go any where else than among *us*—for she loves us better than any one else in this world."[21]

When John was appointed to his new position in Nevada, he suggested that Ann go with him and Clara stay behind with the children. Both Clara and Ann rejected that idea. Ann did not want to go with him alone, and "I cannot consent to his going alone." They had another idea: "Clara is anxious to go with him—so I think that is best, too," Ann wrote her parents. "She can do better than any one else except myself for him." So Clara accompanied John to Nevada, and Ann and the children, with George's help, went home to De Witt, then followed to Nevada a year later.[22]

Clara also benefited from being with the Norths. It opened the world to her in some ways she would otherwise have missed. She shared her family's reforming impulse and attended rallies with John, circulated petitions, actively campaigned for her causes. She also had a great adventure in going to Nevada. She and John got there by rail to New York, then sailed down the East Coast, crossed Panama, then sailed back up to California, and traveled overland to Nevada, all of which was easier than going across country. What an adventure—not one that the single Clara could likely have made herself but only one of several adventures that John and Clara embarked on together (including a trip to the Minnesota State Fair).[23]

Clara's relations with Ann and John demonstrate a significant aspect of sibling relations for single people, particularly for a white middle-class single woman in the nineteenth century. The single life for such women posed problems and imposed limitations on mobility, economic self-sufficiency, and engagement in public life. Clara's life with the Norths relieved some of these problems and expanded some of these boundaries. They gave her place, work, position, and family.

Clara also made opportunities for Ann; her presence and her involvement in the family gave Ann more flexibility and mobility. Her presence allowed Ann to go away, to stay at home, to make plans. She became the sister that Ann never had. They all—John and Ann and Clara and George—needed each other and made room for each other in their adult lives. They all benefited.

Ann and John were at the center of this multilayered family. Their story, though, has a sad ending. We know that Ann suffered from John's frequent absences from her and from their family. He too suffered. In August 1861, for example, he wrote from Nevada that it would not be until the next spring that he could get together enough money for her to join him. "You alone, Dearest, can know how hard this separation is to bear," he wrote, and closed with the hope, "*Dearest,* that we shall not become, even *in the slightest degree,* weaned from each other by this unavoidable separation." They had been married for thirteen years.[24]

Ann recognized John's ambition but worried about its consequences. Having him gone for months at a time could not have been easy, even with Clara's help. To her parents she had defended John for years: "You know I've got one of the *best* of husbands but he, poor man, is driven with business." But even her understanding had its limits. "And my good Husband writes me so discouragingly about his [job] prospects," Ann admitted, "that I fear I shall not go at all [to De Witt] this year. . . . That will indeed be a trial of my Christian graces."[25]

She had less and less patience as the years passed and made more decisions to spend more and more time away from John. When in Nevada in 1862 Ann could not find schools good enough for the children, so she took them to San Francisco. When the family lived in Tennessee, Ann and the children spent long stretches of time in De Witt. When John lived in the Central Valley of California in the mid-1870s, she lived in San Francisco, away from the heat, she said. When he moved for a third time within California, Ann declared herself unable (unwilling) to do any more pioneering. She had used up her pioneering spirit. The final blow for her came in 1882 when she was fifty-four. After sewing a wedding dress for their thirty-year-old daughter Emma, Ann could not afford to go east from California for the wedding because John needed all their available cash to buy yet more land for yet another dream in Fresno. First, Ann made a long visit to friends, then she moved into a boardinghouse. He could live in Fresno or Oleander if he wanted, but she had had enough and she was staying put in San Francisco.[26]

Like Albert Janin, the youngest of six as well, John North never quite figured out how to support his family. They both had big ambitions—perhaps a slightly inflated notion of their own acumen—and disastrous financial affairs. Albert borrowed incessantly from his mother-in-law and wife, for just one more speculative scheme. John borrowed repeatedly and heavily from his father-in-law for one more speculative leap too. Both preferred speculation to other ways of earning a living, and both were quite unlucky investors. Both lived constantly on the brink of financial chaos—or over the edge. When he died in 1890, John left his entire estate to Ann, to thank her for her long loyalty. Unfortunately, he died during one of his fortune's downturns, so the estate amounted to more than $3,000 in debt. Merlin Stonehouse's biography of John North concerns itself primarily with North's political career. Ann never merits much attention in his book. Toward the end of John's life, as John's and Ann's lives drift apart, Stonehouse pays less and less attention to Ann. After John's death she disappears. We do not know, for example, how she survived or supported herself, exactly where she lived, or even when she died. The fate of the politician's wife?

In their lives and through their life we see a supreme example of family durability and family making. Ann and John built out of their families a community of people who made frontier life possible and bearable, who took care of each other, helped each other, provided companionship for each other. They were business and household partners, travel mates, surrogate parents for their children, allies, friends. However loving their marriage, though, Ann and John finally could not, as a couple, survive the life they created for themselves. Like many frontier women, Ann stitched a life out of much loneliness. She made connections to others, she developed her independence and her self-sufficiency, but she learned, ultimately, how to live alone. John built a life out of his dreams. His strength seemed to be in starting things—towns, communities, colleges, political parties, families. Ultimately, however, his dreams left him alone.

This family held so many emotions, so much richness, so much variation. In this it truly was a traditional family.

### Notes

1. This chapter is based on the North Family Papers in the Huntington Library, San Marino, California (unless otherwise noted, all letters cited may be found in this collection). The collection is made up almost entirely of letters sent to and from Ann and her parents and her brothers, plus letters from John to Ann's family. There are no letters among John's family members. I have also found helpful Merlin Stonehouse's biography, *John Wesley North and the Reform Frontier.* Stonehouse provides a helpful chronology at the front of the volume that highlights "important" events in John's life. He did not, however, highlight John's marriage or the birth of any of his children. John North's own brief autobiography gives us a flavor of his personality. John W. North, "Random Sketches of a Crude Life," is a typewritten manuscript in the John W. North Papers—made up of two folders—at the Minnesota Historical Society in St. Paul. John and Ann's daughter Emma North Musser published her "Memories of a Frontier Childhood" in three consecutive issues in *Overland Monthly and Out West Magazine* in the issues of August, September, and October 1924. She recalled that she "came to realize . . . a most touching grace which [her mother] had always conferred on the crude conditions around her" (340).

2. Stonehouse, *John Wesley North,* 17.

3. Patricia C. Harpole and Mary D. Nagle, eds., *Minnesota Territorial Census, 1850* (St. Paul: Minnesota Historical Society Press, 1972), viii; June Drenning Holmquist, *They Chose Minnesota: A Survey of the State's Ethnic Groups* (St. Paul: Minnesota Historical Society Press, 1981), 21.

4. Ann Loomis North to her parents, Oct. 18, Oct. 28, Nov. 6, and Nov. 19, 1849.

5. Ann North to Charlie Loomis, March 15, 1850, and Ann North to George Loomis, May 27, 1850.

6. Ann North to George Loomis, May 27, 1850, and Ann North to Charlie Loomis, Jan. 25, 1852.

7. For example, see Ann North to George Loomis, Dec. 7, 1851.

8. Ann North to her parents, April 10, 1853; Ann North to George Loomis, Dec. 11, 1853, and Dec. 7, 1851; Ann North to George Loomis, May 27, 1850; Ann North to Charlie Loomis, May 28, 1850, and May 25, 1852.

9. Ann North to George Loomis, Dec. 7, 1851.

10. Ann North to her parents, July 15, 1851, March 14 and Nov. 12, 1853; Ann North to Charlie Loomis, Jan. 25, 1852; Ann North to George Loomis, Dec. 11, 1853.

11. Musser, "Memories of a Frontier Childhood," 339.

12. See Stonehouse, *John Wesley North*, esp. 22–89.

13. Ann North to her parents, March 21, 1858.

14. Ibid.

15. Ann's letter to her parents was printed in a newspaper account of Charlie's death. The clipping, which is not identified by place of publication or date, is contained in the John W. North Papers at the Minnesota Historical Society.

16. Mary Ann Loomis (Ann North's mother) to Ann Lewis (Ann North's grandmother), May 29, 1858.

17. Ann North to her parents, May 27, 1848, Dec. 11, 1853, and Oct. 28, 1849.

18. Clara North to Ann North, July 7, 1861; George Loomis to John North, Feb. 11, 1866; John North to G. S. Loomis, Jan. 6, 1860.

19. Ann North to her parents, April 29, 1851.

20. Ann North to her parents, March 31, 1858. Stonehouse thought Ann a terrible gossip and quite a complainer. He saw John as his wife's editor, censoring her letters, correcting her complaints. Her letters don't strike me that way but instead appear to portray a woman alert to the world around her and in conversation with her parents—and confident of her parents' interest—in the dailiness of her world (Stonehouse, *John Wesley North*, 21).

21. Clara North to Ann North, July 7, 1861.

22. Ann North to her parents, April 8, 1861; Clara North to Ann North, March 18, 1866; Stonehouse, *John Wesley North*, 229, 131–49. See also North, "Random Sketches."

23. Ann North to her parents, April 4, 1861.

24. John North to Ann North, Aug. 13, 1861. Theirs had not been a marriage of convenience but of love and passion. Their early letters survive but in severely edited form—scissored, actually. Some prudish reader (Ann herself? or John?) found too intimate the conclusion of a sentence that began "Dear Ann, I did not express what I said" or another that began "How often have I wished that you were here to enjoy [Boston] with me" (John North to Ann North, June 30 and June 25, 1848).

The historian Karen Lystra points to the Norths as an example of loving nineteenth-century relationships. See Lystra, *Searching the Heart*, 202.

25. Ann North to her parents, Nov. 8, 1852, and March 25, 1861.

26. Stonehouse, *John Wesley North*, 238–39.

SEVEN

# The Curtises:
# Broken, Remade, Broken Again

No one ever named a town after the Curtises. None among them claimed—or aspired to—a national reputation for anything. They did not have parents famous for anything. In this way they were not like the Putnams or the Arthurs. Like each of the families here, though, the Curtis family had its own culture and tells its own story. The Curtis story is one shaped by death, three deaths, really: their mother's, their father's, and that of Ben, the youngest brother. In this they were like the Arthurs, whose parents' deaths changed their lives and weighed heavily on their emotional selves.[1]

The seven Curtis siblings were born in Ohio between 1832 and 1847; only four survived to adulthood. The oldest, Mary, lived only until she was fourteen. Sarah Henrietta (Etta) was born in 1835, James in 1838, Delia Augusta (Gussie) in 1841, and Benjamin Wisner in 1847; twins Laura and Clara were born and died in 1844. When their mother died in 1849, the four surviving children were fourteen, eleven, eight, and two. Three years later their father died.

The death of a parent has complex consequences within a family. Even when the child is grown, a parent's death is significant. For years after her mother died, my mother found herself wanting to tell her something or to ask her something else. She was so used to having her around. With the exception of the two years that my father's work took us to St. Louis, my mother always lived within a couple of miles of her mother. As my mother declines now, she finds herself thinking more and more about her mother and remembering things she said and how she looked, even

*The Curtises*

Henry James Curtis (1798–1852)
m. 1831    Clarissa Fisher (1809–49)
            Mary (1832–46)
            Sarah Henrietta (Etta) (1835–1908)
            James (Jamie) (1838–1907)
            Delia Augusta (Gussie) (1841–1915)
            Laura (1844)
            Clara (1844)
            Benjamin Wisner (1847–92)
                m. 1885    Mary E. Hocker
                            two children

what dress she wore on some occasion or another. My mother was forty-nine when her mother died, and at seventy-nine she still misses her.

How much more wrenching and deep a loss—whether the relationship was good or difficult—when the father or mother is young and the child still at home. When, in addition, a child loses both parents, the loss is both emotionally paralyzing and physically centrifugal.

Parents hold the main ties—emotional, financial, physical—that bind families together. When parents die, or are otherwise absent, these bonds slacken and children are sent spinning emotionally, financially, and physically. The velocity of the spin depends on the age of the children, how close relatives are, the children's gender, and their financial circumstances. After the death of his father Alan Arthur simply took off. He was old enough to be on his own, had the resources to take care of himself, and he was male. Each of these factors gave him some choices about what would happen to his life. He could not choose to bring his parents back, but he could decide whether he would stay in school. He did not. He ran off for a long European vacation, though calling it a wake might be a better description. Nell had access to the same resources, but she was sixteen and female; both her age and her gender put her under the care of an aunt. She did not go anywhere for a long time.

For the Curtises age alone would have necessitated that they be put into someone's care. They were simply too young to assume responsibility for each other. Neither resources nor gender mattered. If they had all been boys and all been wealthy, they still could not have stayed put. If they were like other young orphans, they stood by and watched (or were in the other room, completely excluded from any involvement in such decisions) while others made the arrangements. Then they went where they were told.

When the Curtises were orphaned in 1852, there were two main options for their care—county-funded relief or relatives. Fortunately, the Curtises were not cast onto the public benevolence, as it was called. Many nineteenth-century children were. Children in the twentieth century have to cope more and more often with the divorce of their parents, but they have to deal less often with the death of one or both parents. In the nineteenth century, the higher rate of death from childbirth—for women—and accidents—for men—as well as the generally shorter life span meant children more often faced the death of one or both parents. These deaths left children behind in cities and villages and on farms all over the United States. Sometimes such children went to orphanages. A few counties in the United States had orphanages by midcentury and, like hospitals, prisons, schools, and other nineteenth-century institutions, they were known for their harshness. Yet the orphanages were modern improvements over the more common system of county relief—auctioning off orphans to whomever offered to care for them at the lowest cost to the county.[2]

Public or private agencies made efforts to place orphans in other families. Reformer Charles Loring Brace sent hundreds of East Coast girls and boys by train to the American West to find them new families and parents. These "orphan trains" sometimes carried children to loving adoptive homes but often to the hard and harsh circumstances common on the frontier or to the equivalent of penal servitude.[3]

The Curtises were spared this fate. They were taken in by relatives. Four children were too many (and probably too much) for any one relative. Whatever duty and/or love the relatives felt, no one family of relations could take in all four. The Curtis children, then, were divided up and taken in by various aunts and uncles. All the arrangements were temporary and changed with some frequency. Some Curtis relatives lived in New England, where both parents had come from; others lived in Illinois and Ohio, still others in Memphis. The children lived with whomever could manage them at the time, for longer and shorter periods. They did not, however, live together again. They lived in separate households in different states. They lost first their mother, then their father, then each other.

Every family has its defining moments, those events from which all others are measured. It can be a move, a job change, a birth, a disaster, a death. The event becomes one of the ways that a family tells time. It has been one day, one week, one year, five years . . . since . . . Whatever each family member's particular experience, these common events define the family and set its common memories. The public sphere is defined by such common events and memories too: what you were doing when Kennedy was shot or the *Challenger* space shuttle exploded. How much more powerfully private events define people's private lives.

And so the deaths of their parents defined the Curtises and in the process redefined them as orphans—no longer as sons or daughters. Five years after their father's death Jamie commented on that redefinition and its effects to his sixteen-year-old sister Gussie: "This is also the day of the month that our dear Father died, and as oft as it rolls around will it bring to mind the reccollection [*sic*] of that sad event which made us Orphans, and threw us Fatherless and Motherless upon the rough waves of the cold world, and since that time (I at least) have not had the dearest of all earthly blessings: 'Home.'"[4]

Late twentieth-century fiction is full of stories about families "broken" by divorce—attesting both to its common and its disturbing nature in American culture. Late nineteenth-century fiction, by contrast, is full of stories about orphans.

Many of Horatio Alger's heroes are orphans—torn away from parents and other supports, they had to make their own way with no parents at all. (In American popular culture they are reputed to have made their way by dint of hard work and determination. That was how they became "self-made men." In the Alger books, though, the heroes made their way through luck, good fortune, wiles, a well-conceived marriage, sometimes subterfuge and manipulation.) Willa Cather's Jim Burden—the narrator of *My Ántonia*—was orphaned in Virginia, then sent west to be raised by his grandparents in Nebraska. While they might have been a little stiff and formal, they offered him love and care, warmth, and Christmas parties.[5]

These were fictional characters, orphaned for literary reasons. As a metaphor it must have struck home with many nineteenth-century Americans who left family and friends behind as they traveled in search of new opportunities. Perhaps the stories mirrored the fate of a land so recently cut loose from its "mother" country. Perhaps it also simply reflected the all-too-common fact of children without parents.

But the Curtises were not literary characters, nor was their parentless state metaphoric. It was real, no doubt all too real for them. At their father's death their family home was dissolved and their belongings divided up.

Etta, the oldest, was seventeen when their father died, on the cusp of being a child at home and an adult in the world. She was moved from Ohio to Tennessee. Others of her age were courting or thinking of marrying. If the thought crossed her mind, it rarely came out of her pen. Boys take up virtually no part of her letters. Instead, she earned a teaching certificate for herself and started teaching. Her letters are full of news of that life and of family things. She put words to what proved to be a lifelong theme among the Curtises: "How pleasant it would be," she wrote, "if we could all have a home together."[6] Nell Arthur had expressed a similar wish to her brother, Alan, and occasionally the Putnams had talked about wanting to spend more time together. The Channings did not, and Albert Janin did not once express any wish to gather his brothers together in the same household. But the Curtises repeatedly expressed the wish, even longing, that they should live together.

Jamie, fourteen when their father died, went to relatives in Tennessee; Gussie, eleven, to relatives in New England. Through the 1850s and into the 1860s they both went to school. Gussie, like her sister, trained to be a teacher. They both moved around—or were moved around. Their letters came variously from Boston, Memphis, Lacon in Illinois, and Cincinnati and Hamilton in Ohio. After leaving school, Jamie worked mostly as a store clerk in various and many different stores. He never stayed too long in one job.

The Curtis children could not prevent their household's dissolution, but they did not allow their separation to disconnect them. In fact, they made a special effort to stay connected across the distances.

They also tried to take care of each other. Initially, and not surprisingly, the three oldest focused their attention on Ben, the youngest. All three of his older siblings paid attention to his situation and to his progress. Jamie and Etta spoke of him in an unnatural, stilted adult language and tone. Nineteen-year-old Jamie reported that Ben was "getting along finely with his studies." He had gotten a letter "from the dear boy himself," and, he bragged, it "was quite a letter from a youth his age."

Even when older siblings try to become parents to younger ones, or are forced into responsibility for younger ones, they cannot quite make the shift. Jamie, for example, might try to talk as he imagined a father would, but he was not old enough to carry it off. Siblings have a claim on each other but rarely real authority. "You're not my mom!" They could care for each other and take care of each other but rarely became parents for each other.[7]

When their father died, Ben was five and was sent to live with his uncle William in Lacon, Illinois. Perhaps he did not hate it from the beginning, but he did soon enough. In 1857, when he was nine, he ran away. He was found and returned, but his rebellion put his siblings on alert. They consulted with each other about his circumstances and what they ought to do. Jamie explained that in their uncle's household Ben did not have "those ties of friendship existing which would bind one to a home—and to those that would love and take a kind interest in him." More generally, Jamie feared, Ben was "not receiving the attention both socially and intellectually that one of his age should." Together Jamie and Etta, as the two oldest (nineteen and twenty-two, respectively), decided that something had to be done for Ben and they devised a plan. Etta was delegated to carry it out: "Etta will go to Lacon . . . and if she sees that our fears are well grounded, she will ask of Uncle Wm the privilege of bringing him down here, if he is not willing to grant her the request and she thinks it is absolutely necessary that he should be removed from there she will demand it and bring him away."[8]

They used the language of privilege, but they did not really mean that. Jamie and Etta clearly believed that they had rights—and an obligation—to do something for their brother, even if it ultimately meant defying their uncle. More to the point, to their minds Etta had the final say. She was the oldest. It was her job. Apparently, Etta did go to Lacon and made other arrangements for Ben, since before long he was in Covington, Tennessee, where Etta was living with other relatives.

Ben resisted that too—not Etta but living with relatives. As soon as he could, he struck out on his own. He did not want to depend on relatives any longer than absolutely necessary. Like many men in many generations, Ben found in the army his transportation out. Unfortunately, the armies of his day were at war. In 1862, at the age of fifteen, Ben joined the Union Army and was assigned to the gunboat *Indianola*. The Confederates captured the *Indianola* in February 1863 (Ben could not have been on board more than a few weeks) and imprisoned the crew at Vicksburg. Because he was so young, he was soon released, and within the year he was released from the service as well. He did not go back to his uncles and aunts and never lived with or "off" relatives again.

The Curtises all seemed determined to help each other and to save each other from going outside the family for help. This desire seems like a long-term effect of their being orphaned so early in life and made to depend on others, outsiders. They had all felt the sometimes cold charity of others and longed especially for the warm support of each other.

Jamie took a different route than Ben in relation to the Civil War. He was twenty-three when the war began and found himself in a dilemma. He was not sure of his loyalties, ideologically or geographically, as he had one foot (and relatives) in Ohio and one (more relatives) in Tennessee. Moreover, he did not want to fight—he wanted to work so that he could "provide for at least some of you," he wrote to Gussie. "If I can help it I don't want any of us to be dependent on our friends or relatives." We might think that he simply wanted to avoid the dangers of war, but the theme of taking care of each other rings so loudly through the letters that his sentiment here rings true. They all felt economic responsibility for each other. Ben lamented that he had never shown his love for his sisters "by assisting you pecuniarally," nor had he been able to help Jamie "who has helped me so much." Etta too offered financial help, encouraging Gussie to "let me know when you need any more money." All four saw themselves living in a shared economy. They offered what they had when they had it and took help when they needed it—from each other.[9]

Another long-term effect of their parents' deaths was that all four children developed an intense loyalty to each other that persisted into their adulthoods and were dedicated to reconstructing their family as a unit. When Jamie was having some trouble, Ben wrote that he would "sacrifice everything I have here" for him. On another occasion Etta vowed that she would "strive to forget self entirely" in the interests of their all being happy together. They all talked and worked in various ways to make a home with each other.[10]

Home, Ben wanted a home. Not his own home but their home. Like his sisters and his brother, he paid little attention during his teens and his twenties to looking for a wife. He seemed simply not interested and much more interested in making a home with and for his siblings. He preferred nothing more than being with Etta, he told Gussie, and he worried that they were becoming strangers because it had been so long since they had seen each other.[11]

Within a few months after his army service, Ben was clerking in the same store as his brother Jamie and had taken a room next door to his. Within another few months their sister Etta had joined them in Memphis, taking a job as a governess to be able to be near them. Only Gussie was away, still in New England, and Ben wrote her, expressing the wish she could be with them too. Ben visited Etta so often at the place where she was a governess that he felt at home there and got hired on to do odd jobs around the house.[12]

Ben's day job as a mail agent put him on the road between Memphis and Bowling Green, so he came to spend at least half his time away from Etta and Jamie. Then he took a job in the Omaha post office. He was looking for the right place. It had not been Lacon or Covington or even Memphis. It did not turn out to be Omaha, either. By the early 1870s, however, he was in California and that came closer. Once there he started a campaign to get his sisters and brother to join him there. He was sure that Etta could get a job as a teacher and Jamie would like it and the climate would be better for Gussie. Writing at Christmas 1872, he hoped that by the next Christmas they would all be together again. Six months later Ben reported to Etta that he had become a "regular old Bach[elor]" and rarely went out, "tho I think if you and Gussie were here I would find some [company] that would be very agreeable." Three weeks later: "I fully believe that ere another year we will be comfortably settled here, and then we can work for ourselves and make a home.[13]

When one aunt died and left a small bequest to each Curtis, Ben gave his to Etta to fund her move to California. She came. Eventually, Jamie joined them. They lived together for two years, before Etta moved to San Diego and opened a school. Gussie joined her the next year, and they ran their school together. Ben went to Arizona where he made enough money in mining to buy property and go back to California to try fruit growing in San Diego County. His sisters did well as teachers, Ben not so well in farming. He lasted only four years before he sold out and went to Arizona in late 1884.[14]

He found more than a farm in Arizona. Within six months he had made the acquaintance of "one of the best dispositioned girls I have ever met," had proposed to her, and set a wedding date. He was thirty-eight. Mary E. Hocker was twenty and lived on the farm next door. He made a home with her.[15]

Etta and Gussie welcomed her eagerly. When Ben and Mary married, Etta and Gussie sent welcoming gifts— wedding gifts, of course, but they were specifically for Mary and specifically to welcome her. After the birth of Mary and Ben's first baby in 1886, the sisters sent presents for the baby: flannel, more flannel, and more flannel; some linen, baby shoes, other "goods." They offered her the loan of their sewing machine. They sent her, in addition, a silk handkerchief just for her. In another thoughtful and affectionate gesture Gussie sent Mary a picture of Ben when he was small. It is telling that the sisters had such a picture, kept it, then sent it on.

Mary was grateful for it all. In response to the little gifts she enthused, "Gussie knows what I wanted for that is just exactly it." Or, as Ben reported, Mary "wonders how you know so much about what mothers like," he wrote, "she thinks you are pretty well posted on that subject."

In thanks for the photo Mary wrote that she had "always had a desire" for such a picture. Of course, some of these expressions were conventions, expressing the form rather than the substance of affection, because she had not yet met the sisters. But the warmth of the letters is contagious. Mary made other contributions as well to good feeling among the Curtis women. Even before she had met the sisters, Mary wrote her own letters to them, chatty family letters of domestic life, and signed herself "your sister, Mary." She displayed photographs of Etta and Gussie so that the children would know them and recognize them—perhaps so that she herself would know them. She wrote them charming stories of her daughters Delia and Rena and how much they would like to meet their aunts.[16]

Neither Etta nor Gussie ever married, but they settled into their school and made a success of it. Ben and Mary settled into family and farming in Arizona. Jamie was the only one who remained unattached, to a mate or a sibling.

The Curtises always had a special concern for whichever of them was alone. Jamie's "old bachelorhood" seemed to concern them all (including Jamie). In Jamie's case, his worry might have been premature, even if heartfelt. When he was twenty-seven he mourned the marriage of his roommate and his own fate: "Mr W has been my room-mate almost ever since I came here [Memphis] and being left alone now I am almost disconsolate," he wrote to Gussie. "I had begun to think I was a quite contented old Bachelor. But I find I have yet to learn to be without a mate of some kind." Almost twenty years later Jamie was still unmarried, and both his brother and his sisters tried to draw him to them. Ben wanted Jamie to come live with his family and get to know Mary: "I wish I could think of you as being with your family, instead of an old bachelor." Or, as Gussie put it about the same time: "If you [Jamie] could be here with us too, we would be very well satisfied & contented here, but it don't seem right to have you so far away from us."[17]

Jamie talked about joining up with his sisters in particular and sometimes seemed to desire it, but he also expressed some ambivalence. In 1890 and 1891 he made a series of gestures toward coming together (all were then living in California but far from each other): "I wish I could be with you." Six weeks later: "I would gladly give up here [Fall River Mills] altogether, if I could dispose of my property." Six months later: "I would like very much to join you in anything that seems practicable and for your benefit. . . . If I could sell my property here, I would not hesitate to go to you and take the chances of getting into something by which I could obtain a livelihood there. But as there is no prospect of selling my place at present . . ." He rejected the other alternative: "If it were not for the severe winters here I would suggest uniting our forces here."[18] These passages do not make me doubt Jamie's love for his family, only whether he actually wanted to live with them. Like Alan Arthur, Jamie talked about living together but found himself reluctant to make the commitment.

That the family had been fractured by their parents' deaths intensified the siblings' commitment to family and perhaps their sense of duty about keeping it intact. That sense of duty may well have been what kept Jamie promising to live with family, while his behavior demonstrated he had some reservations too.

The deaths of their parents had sent the Curtises spinning outward. Throughout their lives they made various attempts to spin back inward. Ben's death finally brought his siblings together under one roof—his lifelong dream (and perhaps part of his plan?).

Ben had tried fruit farming in California and failed at it. He succeeded for a time at mining in Arizona, but his farm life there failed in 1892. When this enterprise collapsed, mostly as a result of a flood, he packed up his family and moved them all back to California and in with his two sisters, his other family. The sisters were delighted to have Ben and his family and welcomed them enthusiastically. Everyone was happy—it seemed.

Shortly after moving his family in with his sisters, Ben took a walk to the beach and never returned. His body was recovered from the ocean several days later. It has all the hallmarks of a suicide. He was forty-five, his ranch had failed, he had moved his family into the care of his older sisters.[19]

From the letters it is not possible to see Ben's suicide coming. Even rereading the letters with the certain knowledge of his death, one cannot see many hints of it. He may have been depressed by his failure to make a go of his ranch (again). He may have felt unable to ever quite get ahead. His siblings, who had given him so much loving and parenting, would embrace his wife and children. They had already. In any case, he did not hint to his sisters in writing and probably did not in person, either.

The nineteenth century was full of suicides—of one kind or another. Because some regarded suicide as a sin, such events were usually deeply shameful and kept secret if at all possible. Today these taboos have lifted slightly. People more often admit to suicides within their families and seek counseling, join support groups, tell enough of the truth that friends and neighbors know, but many people still keep secrets around suicide. Spare the family, protect the person's reputation, do not tell.

On the day of Ben's death, before they knew, Gussie was still playing the big sister, complaining to Jamie that she had to nag Ben to do something or another, "but I think he will do it soon as I will remind him until he does." And she again urged Jamie to join the family circle: "I think it is time you began to think of the comforts of a home. We have a room here for you, even with Ben's family, and wish you were here to occupy it" and "Now if you will come down too, we will all be together, and we can be very happy." Gussie defined happiness as family solidarity. As she said so poignantly: "I feel we have something to live for in these children." How much more poignant the letter appears when we know that perhaps even as she wrote, her brother was launched on his walk.[20]

Shortly after Ben's death Jamie finally made a home with his sisters. Ben's death, then, brought his family together, finally. His wife and children stayed with Etta and Gussie and Jamie. If it is the function of the youngest to keep the family together, Ben did his job successfully, if tragically.

Like so many families in the past, the Curtises lived out their lives, went about their daily routines, made sense out of their own experiences within a small orbit, known to relatives, close friends, perhaps neighbors. Not much beyond. They are nonetheless remarkable, especially in the strength of their family feeling. They did not have parents who kept them together, who negotiated their connections. They kept themselves together once they had the opportunity to do so, that is, once they became adults. But they could not do everything for each other. They could not save each other—at least they could not save Ben.

This is a story that makes us think about the relationship between one death and another. About suicide and its causes. What happened to Ben? In that letter that Gussie wrote to Jamie on the day of Ben's death, she had said of Ben that he was "most too easy about things generally." Was he so easy because he could see a solution, because he could trust some people he loved to take care of the other people he loved? He knew the effects on children of parental death. He knew what it was like for children to be delivered into the care of their parents' relatives. In an odd way Ben's children replicate an essential part of Ben's experience. Ben must also have trusted that his sisters would do for his children what he no longer could.

This family's story is the most unsatisfying of those I tell here. It is the most promising and the most incomplete. It leaves me with the most sadness and the most questions—much the way that death often does, especially a suicide.[21]

## Notes

1. The Curtis family letters were collected largely by Delia Augusta (Gussie) Curtis and are housed at the Huntington Library, San Marino, California. Not surprisingly, there is no secondary literature on this family. A descendant of this Curtis family—probably the granddaughter of Ben and Mary—has written a helpful guide to the papers. See Elizabeth Curtis Reinbold MacPhail, "Curtis Family Letters," in two parts: "Part One: 1820–1868, Letters Written in East and Midwest, Including Civil War period," and "Part Two: 1871–1875 & 1890, 1891, Written from Shasta County, California, and Environs," with the papers in the Huntington Library. Thanks to Elliott West, who helpfully steered me toward these papers.

2. See D. Rothman, *Discovery of the Asylum;* Cmiel, *Home of Another Kind;* Dulberger, *"Mother Donit fore the Best";* and Zmora, *Orphanages Reconsidered.*

3. Holt, *The Orphan Trains;* Warren, *Orphan Train Rider.*

4. Jamie Curtis to Gussie Curtis, April 3, 1857.

5. See, for example, Alger *Ragged Dick* and *Mark, the Match Boy.*

6. Etta Curtis to Gussie Curtis, Jan. 7, 1864.

7. Jamie Curtis to Gussie Curtis, April 3, 1857. As Walter Toman suggests, "An older sibling is likely to take on a role of responsibility, guidance, and care vis-a-vis the younger one." He continues: "A younger sibling, on the other hand, has ordinarily never been without the older one. The younger is likely to become dependent upon the guidance and care of the older sibling" (Toman, "Basics of Family Structure," 48).

8. Jamie Curtis to Gussie Curtis, July 9, 1857.

9. Jamie Curtis to Gussie Curtis, May 16, 1861; Ben Curtis to Gussie Curtis, 1876; Gussie Curtis to Etta Curtis, Jan. 4, 1864; Etta Curtis to Gussie Curtis, Jan. 7, 1864.

10. Ben Curtis to Etta Curtis, Oct. 24, 1873; Etta Curtis to Gussie Curtis, Jan. 4, 1864.

11. Ben Curtis to Gussie Curtis, August, 1867.

12. Ben Curtis to Gussie Curtis, Nov. 21, 1865.

13. Ben Curtis to Etta Curtis, June 2 and June 29, 1873.

14. See MacPhail, "Curtis Family Letters," part 1 passim.

15. Ben called on his sisters to find just the right breast pin for him to give to his new bride. The granddaughter of Ben and Mary reported that Mary wore that pin often and that it had passed to her (Ben Curtis to Gussie and Etta Curtis, May 20, 1885).

16. Mary (Hocker) Curtis to Gussie Curtis, Feb. 13, 1891; Ben Curtis to [Gussie Curtis], Sept. 3, 1886; Mary Curtis to Gussie and Etta Curtis, Feb. 13, 1891.

17. Jamie Curtis to Gussie Curtis, July 2, 1865; Ben Curtis to Jamie Curtis, Nov. 16, 1891; Gussie Curtis to Jamie Curtis, June 20 and Oct. 24, 1883.

18. Jamie Curtis to Gussie Curtis, July 9, 1857, May 16, 1861, and July 2, 1865;

Jamie Curtis to Etta and Gussie Curtis, July 23 and Sept. 14, 1890, and July 19, 1891.

19. In her notes on the Curtis family letters, Ben's granddaughter says she too believes that Ben took his own life. She must have learned something of it in the family, but she does not say.

20. Gussie Curtis to Jamie Curtis, May 30, 1892.

21. One lesson of the Curtis family is that families' catastrophes and tragedies are often concealed and hidden in the past, particularly when they're felt to be shameful. When his wife, Clover, committed suicide, Henry Adams completely hid it. He razored the pages out of his otherwise extensive and copious journal. And he wrote an autobiography in which she did not figure at all. See Adams, *Letters of Henry Adams,* and *Education of Henry Adams;* also Frederich, *Clover.*

# EIGHT

# The Blairs, Part 1: The Center of Attention

The Blair family was organized from first to last around politics and ultimately around the political life of Francis Preston Blair Jr., the youngest of the four siblings of this nineteenth-century family from Kentucky and Washington, D.C. One biographer in the 1980s compared the Blairs to the Kennedys. An earlier biographer, reflecting a different historical context, declared them second only to the Adams family "in their political influence on the course of American history." He did not exaggerate when he declared that "they were participants in some way in almost every important event in the history of the United States between 1828 and 1876."[1]

Few other families in American history have been so fully engaged in politics, but other families organize around other common enterprises—a farm or business, a collective aspiration, a difficulty, a talent. In each of these quite different kinds of cases the family resources and the lives of all the family members become focused, if not on, then in relation to, that central concern. The Blairs powerfully illustrate how one family organized itself around a common goal—to provide the United States with a president—and ultimately around one person key to that dream.

Located just across the street from the White House, Blair House at 1651 Pennsylvania Avenue serves as guest house for important government visitors (including the president-elect the night before the inauguration), as museum, and as fitting reminder of the Blair families who once lived there.

This well-known (and well-studied) family included Francis Preston Blair Sr., Eliza Violet Gist, and their four children: Montgomery (1813–

---

*The Blairs: Older Generation*

Francis Preston Blair Sr. (1791–1876)
m. 1812    Eliza Violet Gist (1793–1877)
            Montgomery (1813–83)
                m. 1836    Caroline Buckner
                            two children
                m. 1846    Mary Elizabeth (Minna) Woodbury
                            five children
            Juliet (1814–16)
            Laura (1816–19)
            Elizabeth (Lizzie) (1818–1906)
                m. 1843    Samuel Phillips Lee
                            one child
            James (1819–53)
                m. 1846    Mary Serena Jessup
                            four children
            Frank Jr. (1821–75)
                m. 1847    Apolline Alexander
                            eight children

---

1883), Elizabeth (1818–1906), James (1819–1853), and Francis Preston Jr. (1821–1875).[2]

Frank Sr. was born in Virginia in 1791 and raised in Kentucky. He trained as a lawyer but rarely earned his living from the law. First he tried farming. Few men have been less suited to an occupation than Frank was to farming. He did not last long at it. He preferred land speculation, although he was barely more successful in that work. He also served for eighteen years as a circuit court clerk.

He really found his life's work, however, in writing—political writing. He took on various issues that caught President Andrew Jackson's eye, and in 1830 Frank moved his family to Washington, D.C., to take over the editorship of the *Globe,* a fiercely partisan Jacksonian newspaper. The Washington to which he moved was a small town, and Blair quickly became a big fish. He moved freely among its residents, especially with Jackson himself. He was a member of Jackson's inner circle of advisers, his Kitchen Cabinet. The president valued Blair's loyalty, and he took to the Blair children, especially Lizzie and Frank Jr. Frank Sr.'s writing guaranteed that he was involved in political contests through the 1830s and 1840s; in the 1850s he became active in the formation of the

Free Soil, then the Republican, Party, the party of Abraham Lincoln. He established a close personal and political friendship with Lincoln but one strained by Blair's own Southern sympathies. After Lincoln's death and the conclusion of the Civil War, Frank realigned himself with the more sympathetic Democrats. He took an active part in promoting (or attacking) candidates for another ten years, although more from the edges than from the center, until his death in 1876.[3]

In 1812 Frank Sr. had married Eliza Violet Gist, a woman who also took an interest in politics. The success and the prominence of the *Globe* were partly her achievement. She kept track of editorials in other papers, entertained political friends and foes alike, and oversaw the *Globe* itself when Frank traveled—which was not infrequently. She certainly had opinions, and while the political climate of the day precluded her taking any public role, she contributed to the political climate of her household and acted indirectly in the public arena of her husband and sons. In addition, she created helpful and politically wise social settings for her family and their political friends—a contribution of no minor importance.[4]

Both Frank and Eliza came naturally to politics. Frank was the son of a Kentucky attorney general. Eliza was the stepdaughter of a Kentucky governor and related by marriage to Henry Clay, one of the most important political figures of the nineteenth century. Frank, twenty-one, and Eliza, nineteen, spoke their wedding vows in the Kentucky governor's mansion. They were married for sixty-four years and had four children who survived to adulthood. They loved them all, but one became the center of their attention.

When I was growing up, we practiced reciting our family names in order. We also had—and from time to time still do have, I have to admit—contests to see who can name us all the fastest: *robertajudylinda-susanmichaelannettepeggytommarybetsyteresasteven.*

Always from oldest to youngest and each of us always includes our own name, of course. If the contest were to work, we all had to say all twelve names. Without ever discussing it, we did not include the name of the brother who died at birth—though we all knew it and visited his grave from time to time—but we did and do include Peggy, who was twenty-one when she died in 1974. I can't say the family names in any other order without stopping to think and then I often stumble.

We also valued a kind of rough equality. We paid close attention to any signs of favoritism; because they happened so rarely, they live in the family memory. When my third-oldest sister, Linda, was four, our grandparents took her to Florida. We still give her a hard time about it—the rest of us didn't ever get to go, and I wasn't even born yet—and some even still feel a little resentment. It is dim and distant but still there. (I suspect that she still feels a little special about it too.) The older ones also complain about how easy the younger ones had it. We had to take the bus, they got to use the car. The younger ones always had more clothes, more money, more of everything (except discipline, rules, and photo-graphs) than the older ones did. Not fair, we grumble good-naturedly, sort of.

So when I get to the Blairs, I'm naturally inclined to introduce them—as I have most families in this book—in order of age and to try to give them equal treatment. It does not suit the Blairs, however. The family culture requires that Frank, the youngest, go first and get the most.

Francis Preston Blair Jr. was born in 1821. In the late twentieth cen-tury, if parents call a son after his father, it is most often the firstborn. This was not so often the case in the nineteenth century. Among the Blairs it turned out to foretell the family arrangement. It was Frank Jr. who car-ried out his father's—and the family's—ambition. Frank Jr. was the star; he was also the baby of the family.

In birth-order talk the "baby" often enjoys the most congenial at-mosphere, an incubator warmed by the attention of older siblings as well as parents. The youngest is most in need of help when there is the most help around. Growing up the baby might cause some lack of self-confi-dence (someone else is always more experienced, more knowledgeable, and willing to give advice and direction), but the baby is also never "de-throned," never displaced by another, and so basks in the family atten-tion, often for a lifetime. The baby gets used to being the center of at-tention. Some babies react by trying to prove themselves, some just accept this care as evidence of their specialness and enjoy it. Frank—as a child and as an adult—fell more into the second category. One unsympathet-ic historian called him the "spoiled darling of the Blair family," but even a sympathetic one agreed that Frank was "generally overindulged."[5]

Frank did not take too well to school. After a couple of false starts—maybe because he was overindulged, maybe because, as one brother suggested, he was homesick—he graduated from Princeton but not with honors as one piece of campaign propaganda alleged, and not with his class, because some shenanigan got him barred from the ceremony and deferred the conferral of the degree for a year.[6]

After Princeton he attended Transylvania University's law school, following in the footsteps of his father and his older brother Montgom-ery. Then in 1842 he settled in St. Louis where Montgomery and his first

wife, Caroline, were living and he was the mayor; she died in 1844. After a two-year journey to the West, Frank Jr. returned to St. Louis and
married Apolline Alexander in 1847. They set up house next door to
Montgomery and his new wife, Mary Elizabeth, known as Minna. The
wives, Apo and Minna, formed an alliance almost as close as the husbands'.[7]

Frank and Apo had eight children, seven of whom lived to adulthood.
The family resided officially in St. Louis, but Frank's political life kept
him away and in Washington, D.C., for huge blocks of time. When they
were in Washington, they stayed either at the Pennsylvania Avenue house
with Montgomery and his family, or in Silver Spring, Maryland, the senior Blairs' summer home that had become their permanent residence.

Frank Jr. practiced law for a few years but without too much enthusiasm. It was a life in politics that he craved and created. He embarked
on his political career first in the Missouri state legislature (1852–1856),
then in the U.S. Congress. He served both in Congress and in the army
during the Civil War. Although he was not a graduate of West Point
(Montgomery was), he was temperamentally quite suited for war duty,
rose to the rank of major general, and served honorably and prominently
with generals William T. Sherman and Ulysses S. Grant. He was with
Sherman when the Union Army marched to the sea and with Sherman
again when Robert E. Lee surrendered the Confederate cause in 1865.
Frank's early support of Lincoln—as well as his family connections—gave
him a voice at the White House, a voice certainly taken more seriously
than had he simply been a congressman from Missouri. His father's and
brother's positions enhanced and raised Frank Jr.'s profile.

His active role in party politics—in a period of party realignments—
resulted in his nomination in 1868 as the Democratic vice-presidential
candidate on the Democratic ticket with Horatio Seymour; they lost to
Grant and Schuyler Colfax. In 1871 Missouri sent Frank Jr. to the U.S.
Senate to fill an unexpired term. He was in heaven. He would have to
move his whole family to Washington semipermanently. He could be near
his parents and his siblings and at the center of Washington political life.

In 1872 he ran for a full term in the Senate and lost; shortly thereafter he had a stroke that left him partially paralyzed on his right side.
Ever determined, he taught himself to write with his left. His health
deteriorated and in 1874 he suffered a more serious stroke and died the
next year. He was only fifty-four. His death left the family emotionally
devastated and without its central purpose. Montgomery, especially, felt
the loss.

Montgomery, Frank's oldest sibling, was born in 1813. Like his father and grandfather, he aspired to the law, but at his father's insistence he instead attended and in 1835 graduated from West Point. Then he served honorably in the Second Seminole War. As soon as he had fulfilled his duty, he resigned from the army and resumed his law studies. He settled neither in Kentucky, where he was from, nor in Washington, where his parents were, but in St. Louis, where he opened a law practice. At twenty-nine he was elected mayor, then became a judge at thirty-two.

He stayed away from the East Coast, it seems, for as long as he could resist his parents' entreaties to join them. He succumbed—for a time—after Caroline died in 1844, then went back to St. Louis. In 1853 his parents, his father, especially, prevailed upon him to move to Washington. He, his second wife, and their several children moved into the house on Lafayette Square that his father had bought in 1836 and stayed. Montgomery thrived in the Washington world of politics, and his father gave him Blair House in 1854. Montgomery continued to practice law and argued various Supreme Court cases. He represented Dred Scott, the runaway slave who sued for his freedom and lost in 1856 in one of the most important—certainly incendiary—U.S. Supreme Court cases of the nineteenth century.[8]

Like his father, Montgomery was an early and loyal supporter of Lincoln's and was rewarded with appointment as postmaster general (although both Franks had lobbied Lincoln to appoint Montgomery secretary of state). He did the work of that position well, standardizing postage rates and bringing greater efficiency and speed to the delivery of mail. He also took as part of his mandate as a cabinet member the advising of the president on matters outside the post office. He cared especially about the issues that would dominate Reconstruction: treatment of Southern whites and of freed slaves. His opposition to slavery, before and during the war, put him firmly in the Republican camp. His opposition to enfranchisement of black men put him, after the war, firmly among the Democrats. His career focused mostly on party politics from the 1860s until his death in 1883.[9]

He and Caroline, married in 1836, had had one daughter, named Betty after his sister. Caroline and their second daughter died in childbirth in 1844. He married again in 1846 to Mary Elizabeth Woodbury (Minna), the daughter of Levi Woodbury, a Supreme Court justice from 1845 to 1851. Montgomery and Minna had five children. Betty lived with her paternal grandparents after her mother's death, and they formally adopted her when her father remarried. She grew up in Silver Spring and at Blair House and stayed with her grandparents even after her father moved his second wife and family to Washington.

Lizzie, the only sister of Frank and Montgomery, was born in 1818. The Blairs thought her of delicate constitution, though she is reported to have been tomboyish—almost inevitable for the only girl in a household of boys. Frank may have been the center of attention, but Lizzie was clearly very special to her parents and her brothers. They told her secrets and then told her, "Don't tell anybody," or "You all will ruin me by telling every thing I confide to you & therefore forbear for the sake of your afft. brother," or "*entre nous.*" She kept the secrets but passed on the news. She wrote hundreds of letters and kept people variously informed about each other. "Sister tells me" provides the beginning for dozens of Blair letters.[10]

Her letters reveal a warm, charming, engaging girl, then woman. When her parents first moved from Kentucky to Washington, D.C., they left their boys with relatives but took Lizzie with them. She was not the youngest, but she was the only girl and precious because of that. The widowed and childless Andrew Jackson took a special liking to the senior Blairs as well as for Lizzie. She was welcome to play in the room while her father and the president talked. She copied letters and did small jobs for Jackson. When the family first moved into the house on Pennsylvania Avenue, it was in need of some repair, and Jackson insisted that Lizzie live at the White House until the repairs were completed. Better for her health, he thought, and, no doubt, a pleasure for him too.[11]

In 1839 she met Samuel Phillips Lee, a naval officer—and family opposition to any match. Her health worried them—perhaps she should not marry at all—and her intended worried them—a naval officer? In fact, when Lizzie finally insisted on the wedding four years later, even without Montgomery's approval or her father's presence, the match turned out to be perfect. Lizzie and Phil were happily married for more than fifty years. And because he was in the navy and often away from home, she made her home with or near her parents for their lifetimes.

Her parents gave each of her brothers a start-up stake of $10,000 (politics apparently had its rewards in those days: the Blairs had arrived in Washington with no savings and little cash) and offered one to Lizzie as well. She declined the money in exchange for the right to live at home. This arrangement suited everyone just fine; even Phil grew into it as the Blair family warmed up to him. When he retired from the navy, he joined her in Silver Spring or at Blair House for another twenty years.

This arrangement kept her close to the vitality of her family and at the center of American political life. Like her brothers, she had been steeped in the Blair passion for politics. She did not want to leave it. She numbered among her friends most of the important political figures of her time. Jackson was only one of several presidents Lizzie knew well. Her home was full of politics and politicians. Her son, Blair Lee, was the only politician of the next generation. He served in the U.S. Senate from 1914 to 1917.[12]

James, the second of the three Blair brothers, was born in 1819— between Lizzie and Frank Jr. He was the only Blair not much interested in politics. He jumped ship and joined the navy. He proved a worthy sailor and an astute businessman. He took a leave of absence from the navy and went to California to make his fortune. He did too. He was a genius at timing, anyway—the year of his California adventure was 1849, the year in which thousands of fortunes were made (and lost) in the gold rush, most not in gold but, like Jim's, in support services. He rented out property and sailed steamboats. He made a bundle. At the end of his leave he took up his naval duties in California and stayed there for the rest of his life. Unfortunately, it was only four more years.[13]

Jim married Mary Serena Jessup, a woman with a long and honorable political lineage, in 1846. Like his brother-in-law, Phil Lee, Jim spent months at a time away from his wife and found it best to make a home for her near both their families in Washington, D.C. Then he had a house built for his family near his parents' house in Silver Spring. Jim and Mary had four children; their firstborn was Violet—the indomitable Violet who married Albert Janin.

In 1853, while he was still in California, he died. It was nearly a month before word reached Washington. Frank Jr. volunteered, but it was Montgomery who went to California to settle his brother's affairs and to bring the body home. Mary was pregnant and gave birth within days of hearing of her husband's death, so it made sense for Montgomery to take care of Jim's affairs. Nonetheless, this was one of many occasions when the Blair family picked up what might have been the work of the marriage family rather than the birth family. Mary proved to be a loyal and central member of the extended Blair family, though she was quiet and, like her husband, not especially political. She lived more than sixty years after her husband's death and did not remarry.[14]

This, then, was the Blair family, although it feels more accurate to call it the Blair clan. Many of their dealings are characterized by their loyalty, affection, and connection. When Montgomery's daughter Mary died in 1862, he could not bring himself to write, telling Frank, probably then away at war, "I have been too heart broken to write about anything." But otherwise the family members wrote openly. An especially striking example is Montgomery's description of his second wife's labor and delivery. Minna took chloroform, and removing the placenta was difficult, he reported. "The Dr. had hard work to take it away but finally succeeded but giving great pain & followed by considerable flowing. Fortunately however that was arrested, by applying cold & wet cloths to the abdomen, by raising the feet considerably & by using other appliances promptly." He wrote as one who shared a sphere with his wife and his sister that allowed him to write frankly and openly about private matters.[15]

They did have a contentious side, these Blairs, even among themselves. They all had strong reactions to each other's marriages and spouses. Lizzie's father could not bear to "'resign my rights in you to anyone,'" and Montgomery refused to give his approval at all, agreeing with their father, according to Phil Lee's biographers, that "'no one could ever love Lizzie as her parents did.'" They could not bear the thought of losing her. Her father did not attend the wedding—held at Blair House—and Montgomery remained opposed. The marriage, however, went ahead when mother Eliza and Frank Jr. consented.[16]

Montgomery's own marriages sent some ripples through the family. When Montgomery was courting "C"—certainly Caroline Buckner, his future wife, but she was not named in the correspondence at the time—he used Lizzie as go-between to deliver messages between Montgomery and "C" and as fire wall between the couple and the senior Blairs. He also drew on Lizzie's support: she rejoiced in his "heartfelt joy" when he was happy and agreed when he was not that, yes, women were fickle. Even so, as the wedding approached, Lizzie worried about losing her brother. His reassurances that he did not want "to give up my little sweet sis" may not have reassured her in the face of his romantic euphoria. "What are the friends & scenes of my early years to the gentle darling being in whom my pride, my ambition, my happiness, my love my life itself all are centered." Montgomery did take one more crack, however, at meeting his family's worries about his loyalty. "Mother always said . . . that when I got married there would end my home loving &c but you cant imagine how much I have left yet & how anxious I am to . . . go homewards. The truth is, that I shall never outgrow or outlive that disposition." He never did. That disposition was what drew him back to Washington, to the house next door to his sister's, to a summer house next to his parents', down the road from his brother's family.[17]

Weathering conflict within the Blair clan must have been difficult because so many family members lived so close together—or with each other—for so much of their lives. When Montgomery moved back to Washington in 1852, he moved into the Blair house on Pennsylvania Avenue. By that time his parents were living for most of the year in their home in Silver Spring, Maryland, but they liked to spend the winters in Washington, so they stayed with Montgomery. Because Lizzie lived with her parents even after she was married (and while her husband was on active duty in the navy), for most of the 1850s she too would have stayed with Montgomery when she was in Washington. In 1858–1859 her parents had a house built for her right next door to Montgomery's. His address was 1651 Pennsylvania Avenue; hers was 1653 Pennsylvania Avenue. They were nearly identical houses and, according to one historian of the Blair House, the two were "occupied as a unit." I cannot determine from the correspondence exactly what that meant, but it is clear that though there was a solid common wall, family members moved back and forth easily, informally, and often. Just to add to the family closeness, Jim's widow and children lived around the corner from Montgomery's Washington house, and both she and Montgomery had summer houses built near the senior Blairs in Maryland. When Frank Jr. lived in Washington and served in the Senate, he too lived in one or the other of the Blair houses, as did his family (though his wife, Apo, made sure that such family visits were never long.)[18]

Minna, Montgomery's second wife, would have had an easier life if she had lived a greater distance from the Blair clan. She and Eliza did not get on, nor did she and Lizzie, nor did she and her stepdaughter, Betty. For various periods of time at various times Minna was not on speaking terms with one or another of the Blairs. One biographer suggested that her Northern ways clashed with their more Southern ones.[19]

Jim had troubles too. He was one of the strongest opponents of Lizzie's marriage to Phil Lee: "Avoid intimacy with him by all means, for I do assure you upon my honor that he is neither honest or virtuous." When, however, Lizzie objected to his choice, Jim commanded her approval: "Retire your position smoothly & give me Mother's & your written consent." And, he demanded, write it "*cheerfully.*" He also told her to make sure that their father knew that Jim "would desert my *home* . . . and all I love" if the family put itself in the way of his marriage. In fact, the family did put itself in his way and ultimately so did the woman's family. Jim did not really abandon his home over it, but his navy career did keep him away. Three years later he found someone more suitable and one more agreeable to the whole family. Good thing too: she lived among the Blairs for more than sixty years after he died in 1853 after only seven years of marriage.[20]

Frank's marriage to Apo occasioned less opposition, but she was not a woman of Washington, D.C., and they courted and married in St. Louis. Moreover, Frank and Apo were cousins. The family more easily accepted her than others of the in-laws, but Apo kept herself a little separate from the Blairs. Perhaps she felt the gravity pull of their affection for each other, and she strained against it. She wanted Frank to be at the center of their family, but he was much more powerfully drawn to the center of his.

The most telling example of this conflict between Frank's birth family and his married family occurred when Frank had a stroke in the 1870s. He went to a hospital–health spa in Clifton Springs, New York. He was lonely, frightened, and knew that he was dying. He and Apo agreed that he would go home to St. Louis. Montgomery absolutely refused. He insisted that Frank stay, and he paid the expenses. Montgomery was desperate to try everything and certainly terrified. He could not face the prospect of Frank's death. His will prevailed. He was the older brother. He had dedicated his life to his brother. Apo was furious at Montgomery, but Frank apparently consented because they stayed in Clifton Springs until even Montgomery had to agree that nothing more could be done. Only then was Apo allowed to take him home to St. Louis.

Apo had never fit happily into the larger Blair family, and she always worked to keep her distance from them. She might have moved to Washington when Frank was serving in the Civil War or when he was in the Senate or afterward, when maintaining a legal residence in Missouri did not matter. She never made the move, however. She may have been able to stay on cordial terms with the Blairs only by keeping several hundred miles between her family and the rest of Frank's family. Even after his death she remained in St. Louis. To the Washington Blairs this must have seemed odd, if not hostile. Apo's and Montgomery's disagreement about Frank's treatment typified her relationship with the Blairs and proved to be yet another instance when Frank's loyalty to his birth family trumped Apo's wishes and even his own. Apo deeply resented it and let Montgomery know it.[21]

Another family conflict is especially telling (and it's complicated to tell). In some gossipy moment Betty, Montgomery's daughter by his first wife, commented critically to friends outside the family that Frank Jr. had made a habit of borrowing money from his parents, leaving them in financial straits. Word got back to Frank, and he chided her for providing grist for his enemies. He also pointedly reminded her that she too had benefited from his parents' generosity.

We can imagine the layers of emotion that got scratched in this exchange. It has a little whiff of sibling rivalry between this uncle and niece whose relationship in the family changed when his parents adopted her— he had been the youngest, now *she* was. After their exchange about his borrowing, Betty broke off contact with Frank and refused to visit when he was at home. When Betty found herself pregnant some time later, she wrote and asked her grandparents whether she could come home to Silver Spring for her delivery. She yearned for the comfort of her old room. Grandfather, grandmother, and Lizzie refused. They would have had to move one of Frank's children out to make room for her. Several weeks after her due date, her husband finally wrote to inform her family that she had died in childbirth. He had not informed anyone even of the funeral plans.[22]

The story is nearly too poignant to tell. The pain on all sides still seeps across the years. At the heart of it, however, is that Betty committed a very bad offense in the Blair catechism: she had been critical of Frank outside the family in an arena where he might be harmed politically. Her request put the family loyalties to the test—Betty or Frank— and the family chose Frank. Given Frank's place in the family, this was, I think, inevitable.

This loving, contentious, loyal family was also a deeply, fundamentally, essentially political family. The politics of their times were central and abiding—the consuming interest of the Blair family for fifty years.

Politics fill up their letters. They have and express opinions and views and give advice. They interweave the political and the family news—which is how they took their politics, as part of the fabric of their lives. They drew no stark distinctions between the public nature of politics and the private nature of family life. Their collective family dream was to get Frank Jr. elected president—and they almost succeeded.

The central puzzle of this family is why the senior Blair did not himself seek political office. He completed law training but decided not to practice law because of concerns about his health. His failed attempt to serve the United States in the War of 1812 proved his fragility. He enlisted in the army in 1812 and was sent to Canada. He made it only to Indiana before he collapsed and had to return home. A man of Frank's pride and drive was at the least embarrassed and more likely humiliated.[23]

Moreover, Frank Sr. suffered from what his 1933 biographer called "an unfortunate deficiency in his vocal powers." This offers a tantalizing hint for understanding the Blair family. If Frank Sr. could not command the speech that was central to his ambition and if he could not abandon that ambition—which he obviously could not—he had to find another way to express that drive. So he practiced his politics behind the scene and in print, writing and advising. It did not ultimately satisfy him.[24]

In addition, because of the gender restrictions of the time, Eliza also would not have had a direct expression of her political interests. She was a Southern lady, however, and knew how to exercise power indirectly. She might have been an excellent teacher in the practice of politics.

Both pursued their ambitions as much as they could and encouraged and cultivated that ambition in their children. Montgomery took it up, but he had inherited his father's "deficiency in vocal powers." He also may not have had the personality for elective office. He was often abrasive and "temperamentally combative and obstinate," according to one biographer. Even his obituary writer breached the form's protocol and reported that "his opponents considered him unnecessarily bumptious," and "his incessant letter-writing and prodigious 'scolding' were less effective than he supposed."[25]

Montgomery took an active, but primarily appointive, role in politics. His most important post was postmaster general in Lincoln's cabinet. He also served as adviser to presidents and as a shaper of the political parties of his time. He did serve as mayor of St. Louis in 1842–1843 and ran halfheartedly and unsuccessfully in 1874 for Congress. Only after both his brother and his father were dead did Montgomery turn seriously to elective office. He served in the Maryland House of Representatives and, in 1882, ran for Congress. He was defeated.

Lizzie too took politics seriously. Her Civil War–era letters to her husband are remarkably astute accounts of Washington politics. More than a reporter, she actively advised him and lobbied on his behalf. She also transcribed letters and took notes on speeches and for speeches—an unpaid staff person for her brothers and father. Whatever her political acumen, she could not be the family candidate. She was female. She could not run for elective office. She could not even vote for someone else who ran for elective office. She might have picked up the standard of feminism that was being raised in her day by other politically engaged women, but that was not her or the Blair style. Given her acuity and the family's political interests, the Blair family might have carried the torch for woman suffrage. (The Putnams would have.) Instead, Frank Jr. openly spoke against it and Lizzie showed no interest. So, like her father, her mother, and Montgomery, she worked behind the scenes.[26]

Montgomery openly expressed his worries about his sister's management of her emotions. When he was thirty-six and she thirty-one, he bid her to have "some sense" and chided her not to be "carried away so entirely by your feelings." He went on: "Anybody who seems to take an interest in you carries away your affections & with them your judgment." Several years later he again pronounced that Lizzie's "errors lie on the side of her affections and betray her, in her eagerness to make others love those she loves is the greatest of her faults." A woman who got "carried away" by her feelings—or whose brother believed she got carried away—could certainly not carry the family ambition.[27]

Jim might have carried it but did not. Perhaps his family did not think him able enough. More likely, Jim was not interested. He organized a life for himself that could not lead to that outcome. A naval career took one away from Washington, D.C., and away from politics, by definition. Child development literature offers some help here. Sometimes children, sensing the danger of an intense sibling rivalry, go off in quite separate directions so that they do not find themselves competing. Psychologists call this "de-identification" and describe its occurrence most often between same-sex siblings who are close in age—an accurate description of Jim and Frank. Jim could avoid conflict, perhaps even comparisons, with the favorite son by defining a life for himself completely separate from politics. He could be, and was, successful. He was loved. He did not compete with his brother. The cost: a life outside politics. It may not have seemed a high price, all in all.

Then there was Frank. He was just the one. Where Montgomery's personality alienated, Frank's endeared him to many. Where both could be opinionated and dogmatic, even vitriolic, Frank could also be charming, even charismatic. All the spoiling also gave him the impression that the world was happy to revolve around him, and he acted accordingly. Frank had only a minor case of the family voice problem and could function effectively on the stump and in the various houses of government.[28]

Other circumstances too favored Frank's political promotion by his family. Most important—by the time he came along, the family was ready to mount its first full political campaign. When Montgomery was born his parents were twenty-two and nineteen—newly married, unsettled about Frank Sr.'s career and worried about his health, and financially insecure. When Jim was born, his family had just endured the deaths of two children, a two-year-old who died in 1816 and a three-year-old who died only two weeks before Jim's birth in 1819. The household must have been saturated with sadness.[29]

By the time Frank was born—and growing up—the family was ready for its destiny to be fulfilled. The senior Frank was in good health, his career was settled, his finances on their way to prosperity. The Blairs were making strong political connections, they had important friends, and they were settling into a secure place in Washington.[30]

No doubt, each child was special, but Frank was the child of plenty, the boy destined for really great things, the one at just the right time, with just the right personality. He was his father's favorite son, and the family looked forward to Frank's success. As Montgomery wrote to Lizzie, Frank "will be the 'crown & glory of our house.'"[31]

There was just one problem—when Frank was eighteen, his family may have been ready for him to act on the family ambition, but he was not, decidedly not. Used to being the favorite, to getting his own way, he was not ready for discipline or application or hard work. His education did not begin auspiciously. He turned up for college at Yale in the fall of 1837 but made it through only the first semester before the school tossed him out. He also got bounced from the University of North Carolina. He finally graduated from Princeton (where his father's connections had gotten him admitted—this was Alan Arthur's alma mater too).

The whole family paid attention: they interceded for Frank Jr., took his part, defended him, worried about him. All three of his siblings wrote back and forth about their little brother. They complained about his erratic letter writing, his "intolerable habits." When all else failed, they still found things to compliment—even if they did have to stretch. To Eliza: at least Frank "writes an excellent letter." Montgomery agreed.

In a wonderfully patronizing tone the nineteen-year-old Jim complained to Lizzie that Frank was "extremely wild and has a number of very bad ways," which he hoped Frank would "correct when he grows older." Or, Jim complained about Frank's airs, his big head ("although it is very small"). At the same time, Jim entreated Lizzie to "treat him [Frank Jr.] kindly for my sake and persuade father not [to] scold him for he knows what he has done as well as any body and feels for it, I assure you now that he has had a great lesson, he certainly will do well." Frank Jr. apparently had to learn lots of lessons—especially about women. "I am at a loss to account for the conduct on the part of Frank," Montgomery complained when Frank was writing love letters to two different women. After he married one of the two, he had other troubles from his family's point of view (an affair is suggested) that caused turmoil for

Frank with his parents and siblings. Jim hoped that "the unpleasant difference heretofore existing will be extinguished by the real love & affection that has always existed among you all." It was extinguished.[32]

Montgomery's worries suggest his own investment in Frank's future.
He objected to Frank's going into the military because it required "fits
of activity with long intervals of idleness," a tendency that, if developed
any further in Frank, would mean that Montgomery would have to "bid
adieu to all my hopes of his distinction except by some lucky turn of
military life."[33]

While they attended to Frank Jr.'s personal life, his relatives also took
an active part in the development of his professional life. After finishing
law school—at his father and brother's alma mater—he joined Montgomery in St. Louis, in his home and in his law practice. When Frank took it
into his head to go west, he relied on Montgomery to keep the office
going without him, which he did.

While he was away, Frank asked Montgomery to keep track of Apo
and to remind her of Frank's love. He did it. When Frank returned to
St. Louis and married Apo, the new couple shared living spaces with
Montgomery and his wife.

Frank had money problems all his life—he made too little and spent
too much. Apo urged him to leave politics and practice law instead. He
could make more money and he could be at home more. He responded
with some impatience that he had to "make bread for you and the children," and he could do that only with a "public career." Unfortunately,
he never made quite enough bread to support his growing family. He
turned to his family for help—often and repeatedly. He borrowed money from his father, from Montgomery, and from his brother-in-law. He
repaid it when he could but without speed or panic. When his affairs fell
into disarray, he appealed for help in sorting that out as well. In 1860
Phil Lee traveled to St. Louis to help Frank untangle his finances. Even
as Frank was dying, he had to appeal to his family for funds to support
his stay at Clifton Springs—part of what gave Montgomery cause to think
that he could decide what Frank ought to do was that he was helping to
foot the bill. It was also Frank's financial dependence on his parents that
contributed to his break with Betty.[34]

The family, then, rallied its moral forces to contain Frank's excesses.
They focused their financial resources on him. They also focused their
energies on him. Both Frank Sr. and Montgomery kept their eye on
Frank's career. Frank could deliver speeches. He could generate the right
level of passion. He could move people. He was not very good, howev-

er, at writing the speeches. So Frank Sr. wrote virtually all Frank's speeches. Lizzie did some of the research and a lot of the transcriptions. She also learned how to offer a respectable facsimile of his signature so she could sign his letters for him. She gave more than one strategic dinner party, either to invite or to solidify some political interest of Frank's. Frank rarely took a political position or political move without first consulting with Frank Sr. and/or Montgomery. In 1871 a sitting senator from Missouri was nominated for an appointment that, if confirmed by the Senate, would leave his seat open. Frank wrote to Montgomery to tell him to lobby for the man's confirmation so that Frank could finish out the Senate term. That is what happened.[35]

In 1862 Frank Blair Jr. and John C. Frémont—both military men in St. Louis, where Frémont headed the military district and Frank was a soldier—had a falling out (something of an understatement). The whole event shows in sharp relief the centrality of Frank in the Blair family.

Frank, upset by various actions taken by Frémont, wrote to his brother Montgomery, the postmaster general, urging Frémont's removal. Frank was fully confident that Montgomery would pass the letter on to Lincoln, which he did. When he heard of the letter, Frémont had Frank arrested. Montgomery (with no particular authority) ordered Frémont to release him. The story has several other contortions, but Lincoln did remove Frémont.[36]

On a quick telling, it is a simple story of political and military conflict. But it involved virtually every member of the Blair family. As such, it requires a little background. When Montgomery was in Missouri, he had made a personal and political friendship with Sen. Thomas Hart Benton. The two men shared a common interest in politics and many common positions. Benton was helpful to Montgomery. He also proved helpful to Frank and the advancement of Frank's career. In addition, members of the two families became friends, including Lizzie and Jessie Benton, the only daughter of the senator. The two women were faithful and loving correspondents for twenty years, before and after Jessie's marriage to John C. Frémont.[37]

When Frank attacked her husband, Jessie, every bit the politician that Lizzie was, took herself from St. Louis to Washington to answer Frank's criticisms. She visited President Lincoln first, then Frank Blair Sr. She left these meetings angry, hurt, and feeling that her lifelong friends the Blairs had betrayed her, her family, and their lifetime of friendship.

She was certainly right that this was a feud with THE BLAIRS, not just Frank Jr. Montgomery had carried Frank's letter to Lincoln. Frank

Sr. had defended his son's position, without any firsthand knowledge of the situation. As the Blair-Frémont feud escalated, Frank Sr. and Montgomery focused especially on protecting Frank's career. Lizzie turned her back on her long-time friend. When their families' political interests conflicted, they broke all ties with each other. As best we can tell, the two women did not speak to each other again, and the two families ceased all direct contact with each other.[38] All for one and all that.

Jessie's biographer, Pamela Herr, reports Lincoln's comment that "when the Blairs go in for a fight . . . they go in for a funeral" and recounts that the Blairs did not turn quietly away but turned bitter and vindictive. Lizzie regretted that she had "bolstered up such unworthy people for so long." According to Herr, the Blairs also whispered to the press that Frémont took opium and that he aspired to rule an independent West.[39] Whew. This is not a family I'd like to have against me!

Frank had the ability and the fire for politics. He had all the right credentials: law, army service, money, connections. He had the complete and total support of his family. His career moved along well: from the Missouri House of Representatives to several terms in the U.S. Congress to a vice-presidential nomination (a defeat that he could come back from). There were various bumps on this road, contested elections, appointments rejected by Congress, political enemies. Even so, Frank's political career was still on the upswing when his first stroke hit.

His premature death at fifty-four hit the family hard. Frank was so special to all of them that his death would indeed have been devastating in any circumstances. In this case, though, when he died he took his family's ambitions with him. Without him they lost their center. His father and mother had been healthy though aged, but both rapidly and visibly declined after Frank's death. Frank Sr. died the next year and Eliza the year after that.

While Frank was sick, Montgomery had taken a run at a congressional seat but halfheartedly and unsuccessfully. I suspect that he did it to try to distract his parents from Frank's decline. After Frank's death Montgomery did, however, remain active in politics, though he must have felt like one hand clapping. He spent more of his time with his family: Lizzie was still at Silver Spring, and Montgomery was interested in the careers of his four lawyer sons. He died eight years after Frank, in 1883, only seventy and not an old man.

Lizzie mourned openly and deeply. First, Frank, then her father, then her mother. One consolation was that Phil Lee had retired from the navy and moved home to Silver Spring; they lived together there until Phil died in 1897. Jim's wife, Mary, lived close by with her daughter Violet. Apo had never felt at home with Frank's family; she withdrew more and more into her life with her children.

Sibling relationships can have an oddly unchanging quality about them. One might think that we're children when we're young, but when we leave home, we leave behind our childhood selves. The Blairs show us how much this is not true. Once the "baby," always the baby. But not just Frank. Montgomery was the oldest, and he remained the adviser, director, and bossy older brother all his life. Jim was the rebel and outsider from beginning to end. Lizzie was the loving middle child.

Lizzie had never been alone. She'd always been surrounded by family. But she outlasted them all. She lived to be eighty-eight. When she died in 1906, she had survived Frank by almost thirty years. She, the frail one. How lonely she must have been after they were all gone. She had made her whole life in the middle of her family—physically and emotionally—and then she was the only one left.

She had her son, Blair, nearby and her niece Violet Janin. Montgomery's children lived in Blair House—but theirs is the story of the next chapter.

## Notes

1. W. E. Smith, *Francis Preston Blair Family*, vol. 2, 495; Parrish, *Frank Blair*; E. B. Smith, *Francis Preston Blair*. See also the fictionalized version of Frank Blair Jr.'s life (he did not graduate with honors from Princeton University as a precocious nineteen-year-old, for example), prepared for the 1868 campaign when he was the vice-presidential nominee (see Croly, *Seymour and Blair*).

See also Laas, *Wartime Washington*; Herr and Spence, *Letters of Jessie Benton Frémont*; Herr, *Jessie Benton Frémont*; and Cornish and Laas, *Lincoln's Lee*.

This chapter is based primarily on the correspondence among the Blairs in the Blair Family Papers at the Library of Congress, Washington, D.C.

2. All four of the children were born in Kentucky and raised with at least one slave in the household and with other black people in their world. Like many of their generation, they were serious racists and their attitudes about black people accounted for several of their fiercest political battles—but that was still some years ahead. They had "favorite" slaves who stayed with them after the Civil War. The race dynamics of this household would prove a fascinating research topic.

3. See Parrish, *Frank Blair*; E. B. Smith, *Francis Preston Blair*; W. E. Smith, *Francis Preston Blair Family*.

4. Some years later another quite active political wife—it would be anachronistic, though completely accurate, to call her a politician herself—Jessie Benton Frémont, wife of the Free Soil Party's presidential nominee in 1856, John C. Frémont (and daughter of Sen. Thomas Hart Benton of Missouri), alluded

to the difficulty of being a woman with political opinions that she expressed. "Strange, isn't it, that when a man expresses a conviction fearlessly, he is report-ed as having made a trenchant and forceful statement, but when a woman speaks thus earnestly, she is reported as a lady who has lost her temper" (see the excel-lent biography by Herr, *Jessie Benton Frémont*, 339).

5. Adler, *Social Interest*, 238–39. The unsympathetic historian is Herr, who saw the Blairs in general and Frank Blair Jr. in particular as responsible for the re-moval of Frémont as head of the military district of Missouri during the Civil War (Herr, *Jessie Benton Frémont*, 331). The most sympathetic historian is Par-rish, *Frank Blair*, 3.

6. The Parrish biography gives the most play to Frank's college difficulties. See Parrish, *Frank Blair*, 4.

7. Their alliance proved helpful to both, especially after Minna and Montgom-ery moved to Washington and Minna found herself so often at odds with her in-laws. Apo was her ally in this family configuration, because she too could also be at odds with the senior Blairs. See Parrish, *Frank Blair*, 31ff.

8. Fehrenbacher, *The Dred Scott Case*.

9. In addition to the three Blair biographies, see Cullum, *Biographical Regis-ter*, vol. 1, 597–603.

10. James Blair to Lizzie Blair, June 16, 1842, and June 15, 1843; Montgom-ery Blair to Lizzie Blair, July 18, 1837.

11. W. E. Smith, *Francis Preston Blair Family*, vol. 1, 96–102.

12. See E. B. Smith, *Francis Preston Blair*, 182; Parrish, *Frank Blair*, 13. Liz-zie does not appear in the *Dictionary of American Biography*, but her husband does. See the entry for Samuel Phillips Lee, *Dictionary of American Biography*, vol. 11, 129–30. See also Cornish and Laas, *Lincoln's Lee*, and Southwick, *Presi-dential Also-Rans and Running Mates*, 331–36.

13. Jim gets the least attention in the Blair biographies, which is not surpris-ing because he was both the least publicly involved and the shortest lived. None-theless, one still gets a hint of what Jim's experience of his family might have been. We can imagine him as the one on the sidelines at family gatherings. In his bi-ography of Frank Blair, Parrish, for example, barely mentions Jim. The index includes more entries for Frank's son Jim than for Frank's brother Jim. Jim's wife is even incorrectly identified in the index. See Parrish, *Frank Blair*, 53, 312, 313. See also Laas, *Love and Power*, 1–5.

14. See Laas, *Love and Power*, 2–4.

15. Montgomery Blair to Frank Blair Jr., Sept. 13, 1862; Montgomery Blair to Lizzie Lee [June 1849].

16. Cornish and Laas, *Lincoln's Lee*, 51, 52; E. B. Smith, *Francis Preston Blair*, 179–81.

17. Montgomery Blair to Lizzie Blair, Jan. 2, 1834. Jan. 29, 1836, and July 18, 1837.

18. Crane, *Blair House*, 21. After their parents died, Blair Lee continued to live, at least from time to time, at 1653, and Gist Blair, Montgomery's youngest son, at 1651 Pennsylvania Avenue. In 1942 the federal government bought the two houses and converted them into one unit. What is now called the Blair-Lee House is used as a formal guest house, primarily for visitors to the president. On the

eve of his inauguration the president-elect and his family usually stay at the Blair-Lee House. The Blairs would have been very proud but not surprised to have their house still at the center of Washington political life.

19. See E. B. Smith, *Francis Preston Blair*, 181–82, 189; Cornish and Laas, *Lincoln's Lee*, 83; Parrish, *Frank Blair*, 112 n.

20. Jim Blair to Lizzie Blair, Nov. 24, 1840, and Oct. 20 and Nov. 11, 1843.

21. W. E. Smith, *Francis Preston Blair Family*, vol. 2, 460–61; Parrish, *Frank Blair*, 31–32, 283–89.

22. E. B. Smith, *Francis Preston Blair*, 431–32.

23. Ibid., 48–49.

24. W. E. Smith, *Francis Preston Blair Family*, 19. The later biographers do not mention anything about the senior Blair's speech, nor do they hazard an account of why he did not pursue a different kind of political life. E. B. Smith did say that Frank Sr.'s father-in-law, the governor of Kentucky, "took no pride in a son-in-law of such delicate constitution"; Smith also describes the lung hemmorhage that disqualified Frank Sr. for war service but does not conclude that either cut him off from two important avenues of advancement, especially in wartime (E. B. Smith, *Francis Preston Blair*, 8).

25. Entry for Montgomery Blair in *Dictionary of American Biography*, vol. 2, 339–50; *New York Times*, July 28, 1883.

26. Parrish, *Frank Blair*, 265.

27. Montgomery Blair to Lizzie Lee [May–June 1849]; Montgomery Blair to Mary Elizabeth (Minna) Woodbury, Jan. 24, 1854; *New York Times*, July 28, 1883. The statements by the apparently very emotional Montgomery are remarkable. He was, his obituary in the *New York Times* reported, often carried away by his emotions but anger more than affection. Moreover, I'm struck by the similarity between his complaint that Lizzie was eager to make others love those she loves and the comment in the *New York Times* that Montgomery was "determined apparently to bring others to his way of thinking." Psychologists might call this projection—where he criticizes in her what he sees and perhaps does not like in himself. In fact, all members of the family seemed to err on the side of trying to convince others; of them, however, Betty was quite moderate.

28. Some of this makes me wonder whether the Blair problem may have been a stutter, although E. B. Smith describes it more as a high squeaky voice. Either way, it would not have been a problem in many areas of political life but would perhaps have been considered a hindrance to service in the House, Senate, or the presidency.

29. Death was not less painful to the survivors in the nineteenth-century than it is to us today but might have been less surprising.

30. With the 1830 move to Washington, D.C., Frank Sr. was awarded the lucrative government printing contract. The man who was nearly cashless in 1830 had by 1845 amassed a personal fortune of more than $100,000 (plus his houses) and had already provided his sons with start-up money.

31. E. B. Smith, *Francis Preston Blair*, 191; Montgomery Blair to Lizzie Blair [1841].

32. Jim Blair to Lizzie Blair, Jan. 14, 1838; Montgomery Blair to Lizzie Lee,

July 13, 1846; Jim Blair to Frank Blair Jr., Dec. 15, 1851; Jim Blair to My Dear Mother, Jan. 15, 1838.

33. Montgomery Blair to Lizzie Lee, July 13, 1846.

34. Frank Blair Jr. to Apolline Blair, March 13, 1864; Parrish, *Frank Blair*, 88.

35. E. B. Smith, *Francis Preston Blair*, 420–23.

36. All three Blair biographies recount essentially the same story, both about the events in St. Louis and the repercussions in Washington. See W. E. Smith, *Francis Preston Blair Family*, vol. 2, 53–89; E. B. Smith, *Francis Preston Blair*, 296–303; and Parrish, *Frank Blair*, 112–39.

37. They shared many life circumstances and found comfort and support in each other—they each had exceptionally political families, they each had strong political views of their own, they each took as active a role in that political life as the gender conventions of their times permitted.

38. Herr and Spence, *Letters of Jessie Benton Frémont*, 340–43.

39. Herr, *Jessie Benton Frémont*, 342. As might be expected, this rendition differs from those offered by the Blair biographers. It is Jessie who suffers most at the hand of the Blairites—then and now.

NINE

# The Blairs, Part 2: Things Fall Apart

By the time I turned to Montgomery's children, I had been following the Blairs through fifty years of their history. I felt pretty familiar with the whole family. I'd developed appreciation for Montgomery, affection for Lizzie and a vague mistrust of her husband, sympathy for Jim, and mixed feelings about Frank Jr. I was sorry to see them fade off, to watch them die one by one, to know that there were some things that I'd never know about them. I knew that they had secrets that they didn't tell, confidences that their letters didn't yield up to me. I missed their company.

But then I got to the folders in the collection that contained the letters of Montgomery's children. I was delighted. They too felt familiar, and I liked the feeling of family continuity that came from following the family into the next generation. When I read my way to the end of the last folder of Blair letters, I was very sad to read on the back of the last letter to Montgomery's only daughter from her brother Gist: "My last letter to Minna." She had not died, she had simply refused to answer and in her refusal broke off all contact with her brother. For the Blairs of the second generation, something so important, so basic, so central happened that they could not reconcile with each other.[1]

This book is biased toward loving connected families whose members were involved with each other, who sought each other's company, comfort, sometimes counsel, and connection. The Putnams, the Arthurs, and the Norths all clung to each other, whatever the tensions and hurts. Their lives often took them great distances from each other, but their family ties kept them bonded. The Blairs of the second generation began that way, but they ended up estranged, permanently.

138

*The Blairs: Next Generation*

Montgomery Blair (1813–83)
m. 1836     Caroline Buckner (d. 1844)
                    Elizabeth (Betty) (1840–72)
                          m. 1869     C. M. Comstock
                                      unnamed daughter (1844)
m. 1846     Mary Elizabeth (Minna) Woodbury (d. 1887)
                    Mary Elizabeth (Minn) (1850–1919)
                          m. 1869     Stephen Richey
                    Woodbury (1852–1933)
                          m. 1907     Emily Wallach
                    Mary (1854–62)
                    Gist (1860–1940)
                          m. 1912     Laura Lawson
                    Montgomery (1865–?)
                          m. 1895     Edith Draper
                                      seven children

A study based on letters will inevitably underrepresent broken families. The disaffected and alienated do not often write letters. We do not
see much hate or fury, and we certainly see virtually no mention of incest or sibling abuse. Such letters were probably not written—and if they
were written, they probably were not sent, certainly not saved, and most
definitely not added to a collection for public scrutiny. Families have taken
many such secrets to the grave, sometimes leaving the impression that
such problems did not exist in the past. Clearly, this is not true, but how
many secrets have grandparents not told parents or parents not told
children? It saves face, but it gives a false picture of the past. It certainly
gives a wrong impression about the complexity and sometimes hostility
of sibling relations.[2]

In colonial America the family was in many ways a public institution.
The walls that separated hearth and community were thin, and people's
home lives were not very private. Families had public responsibilities—
education, relief, medicine; communities had family responsibilities—
caring for each other's children and each other's well-being. One effect
of the move into a more industrialized and urbanized society has been
the thickening of the walls between inside and outside, between private
and public. This has meant greater secrecy within families. In the nineteenth century and even well into the twentieth, few people gave words

to stories of incest, adultery, divorce, homosexuality, sexual abuse—let alone committed them to paper.

When I was in the third grade in about 1958 my class gave a program for the PTA about the family. I don't remember anyone else's part, but I do remember reciting from memory a little set piece (largely written by Sister Cecilia) on the theme of family loyalty that urged the keeping of family secrets. In the last forty years the walls between private and public have become thinner again, and such stories are increasingly being told (or shouted, if you listen to television talk shows).

Stories of what families considered shameful—including family break-ups—do not often show up in nineteenth-century letters.[3] The sons and daughters of Montgomery Blair give us at least a glimpse, however, of one family break, and even their story is still shrouded in some secrecy. At the end of this chapter, as at the end of my reading of their letters, we will not know exactly what happened. It is, nonetheless, the one family in my research where an evident and irreparable break did happen, so here is the story of one family in the next generation of Blairs, as far as I know it.

Montgomery Blair married Caroline Buckner in 1836. Together they had one daughter, Betty, named after Montgomery's sister. In January 1844 Caroline and her second child died during childbirth, leaving the widowed Montgomery with four-year-old Betty. Because they were living in St. Louis, far from all his relatives except Frank Jr., he had no child-rearing help, and he could not leave St. Louis because he was the mayor. Montgomery sent his little daughter to his mother and father; his sister, Lizzie, was still living at home and would help. It made sense. Lizzie had been Caroline's close friend. His mother was willing. Montgomery could not manage alone. Betty, then, was raised by her grandparents with the help of her aunt and a neighborhood full of other Blair relations.[4]

Montgomery soon met, courted, and became engaged to Mary Elizabeth Woodbury (called Minna), from another family prominent in American politics. Minna and Montgomery, married in 1846, had five children: Mary Elizabeth, known here as Minn (1850); Woodbury, called Wood (1852); Mary (1854–1862); Gist (1860); and Montgomery, known here as Mont (1865). Thus the oldest was fifteen years older than the youngest. And Betty was twenty-five years older than her youngest half-sibling.[5]

Montgomery and Minna lived in St. Louis during the early years of their married life and moved to the Lafayette Square house in Washington in 1853. Their three sons—Wood, Gist, and Mont—all trained in the law and practiced in St. Louis or Washington. Minn married a doctor and lived in Washington. Unlike their father, none of them achieved prominence in the public arena. In this they were like Nell and Alan Arthur. They lived in the shadow and memory of their father's greatness but did not aspire to it or work toward it themselves.

The two grandfathers, Frank Sr. and Levi Woodbury, had ambitions for their grandchildren. Frank Sr. hoped, no doubt, to establish a family dynasty. Levi Woodbury had had only daughters and hoped for grandsons to carry on his ambitions and dreams. When Minn was born, both grandfathers lamented that she "would have made a president if it had been a boy." Montgomery shared his father and father-in-law's disappointment. "It is a pity isn't it," he brooded to his sister, Lizzie, "that such hopes should be extinguished by the mere accident of sex." Even Minn's brothers, however, without the accident of sex to bar them, did not follow their grandfathers, uncle, and father into politics.[6]

None of the four siblings followed typical marital patterns of the time. Minn was thirty-four when she married in 1884. Like her cousin and close friend Violet Blair, Minn wanted to stay close to home and to her parents, so she delayed marriage until she found a man who was suited to her Washington life at Blair House. Minn's marriage to Dr. Stephen Richey may have engaged her emotions deeply, but her letters provide little evidence of that. Her family's doings seemed her most important hobby. Her parents, her siblings, the Blair reputation, and Blair House took up much more of her attention.

Mont at thirty was the first of the brothers to marry, even though he was the youngest. Like Minn's, his marriage also existed mostly off the stage of their correspondence, and he focused more on his sibling family than on his wife and children, so none of them assumes any shape in Mont's literary life. Wood's and Gist's love lives proved quite the undoing of the Blair family and form the central piece of their family's story of conflict and discord.

When he finally married in 1907, Wood was fifty-five. In that same year Gist, who had been living in St. Louis, moved back to Washington, D.C., and took up residence with Wood and his new wife, Emily. Five years later, when Gist was fifty-two, he finally married. Neither Wood nor Gist had children.

The family's letters do not foretell the falling-out and in most ways are quite like those of other siblings in this book. In the first letter in the collection, for example, a young Mont still at home wrote to Gist, who was at school, about the death of their dog. (He was very sorry and it was not his fault.) These siblings teased each other, scolded, advised, and offered assistance of various kinds and accepted other kinds. They apologized for not writing more often, they chided for short letters. They talked about friends and relatives, what was happening. Minn long played the responsible firstborn. At thirty-five, for example, she was scolding twenty-five-year-old Gist about his handwriting. "If you don't write more carefully," she told him, "you will certainly fall into just such a handwriting as father had, & suffer from all the inconveniences that he did." So, "take pains" to correct it, she directed. The others also behaved predictably. Mont, the youngest, wrote with the bravura of the youngest: "I well know how hard it is for the family to get along without its youngest branch and I concluded that my absence would be felt less severely having two of my photos in the house." Ever the serious one, Wood most often wrote about bonds and income, taxes and insurance, the practical things. Nothing unusual here.[7]

But their letters are remarkable in a couple of ways. One way to read letters is to by looking at what is in them: what do they say, how do they say it, what words, what tone, what meanings, and so on. Another is to look at what is *not* there, to read for absences. In this generation of Blair letters two absences are curious.

First, Betty is missing. Betty, the daughter of Montgomery's first marriage, the half-sister to all these children of his second marriage. She was not so far away. When her half-sisters and -brothers were in Washington, she was in Silver Spring—eleven miles away. The letters make no mention, but the biographies of the senior Blairs make clear that real strain existed between Betty and her stepmother. There is no evidence of strain between her and her half-siblings in the letters because there is so little evidence of her at all.

What is clear is that she did not get blended into her father's new family, and no serious efforts seem to have been made in that direction. Only in one circumstance did Montgomery Sr. envision bringing his two families together. In 1853 his younger brother Jim died in California. Montgomery was assigned to go out and settle Jim's estate and to collect the ashes for burial in the family plot in Washington. The occasion prompted Montgomery to think about his own death. Preparing for his journey, then, he wrote a letter "to be opened in the case of death" and left it with Lizzie for safekeeping. In it he directed that Betty, then twelve, should be raised by his wife, Minna, and not by Lizzie—though he did not explain why. Montgomery survived the trip, however, so Betty never joined Montgomery's second family. When Montgomery and Minna's children talked about their family, they meant the four of them—Minn, Wood, Mont, and Gist. Betty was "family" but in the category of cousins, aunts, uncles.[8]

The second notable absence in the correspondence among these siblings is politics. It is almost not to be found. It had so dominated the letters of their father and his siblings that it is striking to note its near-invisibility in this generation. To the outsider the political world of the Blairs is highly unusual. When Minn writes that she attended a White House reception given by First Lady Frances Folsom Cleveland, it is remarkable to me but not much to her, apparently.[9] She passed the news along with a nonchalance that I would adopt if I were reporting that I'd seen Mrs. Hough, my mother's lifelong friend, or Monsignor McEneaney, a priest of whom my parents are especially fond.

Spending time at the White House was simply part of the fabric of their lives and had been since the 1830s when Grandfather Frank Sr. and Aunt Lizzie spent time there with President Andrew Jackson. As such, these things did not merit much conversation or attention.

Each family creates its own version of a "normal" world, and the power of a family culture is evident in the ability of a family to normalize what to outsiders appear to be the most extraordinary circumstances. What to the outsider may seem completely unusual can, from the inside, feel fine and part of the course of things. It is normal to go to church or not to eat meat, to talk, to express emotions (and which ones), to make your bed, or even to go to the White House.

People tend to write about what is unusual. We do not generally write about eating breakfast or brushing our teeth or going to work unless something out of the ordinary happened. So to the Blairs, politics was generally "normal" and therefore not often commented upon.

That they did not write much about the politics, however, does not mean that politics was not a profoundly important part of their lives. Their family environment was steeped in the political world where appearance, reputation, and public opinion mattered. These the Blair family did care about. The Blairs' most divisive conflicts circled around these issues.

Whether it was true of individual Blair family members or not, the Blairs were a public family living at the center of the nation's capital with a name familiar to a very wide circle of people. They took their social position seriously. Cousin Violet Blair Janin, "always conscious of her social standing," selected her party guests with care and gloried in being a BLAIR—it meant something special and public to her, as it seemed to for most of the Blairs. Minn, Wood, Mont, and Gist were Blairs. They were also Woodburys, another public family protective of its reputation and public standing. On both sides, then, their families were accustomed to being in the public eye.[10]

Sometimes that public eye can be oppressive. The Blairs of their parents' generation—Montgomery and Frank Jr. and Lizzie—had sought the public eye and had cast themselves into the public arena. The Blairs of the next generation—Minn, Wood, Mont, and Gist—had not. They were born into it and grew up in it. As a public family they were perhaps more finely attuned to issues of reputation and appearances. They were certainly tuned to a high emotional pitch in general.

To the Blairs strong feelings strongly expressed were also normal. One might even say that they were a contentious lot. In their public lives the senior Blairs were known for their strong feelings and sharp tongues. Their grandfather's newspaper, the *Globe,* specialized in attack journalism. When their interests and those of John and Jessie Frémont diverged, the Blairs broke all ties with their long-time friends and allies, with rancor and without regret.

The Blairs also expressed strong feelings at home. Their grandfather had refused to attend his only daughter's wedding. Two of her brothers spoke against her future husband, and one remained hostile to his brother-in-law. Minna Woodbury Blair had rancorous dealings with both Eliza Blair and Lizzie Lee, which must have been evident to all her children because they all lived in such proximity to each other in Washington. Uncle Jim ordered Lizzie to be nice to his fiancée and told his sister to warn the family that he would "desert my home . . . and all I love" if the family stood in his way. When Frank Jr. was on his deathbed, the long-time conflict between his wife, Apo, and his brother Montgomery flared into open warfare.[11]

In their parents' generation these strong emotions strained the family fabric at several points, but somehow the family members kept their conflicts from tearing it apart. The tensions in the next generation, however, resulted in an irreparable rip.

They were, interestingly, the same tensions. What had most ignited the Blairs of Montgomery's generation had been their marriage choices. The same held true among Montgomery's children.

Minn took it upon herself to oversee her brother Mont's relationships with women. When Mont was twenty-six and Minn was forty-one, she worried about her youngest brother's relationship with a Miss Hobbes, whom Minn considered "dangerous." She kept Gist, who was in St. Louis, apprised of the situation; the treacherous Hobbes was trying to trap Mont. "I tell you that Hobbes is smart," Minn wrote. "She knows just how difficult it is for a youth like [Mont] to evade such an attack." Minn was reassured that the "young man," Mont, "is not at all inclined to be caught again." Even if he were, she reported, "we keep him very firm in his present mood."[12] She was happy when Mont moved on to other women, which he did before too long. Some years later Mont married a woman who did not elicit much controversy among the Blairs, and he settled down to a fairly conventional family life, including seven children in the next eighteen years.

Wood, though, elicited his sister's continuing worry (meddling?), whether he was escorting women in his sled when he was quite young or having an affair as a thirty-nine-year-old man. The latter proved almost too much for Minn. In 1891 Wood became involved with a Mrs. Marion McKay. Minn, and her mother's sister Ellen (Nell) Woodbury, had a fit. McKay was recently divorced and, apparently, stood accused of various infidelities that her ex-husband was not loathe to publicize. Wood and Mrs. McKay had known each other since his days as a student in Cambridge, Massachusetts, when she had been engaged to one of his classmates. The gossip about her reached back even to those college years, and from his own experience Wood believed those stories to be false. These and other stories were circulating around Washington. Wood did not countenance them and he did not care. He planned to marry her as soon as she finalized child-support arrangements with her former husband.

But Minn and Nell certainly cared a lot. To them Wood was keeping company with a woman of questionable character and reputation, and it reflected badly on all the Blairs. Aunt Nell proclaimed to Minn that she would "leave Washington immediately" to avoid the "mortification" if Wood continued his relationship with Mrs. McKay.

Wood had known that his engagement to Mrs. McKay would cause Minn to be "very much worried and troubled," but he had assumed that because of their brother-sister relationship Minn would at least "refrain from saying any thing disagreeable about her" and would, in fact, even speak in Wood's defense if anything "disagreeable" were said in Minn's presence. That did not happen. Instead, Aunt Nell had Minn worked up "to boiling heat." The two of them campaigned vigorously against the liaison.[13]

Minn took Wood aside and lectured him, as she reported to their brother Gist in St. Louis. She had told Wood of the rumors and gossip going around about him and Mrs. McKay. "I explained how unpleasant it was to have to hear reports which were derogatory to his character, and inquired if he was willing to bring such discredit upon himself and her." Minn was certainly concerned about the discredit it was bringing upon the Blairs, including her.[14]

Wood's brothers stayed out of this controversy as much as they could. "I think your suggestion to keep quiet and let the women do the shouting, is a good one," Mont wrote to Gist. But both brothers had opinions about Wood's love life. Wood suspected that Mont reported to Minn whenever he saw Wood and Mrs. McKay together. Gist also had things to say but did not feel that he could raise the issue until Wood spoke to him. He would speak his mind, if Wood would "give me an opportunity," but, Gist declared, he "seems to be pretty damned careful not to give me a chance."[15]

Everyone in the family had an opinion, and Wood's relationship occasioned a flurry of conversation among all the siblings (and the dreaded aunt Nell who, Wood charged, imagined "that she personally still holds the position she did in Pierces administration"). Wood also asserted that "the family have considerably more feeling and are giving themselves more borrowed trouble than the circumstances justify." Clearly, many conversations were held on paper and in person among all the family members. Mont even offered to talk to Marion McKay himself on the family's behalf (and say what? I wonder).[16]

Some years later—when Gist's love life was getting him into family trouble as well—he recalled how he had supported Wood during this crisis, "at the *risk* & a serious risk it was of alienating from myself the love & affection of those I loved the best." He had stayed loyal to Wood while "other friends that winter dropped & deserted them on every side" and "against the expressed wishes of every woman of my family," suffering in the process "severe criticism of myself."[17]

Wood did not yield to the family pressure, perhaps because of Gist's support. Wood continued the relationship for at least three years, and the family eventually grew resigned and withdrawn. "There is a perfect understanding here with all the family on this subject," Wood reported to Gist, "they have each for himself or her self elected to do what they think best and I have never once interfered or made a suggestion except to clean up misunderstandings. Mrs. McKay owes absolutely nothing to any member of my family they have in most instances been civil nothing more or less."[18]

Wood suffered from this tension. Perhaps reflecting his sense of alienation from his family and feeling the power of their judgments, he hoped that Gist would "someday realize that your old brother is not altogether such a damned fool." He concluded the same letter by lamenting that he "would give ten years of my life to have prevented all that has happened, the experience is dear as it has cost sorrow and soreness to the very few people in the world whom I really love." The family survived. Wood and Marion McKay's romance ended.[19]

Minn often served as the passer of all kinds of family information and gossip. When their cousin Blair Lee and his wife had their baby, Minn sent word and detail to Gist. When there was a "little bit of scandal in [the] neighborhood," she recounted it ("It seems Emily Beale McLane claims to have caught papa Beale in questionable position with Mama Beale's maid"). She also did the family's bidding in other ways. For example, Minn "was told by the united family the other day that I aught to call you [Gist] to an account for the statement made in your last letter that a 'man's wife was usually the smallest part of him.'" Oh, this riled Minn and, should we presume, others in the family? So the family called on her to respond. "I think myself it is time for you to understand that that which we call a wife is not *a part* (either small or large) of *a man* and in this enlightened age she is fast ceasing even to be considered *a part* of his goods & chattels."[20]

Wood did eventually marry, though because of Minn he delayed the wedding for two years. From 1905 to 1907 Minn was going through what she called her "terrible trials" (her husband may have been addicted to prescription drugs). Despite her harshness to Wood around the matter of Mrs. McKay, he postponed his plans for her sake. (Why a postponement helped her is not entirely clear.) Despite their tensions, when she needed his help, he rearranged his life and, she reported, "has been everything to me."[21]

The family approved of Wood's ultimate choice—perhaps in relief the family made a real effort to welcome his new bride, Emily Wallach, even though neither Mont nor Gist made it to the wedding. (All but Gist apparently were living in the Washington, D.C., area but traveled a lot.) According to his new sister-in-law, Gist made it clear that he "approved of me as a sister." Minn too found Wood's new wife "very sweet and sisterly." Wood reported—perhaps also in relief—that "Minna has accepted it very sweetly." Such a remark seemed normal and unremarkable to them, but it is notable to someone from a family that does not voice its thoughts about prospective in-laws. It would not, in my family, be the prerogative of any of us to "accept" another's spouse, but obviously Wood and Minn disagreed. She was allowed an opinion on the subject, and he did care about it. They both agreed somehow that it was her business. She was fifty-seven. He was fifty-two. The tensions of Wood's earlier engagement must have been completely forgotten. Emily—as reported and perhaps interpreted by Minn—"talks as if it was a great pleasure to her to be a member of a family in which we have so much consideration for, and devotion to each other."[22]

It was a consideration, however, that turned sour. Shortly after Wood and Emily's wedding, Gist, then forty-seven, decided to leave St. Louis and move to Washington to live with Wood and Emily and to be just around the corner from his sister Minn and her husband, Stephen. For years the family had wished Gist would live closer. Minn had written him that she was lonesome for him. Wood had written as much as fourteen years earlier: "I personally am willing to make most any arrangement which will bring you East more frequently." Minn was delighted at the prospect of yet another family member's being so close. As it was, she lived next door to Wood and relished the prospect of slipping over in her wrapper and slippers.[23]

Some years earlier Wood, who recognized the strong personalities in his family, had issued a warning against living too close to one another. In that case, however, his worry was about conflict between Minn and Mont. Wood figured they could all live together for three months in the summer, but being in Washington together would not be possible: "The City is scarcely large enough to hold two families with such different tastes ages &c" as Mont and his wife and Minn and her husband. But Gist, Gist would be easy, they thought. He wanted to come. He had so long been in St. Louis and had, in part by virtue of his distance, been the long-time confidante of all his siblings. He would be a welcome addition. Wood and Emily seemed to want him and encouraged him to take full part in the household.[24]

It did not work out very well, though. Gist and Emily clashed, and Gist suspected Emily of trying to turn both Wood and Minn against him. "I am very fond of my brother and am very anxious his affection should not be diverted from me," moaned Gist. But he feared that it was "seriously threatened" as it had not been "in forty years of intimacy." Before this marriage the two brothers had "never had a harsh word." Oh, he went on in a letter to his cousin Ginny, "you do not know how all this has pained me & wounded my heart, for my family have always been first in my affections, and we have stood up for one another not secretly torn one another down." He asserted further his determination that "I do not intend there shall be any open quarrel whatever she does." Gist and

Ginny had once been very close, and he added, "I mean to write as I used to when a child, when you were my confidante." Sadly, Gist felt he could no longer confide in his brother Wood, who had turned against him. Moreover, Gist feared that Wood and Emily gossiped to Minn about Gist's love life, about which Minn had "strict views," in a way "calculated to prejudice [Minn] . . . against me."[25]

By 1910 Gist, Wood, Emily, and Minn had healed this quarrel, but by 1915 Minn was no longer speaking to Gist. No matter his pleadings. In 1912 he had married a woman Minn disapproved of, for reasons not evident in the letters. Why she so strongly opposed this woman is one of the mysteries here. She had accepted Wood's wedding "very sweetly" but not Gist's. She made it known in Washington social circles too that she did not approve. To this Gist especially objected: "Is it not possible for us, children of the same parents to so compose the differences which now divide us as to at least remove them from the realm of social gossip?" Differences were one thing, but to air them publicly seemed to him a real breach. It was as if they each agreed on a basic principle of public propriety, but each felt that the other violated that value. He continued in the same vein: "If, as I believe, you disapproved of my marriage is it necessary or even reasonable to manifest such disapproval by ejecting me from the family circle thereby subjecting all of us constantly to the wagging tongues of many who delight in our family feud." It is here that we see the effect of the family's prominence in Washington life. They cared what other people thought and what they said.

Gist seemed more hurt than angry. To Minn he recalled their lifetime of connection, looking to pull the ties that bound them: "Even should your disapproval be merited is nothing due to the life long affection which until recently we have borne and expressed to each other—is nothing due to the memory of that mother & father who gave us being, nurtured us in childhood & left us a mutual heritage of love—is nothing to be weighed as due to family pride—however wounded we may feel by what may be thought an inconsiderate action on the part of one of us."

He would not, could not, say that she was right in her objections to his marriage and simply apologize. She disapproved of his wife. In a real sense he had made a choice, and he could not undo the choice. Gist and Minn had gotten along fine before his marriage. The letters testify to it, so did Gist's memory: "In years past & up to the time of my marriage there had been no point of controversy or serious disagreement between you and me," he reminded Minn. But that did not keep Minn from turning away.

He also could not recall trouble with Mont, yet he had trouble with him too. "With my brother Montgomery through a life time of intimacy I can now recall no matter of material difference between us. Our relations have always been more than fraternal until recently and never until lately have I failed to respond to any appeal of his." Nonetheless, Mont and Wood joined Minn against Gist.

Estranged from Minn and Mont and Wood, Gist appealed for another chance, for an end to the hostility. He petitioned Minn to pass his letter to his brothers and to urge them toward reconciliation. "I wish to assure you all for my part I am willing to make amends for whatever matters exist of my fault." He continued, "I have been very happily married and the happiness which has come to me has gone a long way in helping me take a natural and normal view of life and life suffering, the greatest of which in my life has been the differences which have existed in our family, and I can not believe you are so differently constituted from me but there is a constant tugging at the heart strings of my brothers & yourself, all of the time begging you all to make up these difference with me & my beloved wife."[26]

This letter to Minn—and the absence of letters to or from Mont and Wood—suggests that the Blair men let the womenfolk carry out the argument or disagreement, as they had when Minn and Wood feuded about his relationship with Marion McKay.

In any case, Minn answered coldly, refusing Gist's overtures for herself and for Mont and Wood: "Their lives are very full and they have no time to brood over wrong or nurse malice. Two years of harmony in our family circle have been very restful and they seem to think we are getting along very well and it is wise 'to let well enough alone.'" Minn had opposed his engagement and seemed to resent that "there was an influence stronger than mine." Gist had earlier suggested a reconciliation, which Minn said he had broken, so there was no room for further reconciliation. "There can be no congeniality between the family and one whose point of view is so at variance with it." In effect, then, she declared him out of the family. The "family" had one point of view, he another, and he therefore had forfeited his membership therein.

She concluded: "I am truly glad that you are happy and have no feeling but sorrow in thinking the days when I made such a sad failure in the roll of peacemaker." Then, after a lifetime of signing her letters to Gist "affectionately yours, Minna," she signed this one "Sincerely yours, Minna Blair Richey."[27]

Gist wrote one last letter to Minn, acknowledging receipt of hers and trying to clear up several misunderstandings, but they had moved beyond the possibility of straightening out misunderstandings. In his draft of this letter he signed himself first "Your brother," then crossed that out and inserted "I sign myself as you do, Sincerely Yours." Her signature, then, had not been lost on him. It was on the back of this letter draft that Gist wrote, "My last letter to Minna."[28]

Then, the last letter in the file, another copy, went from Gist to Mont's wife, Edith Draper Blair. He wrote to offer her sympathy during Mont's illness and to tell her that he had written to his sister with the request that all the family forgive and forget. Perhaps he thought that another who was not strictly "family" would help him out. He underestimated her loyalty, however. He notes in the margin that this letter was never answered.[29]

When the final break came and silence separated Gist from his siblings, there are no further letters in the file because Gist was generally the saver of the letters. In 1915 Minn was 65, Wood was 63, Gist was 55, and Mont was 50. Minn lived four more years, Wood eighteen, Gist twenty-five, and I'm not sure about Mont. There is no indication that the family ever reconciled. What a tragedy. What a sadness it must have been. What bitterness each of them must have felt. To break a family bond requires real effort. What is so important that it breaks bonds so tightly woven over so many years? Was it the gossip—perhaps the shame—that Minn hints that Gist brought upon them? This was a family sensitive to gossip and public embarrassment. They could stand anything, but they could not stand public humiliation. But how interesting that each of them seemed to have gotten involved in a situation that invited such public difficulties: Wood with Mrs. McKay, Mont with that Miss Hobbes, Gist with his wife, Laura Lawson Blair, and Minn with her husband, who had "bad habits."

This is a family that teaches us both about closeness and bitterness. It shows both the durability and the fragility of family bonds. It also warns us that breakups can and did happen even in close loving families, even in adulthood.

### Notes

1. Gist Blair to Minna Richey, June 28, 1915. The letters of the Blair family that serve as the basis for this chapter are held in the Blair Family Papers, Library of Congress, Washington, D.C.

2. Stephen Frank also talks about this problem of the overrepresentation of positive relations. In offering an avenue into a particular kind of intimacy, let-

ters inevitably carry an inability to convey the breaks in intimacy. See Frank, *Life with Father,* esp. 183.

3. In fact, stories of family problems have often become hidden in stories of American individualism. American migration patterns have offered useful protective coloration for many a family secret. People have not moved away from home and family always and only because of the pull of adventure and the lure of opportunity. They have also been pushed by family violence, alienation, and pain of one kind or another. They have run away. See Peavy and Smith, *Women in Waiting.*

4. The letters of Montgomery's children make up a portion of the Blair Family Papers at the Library of Congress. All the Blair biographies listed in the notes to chapter 8 speak of some of the details of Montgomery's life but do not pay particular attention to his children, especially once they are grown. The children settled into a life made comfortable by their father's finances and reputation.

5. Montgomery Blair to Lizzie Lee, July 5, 1846.
The names can be quite confusing. There were two Frank Blairs, two Elizabeth Blairs, two Mary Elizabeth Blairs (and one Mary Blair), two Montgomery Blairs. The Blairs also adopted the habit of using last names as first names so that Blair is a first name as well as a last name; Woodbury and Gist are both first and last names, as is Montgomery. In this chapter I'm trying to diminish the confusion by using "Montgomery" to refer to the father and "Mont" to refer to his son; I'm using "Minna" to refer to the mother and "Minn" when I mean the daughter. The family solved the problem of the two Elizabeths by calling Montgomery's sister Lizzie and his daughter Betty. Otherwise, however, the family did not use the name conventions that I have adopted here. They—like every family—had their own ways of distinguishing between people of the same name.

6. Montgomery Blair to Lizzie Lee, June 13, 1849. In the next generation only a cousin, the son of Lizzie Blair Lee—Francis Preston Blair Lee—achieved national political office, serving as senator from Maryland from 1913 to 1917.

7. Minn Richey to Gist Blair [Jan. 14, 1885]; Mont Blair to Minn Richey, Nov. 10, 1885. About the handwriting, Minn was exactly right—Gist's handwriting, like his father's, was nearly unreadable. He should have listened to her.

8. Montgomery Blair to Minna Blair, Jan. 24, 1854.

9. See, for example, Minn Richey to Gist Blair [May 20, 1885].

10. Laas, *Love and Power,* 7.

11. Jim Blair to Lizzie Lee, Oct. 20, 1850. See also E. B. Smith, *Francis Preston Blair,* 180–82, 189; W. E. Smith, *Francis Preston Blair Family,* vol. 2, 460–61; and Parrish, *Frank Blair.* Violet Blair Janin and her siblings also had a fiery relationship. "The relations of the Blair siblings had never been peaceful," biographer Laas writes, "and the wrangling only became worse as they aged" (*Love and Power,* 104).

12. Minn Richey to Gist Blair [Oct. 2, 1887, and Nov. 27, 1887].

13. Wood Blair to Gist Blair, Feb. 25, 1892.

14. Minn Richey to Gist Blair [March 23, 1891].

15. Mont Blair to Gist Blair, March 2, 1892.

16. Wood Blair to Gist Blair, Feb. 25, 1892; Mont Blair to Gist Blair, June 1, 1892.

17. Gist Blair to Ginny [his cousin Virginia Woodbury Lowry], July 28, 1908.

18. Wood Blair to Gist Blair, April 12, 1895.

19. Wood Blair to Gist Blair, April 12, 1895, and Feb. 25, 1892.

20. Minn Richey to Gist Blair [Oct. 24, 1892, and May 20, 1885].

21. Minn Richey to Gist Blair, July 8 [1907].

22. Wood Blair to Gist Blair July 5, 1907; Emily Blair to Minn Blair [July 26, 1907]; Minn Blair to Gist Blair, July 8 [1907]; Wood Blair to Gist Blair, July 5, 1907; Minn Richey to Gist Blair, Aug. 21 [1907].

23. Minn Richey to Gist Blair [March 30, 1896]; Wood Blair to Gist Blair, Sept. 11, 1893; Minn Blair to Gist Blair, Aug. 21 [1907].

24. Wood Blair to Gist Blair, May 26, 1896; Wood Blair to Gist Blair, Aug. 29, 1907.

25. Gist Blair to Ginny Lowry, July 28, 1908.

26. Gist Blair to Minn Richey, June 12, 1915 (Gist's copy).

27. Minn Richey to Gist Blair, June 1915.

28. Gist Blair to Minn Richey, June 12, 1915 (Gist's copy), and June 28, 1915.

29. Gist Blair to Edith Blair, July 21, 1915.

TEN

# The Christies: Our Shared Spheres

I was born in 1950 into a corner of American society where many clear lines were drawn between males and females. Girls played hopscotch and jumped rope. Boys played with marbles and every kind of ball. Girls helped with the dishes and boys mowed the lawn. Boys played sports and girls cheered them on. Girls were the regulators of sexual activity (saying no was our job and going too far our fault). Girls could dream of growing up to be mothers, nuns, nurses, teachers, secretaries, and cleaning ladies. Boys, anything they wanted—as long as it wasn't a nurse or kindergarten teacher or a secretary, or other lines of work insufficiently "manly." My father, like the fathers of my friends, made the money, and my mother never had money that she called hers. My father smoked for many years; so did my mother, but I was in college before I knew it because she hid it from us. In our household, you see, women did not smoke.

My mother violated that gender rule and lots of women and men did, sometimes paying only a small price. Among children, if a girl "threw like a boy," she was called a "tomboy," not a very hurtful label and, for some of us, even a title of some honor, though tomboys rarely moved smoothly into the ranks of datable teenagers. Pals and teammates, yes; dates, no. If, though, a boy "threw like a girl," which implied that either he was ineffectual or homosexual, the charge had, I imagine, quite a bit more sting. That was a higher price. Those who violated the roles often felt out of place and isolated (only occasionally daring). Others who conformed to those roles often paid an even higher and more painful price: stunted dreams, limited opportunities, discouragements, a distorted sense of their own abilities.

154

*The Christies*

James C. Christie (1811–90)
m. 1829    Elizabeth Gilchrist (d. 1834)
           William (1830–1901)
                m. 1865    Mary Beth Aimer
                          eleven children
           Mary (1832–34)
m. 1838    Eliza Reid (1818–50)
           Alexander (1839–41)
           Alexander (1841–43)
           Thomas (1843–1921)
                m. 1872    Carmelite
                          seven children
           Sarah (1844–1919)
                m. 1879    William Stevens
                          four stepchildren
                          two children
           Alexander (Sandy) (1846–1933)
           David (1848–1920)
                m. 1870    Emma Stratton
                          nine children
           unnamed son (1850)
m. 1853    Persis Noyes (1815–87)

This background of gender-specified behavior, attitudes, aspirations, and talents made me deeply grateful for the historical literature on "separate spheres." Barbara Welter's path-breaking article, "Cult of True Womanhood," provided a name and a language for what I already knew so well. Nancy Cott's *Bonds of Womanhood,* and Carroll Smith-Rosenberg's "Female World of Love and Ritual" gave rationality and dignity to what had previously felt mostly confining and frustrating.[1]

This work and a subsequent generation of scholarly work was enlightening, helpful, and encouraging. It helped me answer all those implications of gender roles—that women were inferior or less or not as good as. It gave me a way to understand women's absence from so much of the historical record, and it helped me discover the courage that life had required of so many women in the past. No wonder so many women historians studied pioneer women, even when we were not entirely conscious of why we were doing it. This historical literature helped me to understand women in the past and to understand myself as well.

In 1978, when I was doing research for my doctoral dissertation on agricultural disaster, I read a letter from Alexander (Sandy) Christie to his sister, Sarah, written in 1873. It violated everything I had come to think or know about nineteenth-century gender relations, but it also made complete sense to me too. It conformed to my experience in my family.

This is an excerpt from that letter:

> Dr. Miller's case was undertaken by the district attorney today at Oak Grove before a Justice; and after all the evidence was in, the prisoner was ordered to be discharged, as there was not sufficient basis to warrant prosecution at the next term of the Circuit Court. The legal evidence was quite insufficient; though most people, even his own counsel, have little doubt it was a case of seduction and abortion—the latter very successful. Of course you are aware Dr. Miller is considered a successful practitioner in that line—the women say so and large numbers of them here ought to know. Miller has escaped the clutches of the law, the girl has got through it all right, and has refused on the witness stand to say aught against him. . . . The girl has been instructed pretty well by . . . one adept in obstetrics and will be able to make things appear pretty well, anywhere she is questioned. Mrs. Grundy is coolly told she doesn't know anything: this was a case of false pregnancy—and if the girl chooses to substantiate the tale who can say further.[2]

This letter crossed the boundaries between women and men in a way that I had come not to expect. At the same time, it helped me understand that while gender explained a lot, it does not account for everything. It helped me understand, in part, why not all women—not even all white, middle-class, Catholic, northern European women in Sioux Falls, South Dakota, in the 1950s—were alike. They each came from different families and while gender conventions matter, so do family conventions, and they were not always the same.

Families give and gave permission—or refused it—to violate the gender roles. Families provided money—or refused it—for blue jeans for girls or ballet lessons for boys. Families enforced—or refused to enforce—conventions about what boys and girls ought to do. So gender and family, siblings in particular, were what Sandy Christie's letter sent me off to study.

I have now lived with the Christies for twenty years, and in some senses I know them almost as well as I know my own family. I can pick up any letter in the collection and know who wrote it without checking

the signature. I know each one's handwriting and each of their personalities. I like some of them better than others and have definite opinions
about each member of the Christie family.

James C. Christie was the patriarch. He was loving, hard working,
and close to his own family, as well as opinionated, astringently antireli-
gious, and decidedly stubborn. He was born in Scotland in 1811. He had
three wives and children with two of them. His first wife, Elizabeth Gilchrist, bore two children. Her son, William, lived more than seventy years;
her daughter, however, lived only eighteen months and even at that
outlived her mother. After his wife's death James moved to Ireland to
find better work in the textile mills there, leaving his surviving son in his
own mother's care until he remarried, which he did in 1838. His second
wife, Eliza Reid, bore seven children, four of whom lived to adulthood.
When her fifth child was about a month old, the family, including William, migrated from Ireland to Wisconsin, joining both Reids and Christies who had already made the move. Her sixth child was born in Wisconsin; she and her seventh child died in childbirth in 1850. Three years
later James married for the third time, to a neighbor woman, Persis
Noyes, who raised James Christie's children and bore none of her own.

William, born in 1830 and the oldest of James's sons, was thirteen
years older than his next half-brother, Tom, and eighteen years older than
his youngest half-brother. He served in the Minnesota Artillery from 1861
to the end of the Civil War. He and his wife, Mary, farmed all their lives
and had eleven children. Like his father, William was a strong family man.
He was also politically engaged. As a dedicated farmer activist, he ranted against the money lenders and other villains who were sucking the
blood of the farmers. He was also the family historian, and as he aged
he kept the family memory, which made sense because he had preceded
all of them by so long.

Tom was eighteen when he and William marched off together to enlist
in the army. After the war Tom did not, however, follow his brother into
farming. Instead, he went to school, then Beloit College, then to semi-
nary to become a Congregational minister. Quite out of keeping with
his father's bitter antireligionist stance, Tom had a conversion experience
and spoke of religion enthusiastically to his siblings as well as his con-
gregants. He and his wife, Carmelite, spent most of their lives as mis-
sionaries in Turkey and came home for good only after one of their sev-
en children killed herself and broke her parents' spirits.[3]

Sarah, the next-born Christie, arrived in 1844 and was the only daughter of James and Eliza and the only sister to William and Tom. After the

Civil War and the 1862 Dakota War in Minnesota, the Christies moved to Minnesota. Sarah went to school, took up teaching, opened a dress shop, and taught at Carleton and Wheaton colleges. For part of that time, while Sarah, Tom, and Sandy were all going to school and unmarried, they kept house together. Sure that her ambitions were enough to keep her from being able to marry, Sarah had simply declared that she was unlikely to marry and set off on a path to financial independence and a career. Her debts, however, overcame her and when her creditors attached her salary while she was on the faculty of Wheaton College, she lost her job. At thirty-five she did marry Mr. William Stevens, a widower eighteen years her senior who had four children. Together they had two girls, one who shared her mother's ambition (and her unrealized desire) to become a doctor and one who died of tuberculosis when she was in her late teens. Sarah lived near her father and stepmother in rural Minnesota until they moved to Montana to live with her youngest brother. She stayed in Minnesota. In 1890—the year her father died—she was elected superintendent of schools for her county, then was defeated in her bid for reelection. She stayed on her farm until poor health sent her to live with her daughter and son-in-law, another doctor, in Minneapolis, where Sarah died in 1919.

Alexander (Sandy) Christie was one month old in 1846 when his family moved to North America. Scottish and Protestant, James Christie supported his family by working in mills, not on a farm, so they did not suffer from the Irish potato famine of the 1840s. They nonetheless joined the tide of those who fled Ireland during the famine years. So, like his older siblings, Sandy was born in Ireland, bred among his father's Scottish relatives, and raised in the United States. I wonder what he answered when people asked about his nationality? Alexander was the third of his family to be given that name. The first had lived for eighteen months; the second also died at eighteen months. This Alexander, however, lived until 1933, outliving all his siblings by twelve years. He was eighty-seven when he died. Throughout his life he was variously called and called himself Alex and Sandy.

Sandy's greatest disappointment in life was that he was too young to march off to the Civil War with his older brothers. His greatest joy that he was able, nonetheless, to join up in 1865 at the very end of the war. Like his sister, he had a talent for mathematics; unlike his sister, he went off to Beloit College, then to Harvard University. After graduating, he got a job with the U.S. government that he held for fourteen years until he was dismissed (fired?). He spent the next several decades roaming around—from one sibling to another, one perch to another. He did not marry. He seemed to have been a little unanchored and searching for a home. Sandy spent some time his brother William's family and with his sister Sarah's but seemed most at home, finally, with his brother David. He was a man tortured, troubled, and very emotionally expressive.

David, the youngest, was the only one of the Christies to be born in the United States, in 1848. His mother died when he was two, and he got a stepmother when he was five. Much too young even to think about enlisting during the Civil War, he stayed and helped on the family farm. When his brothers came home, though, he was old enough to help select a homestead in Minnesota. Soon after the move his siblings scattered. William and his wife and baby went to their own farm, while Tom and Sarah and Sandy went to school. David, though, stayed on with his father and stepmother. When he married in 1870, his wife, Emma, was just seventeen, five years younger than her husband. They lived with his parents. In the fashion of the time they did not share his parents' household for long, but in the fashion of some they lived nearby. For the next sixteen years they lived the same life—work, community, friends, family, farm. David's own ill health drove him to move his family—including his seventy-five-year-old father and seventy-one-year-old stepmother to a new farm in Montana in 1886. His stepmother died in 1887 and his father in 1890. David and Emma lived on in Montana for another thirty years.

Historians have used the term *separate spheres* as shorthand to describe the differences between the lives of women and of men in the nineteenth century. They were said to have occupied separate spheres. The Christies certainly did conform to some of those male and female roles or spoke the language that honored them. Sarah, like her brothers, worked on her father's farm, but while the boys worked in the fields, she usually would have worked in the garden and the house. When Sarah looked for her life's work, she looked in a smaller circle than her brothers did. She would not have been admitted to Beloit or to Harvard. She could not have gotten a job with the U.S. Coastal Survey, as Sandy did. She could not, in any case, have struck out on her own. Whatever she did, she would have earned less than her brothers could have.

James Christie, their father, had strong and clear views about women and men. He was not a formally educated man, but he read enthusiastically and carried on highly intellectual conversations in his correspondence. However, these letters were almost exclusively to his sons, even though Sarah was her brothers' intellectual equal, if not their superior. James was a much stronger proponent of education for his sons than for his daughter. He did not willingly and entirely happily send Sarah to school and objected when she wanted to pursue mathematics, judging it to be too masculine an enterprise for her. He did not pay the fees for any of his children to go to school—he never had enough money—but he at least offered to Tom and Sandy moral support and encouragement. He actively discouraged Sarah.

Of course, all the Christies had ideas about men and women. Sandy said them most directly, but then he said most things more directly than others in his family. "Remember," he reminded Sarah, "that I like to hear all the news but not the gossip which pries into other people's affairs. But of course you will declare you deal not in such as will every other woman." Sandy was the worst gossip in the family, but he thought of gossip as a woman's activity, apparently. Some years later Sandy complained about having to "pay the debts of a spend thrift woman." And wondered, "Is my manhood to be wasted in such vain effort?"[4] When they were older and Sarah was running for public office, Sandy advised her to read her speeches—some of which he had written for her—rather than speak extemporaneously—because it was more womanly that way.

Their understanding of women's and men's roles and responsibilities also are apparent in more subtle ways. When Tom and William were soldiering, Sandy could not bear being too young to join up. Tom protested Sandy's eagerness. Having already been in the army for more than three years, Tom certainly had many reasons to discourage Sandy from joining up any too soon, but he stressed especially Sandy's duties to his family. "On your shoulders," Tom wrote, "rests the responsibility of advancing the welfare of the family at home." As Tom saw it, the farm had to be taken care of, and only the boys, Sandy and Dave, were available. He did not consider that Sarah might run the farm. The thought probably did not occur to him. That was a man's job.[5] Sarah's brother William had the gendered idea too that she would write differently to a "very Dear Friend" than she wrote to "a pair of Soldier Brothers," and her female friends would then see "a little more under the surface."[6]

In addition to the evidence of separation, however, the Christies also offer much evidence of a world shared. What does it mean to share a sphere? At one level it means that they spoke in a common language. It was evident in Sandy's letter to Sarah about the abortionist that they lived in a world of much common language and many common experiences. Even if this were the only letter we had between them, we could know that they were close and in close contact because of how little in the letter is explained. Sandy did not identify the players in this drama, except by name: Dr. Miller, the girl, Hilliker and his wife, Mrs. Grundy. He and Sarah knew all of them, no need to explain. In any case, Sandy offers no explanations. There is also the tone of something else shared: judgment, opinion, point of view. Perhaps he was wrong, but he clearly presumes that he and Sarah will see this similarly and have similar judgments because he does not disguise his judgment, defend it, or even call any particular attention to it. He was simply reporting it openly and fairly frankly (we might call it simple gossip). They also shared a space in which discussion of such things was not taboo.

When we move away from this particular letter to their relationships in the correspondence we see a similar blurring of sphere boundaries and lots of evidence of shared family. Family connections mattered enormously among the Christies and in ways that transcended their gender roles.

They lived in a shared economy. Their commitment to helping each other was strong. When Sarah and a friend wanted to open a dress shop, Tom proposed that they all live together. "Our housekeeping would be a model. . . . I shall take my full share in all the housework, & thus leave you plenty of time for everything." He went so far as to say that he would be "associate housekeeper" for her. In a world of separate spheres this is a remarkable statement. It seems, somehow, less so between a brother and a sister. Whatever their father felt about the inappropriateness of education for Sarah, her brothers Will and Tom sent some of their military pay to her to help pay for her schooling. Later, when Tom was in a paying job and Sandy was not, Tom sent him money and the promise of more to keep him there. When he later took time off from school, Sarah was determined that he would get back and go to Harvard and proposed various schemes to help him.[7]

In the late 1860s and into the 1870s Sarah got herself into serious financial trouble; among other things, her dress business went bankrupt. Sandy gave her words to speak to her creditors: "'I don't have it,'" he told her to tell them, "'I am earning it and two brothers are helping me.'" If that did not satisfy them, Sandy wrote, "Let *me* talk to them." Sarah's troubles elicited her family's help, also their annoyance, sometimes their anger. Sandy simply could not understand "how you managed, how you *dared* spend so many hundreds of dollars during two years of 12 mos. each." Her brothers were angry because, as they saw it, her debts were their debts, and her debts were causing problems for her family. "To what extremities do you mean to drive us? Here am I . . . nearly starving to death for want of money. . . . Dave crowded into corners at every turn by the burden you left upon us." Please, Sandy begged her, do something. "I make this last appeal to you as a *brother*."

Sarah's troubles even drove the normally placid Dave to sharp talk—and desperation. He was on the verge of losing his farm because he had taken out a note to pay off her creditors. He criticized her way of doing business and ordered her to send him money immediately: "Now I want to know just what you mean by Such conduct you have got me into a mess which will Ruin the whole consern [*sic*]." What is remarkable is the shared nature of Sarah's troubles. As Sandy wrote to Dave in a similar context: "Your interests are my interests."[8]

The family shared a common commitment to an active intellectual life, evidenced in their father's long and thoughtful discourses about some philosophical issue or another, some religious idea or another. Not everyone in the family engaged in such discourses, but who did and who did not, who went to school and who did not did not reflect gender. Tom, Sarah, and Sandy all went beyond basic schooling; Will and Dave did not. Perhaps because he was so much older, Will did not have the same opportunities. Dave simply seemed disinclined. Sarah, though, like Tom and Sandy, was inclined, and the three of them threw in with each other to get each other through their schooling and launched into lives that suited them. When Sarah ran for political office, Sandy advised her and wrote speeches for her. William and Dave encouraged her. Sarah wrote about being an assistant to Sandy when he was looking for teaching jobs, but she did not do so out of some appreciation for her "proper place" as second but to get around the gender stereotypes that limited her opportunities. (He would get a job as a principal, she would be his assistant; the next year he would return to Harvard, and she would take over the position. Nifty idea.)

Sarah did have friendships with women—at least before her marriage—that were significant and meaningful. She lived with other women when at school and later. They traded help, encouragement, confidences, news, and information, as well as dreams, ideals, hopes, and trials. When she was in her midtwenties, for example, Sarah wrote to her friend Annie about her dreams of opening a dress shop and her feelings. "I hope Lucy [a friend of Annie's] is with you and give her my love. I hope to get a letter from you tonight. If Lucy brought any money send me ten dollars and if you get an money from *any where* send me some, be it ever so little."[9]

Of more centrality to Sarah and to her brothers was a strong kin network generally. Their father had moved to Wisconsin at the urging of his brothers, and they lived near each other. All the Christies had active relations with these uncles, their wives, and children. Except for Will, they also had their mother's mother nearby.

The threads of their lives intertwined tightly. In twos and threes and fours they spent significant parts of their lives together: Will and Tom enlisted and served together in the army; while Will was away, his wife and baby went to live with his family; all four brothers went together to search for a family farmstead; Tom and Sarah lived together, then Sarah and Sandy, then Sandy and Tom. As they got older, Sandy again made his home with or near Sarah and Dave. In their old age Sandy lived with Dave and one of Sarah's stepsons lived next door.

When they were apart, they told secrets to each other. "I beg of you," Sarah wrote to Sandy, "do not say a word of anything I wrote you." Tom asked Sarah not to "say anything about it to anyone, but tell me your candid opinion about it when you write." In another form of family encircling, Sandy instructed Dave to forward his letters to their siblings "to save me the trouble of writing all I wish to say to each individually." When the letters that were supposed to make the rounds did not, the senders got quite annoyed: "Again and again," Tom wrote, "I told Sarah I was sending [the letter] to her that she might have the whole clan read them." She failed to send them, and Tom was "naturally quite troubled by this."[10]

The bond they felt among themselves was evident in the variety of roles, responsibilities, tasks, and emotions that the Christies shared. They gave and took advice from each other without much regard for either gender or age. Tom, for example, asked Sarah's advice about his career when he was in his forties: "In this I want you to help me." He cared what his siblings thought: "Am glad you approve, as Alex does most warmly." They gave unsolicited advice—a category in which siblings can often excel. Do this, do that, don't do some other thing. Some of it was personal advice. Some professional. When Sarah stood for election to the local school board in the 1890s, for example, Sandy advised her how to organize her campaign and then wrote speeches for her. Sarah advised about medicine, sent pills, and instructed Dave to send for the doctor: "Don't neglect this now." They also recognized that they had duties that grew out of their family connections. Sandy to Dave: "I am very much troubled over two things, and as your brother I *must* speak, and as my brother you will forgive me if I had better have kept still."

All this shared area did not mean the Christies were without conflict— far from it. Their anger smolders and flames. I wouldn't like to receive any number of letters that the Christies sent to each other. Sandy wrote furious, vitriolic letters to Tom and about him. Tom responded in kind and in defense: "It is not chance or single expressions in your letters that hurt me in themselves, it is rather the whole spirit and tone of your expression toward me and my course. . . . Although I am a Christian I am not necessarily bound to sacrifice my self respect, even to preserve friendly relations with a brother. . . . Several of your letters . . . are full of arrogance, self-conceit and an ill concealed contempt of me and my principles."[11]

On other occasions Tom threatened never to write again and returned some of Sandy's letters unopened and unread. Sandy reviled Tom to their sister, calling him "cruel, reckless, thoroughly unfair, a *dangerous* man." Back and forth they went, off and on for years. Among the younger generation of Blairs public reputation brought them to a family crisis. Between Tom and Sandy it was religion. It was the centerpiece of Tom's life, and Sandy spoke of it with derision, bordering on fanatic opposition.[12]

When the two of them came to the breaking point, Sarah, especially, intervened. She did not speak at all to the issues that divided them but called on their family ties to keep them connected. Sarah to Sandy: "You must stop feeling so at Tom. It is dreadful! Have you forgotten that the same mother bore you? & that you were babies together?" It was not just Tom and Sandy who fought or criticized, and Sarah did not always defend Tom. "Father needs and craves sympathy & Tom to tell the truth is too selfish to give it, too much absorbed in his own particular ambitions to care much," Sarah complained. On other occasions Sandy ranted to Dave about Sarah, and their father turned to Sandy for help with Tom: "Whether [Tom] will write to me or not I cannot say. I should be sorry if he does not and would like if you would become mediator between us. I said a few plain things to him and may have hurt him a little."

But their communications continued nonetheless. At the end of the letter in which Tom blasted Sandy for his arrogance, he signed off with "My love unchanged to all at home; we are all well." This seems a marvelously accurate example of at least this family's handling of conflict: the harshest words tempered by the commonplace conventions of familial engagements.[13]

The Christies did a poor—or intentionally protective?—job of integrating their in-laws into their family life. In my family we send letters and cards and greetings in the names of both husband and wife. Dear Betsy and Tim or Love from Teresa and Matt and, of course, the handwriting is my sister's. The Christies, however, did it differently. No more than a handful of their letters were addressed to both husband and wife or signed in the names of both. Letters always went from Dave to Sarah or Tom to William. They often included news of their spouses and asked to be remembered to the in-laws but did not address their letters to them.

Moreover, at least Sarah adopted a formal tone about her husband with her siblings, and her siblings followed suit. When she referred to her husband in her correspondence with her siblings, she almost always called him Mr. Stevens. On the face of it, we might think that perhaps Sarah and William had a fairly cool, distant relationship, particularly given that he was about eighteen years older than she. The love letters between Sarah and her husband refute that interpretation. So the form of address does not tell us much about Sarah's relationship with her husband but perhaps about that with her siblings. Perhaps she wanted to push them a little away, to keep them at a little distance.

She wanted to push Tom's wife away a little, perhaps even a lot. Tom's relationship with his wife bothered Sarah. He married around the same time that Sarah was having such financial problems. She wrote him a steamed letter scolding him for talking to his wife about "our private affairs"—the "our" included the Christies but not the new sister-in-law. Sarah continued: "She already is my *enemy*" and "there is no mistaking her enmity towards me arising *without foundation* but in petty jealousy." Then she concluded with a statement of her family philosophy: "There should be *some* things held as sacred between brother and sister Tom, as between man and wife especially after having experienced so much together as we have."[14] Tom and Carmie had been married only four months.

David's wife, Emma, and Sarah also had strained relations. David's attempts to help Sarah pay her debts caused money troubles for him. Emma resented this. After her marriage to Mr. Stevens, Sarah became the lender and David the borrower, but this added further tension, apparently, to Emma's relations with Sarah. They lived near each other for decades, but Sarah and Emma never forged a sisterhood.[15]

Sandy, like Sarah, also had clear sense of the duties of siblings: "Tom never brought a child of his within our circle. Willie's children and yours and Dave's, all seem to me like younger members of father's family. They are all of us and for us. Tom has kept his apart, even in their names. This is unnatural, and to me it is revolting. It is due to several causes. Tom's natural affection for his own kith and kin was always weak, he married a wife having no affinity with us or ours, and he embraced a religion that consigns most of us to eternal damnation."[16] Clearly, both Sarah and

Sandy held their birth family loyalty above all others and expected the others to as well.

Tom did not. His religious commitment and his obligations to his wife and family preceded his commitments to his birth family. He converted from the religion of his family. He took on a powerful religious commitment that distanced him ideologically from his birth family. He also selected for himself a wife who would not be kept out by the family boundaries and rules. She insisted on being included in the family. She wrote letters to all the siblings—not instead of Tom's writing but in addition to his letters—and she addressed her letters to her "sister" and "brother" and often signed them "your sister." The Congregational convention of addressing each other as "sister" and "brother" no doubt fueled this familial language; it was nonetheless the language of the Christie family. Even so, Tom did not break the family convention of addressing singly and signing singly.

Part of the shared life of the Christies had to do with the strong role played by their father. He actively fostered the relationships among his children. In one of his more explicit versions of this he urged Tom to write to his siblings before he wrote to his father. Better to overlook him than them. Their enormous love for him kept them going through much of their conflict. His death had something of the same effect. It elicited tides of emotion. Dave was the only one with their father when he died. Having moved from Minnesota to Montana, Dave and his father lived farther from Will and Sarah and their families than they had previously; where once all their lives (except Tom's) had overlapped significantly, the Montana years were primarily shared only by Dave's family and his father. Sarah responded to her father's death with an anguished lament: why didn't you telegraph me as I had requested, so that I could have come? Dave had not himself realized just how near to death their father was. She also felt what many feel when their parents die: "Very old." "The years have been creeping over me, but I felt young at heart. I never can again. I feel that I am an old woman," she told Dave. She also drew a larger familial lesson: "We owe it to father in gratitude for what he was that we take up our duties with courage & live our lives out in such manner as would please him especially as regards our children." Sandy too thought of his duties, of how to secure his father's land claim for Dave, and of the fabric of their familial relations. "I thought when father died . . . I might cease to have as much interest in those left in this world. But it draws me nearer to you all." Tom too wanted them to "draw nearer together, now that he who loved us all so dearly, and prayed in

his heart so constantly for our true welfare has left us alone in the world."
Tom felt remorse at having hurt his father and asked for Sandy's forgive-
ness: "I wrote him a long letter only last week, in which I spoke of you
as I ought not to have done." Sandy did not know what Tom was refer-
ring to, probably "the old trouble that has kept us all in hot water for 30
or 40 years I suppose." But, he noted, it no longer mattered. Dave also
felt that "Father's death should bring us all nearer to one another. I miss
him so much I used to ask his advice about things sometimes and now
it is all a blank what a mystery it is." Even Carmie echoed this family
feeling: "As our family circle grows smaller and smaller here, I hope we
shall draw nearer together in heart, and be able to know each other better and to be more mutually helpful to one another."[17]

 There had been, in fact, two Christie families. William was the son
of James's first marriage, and the other four were the children of his second. They got blended into one Christie family. The blend was not without its seams. William sometimes felt that he was not a part of the "core"
family, he admitted to Sarah when they were older—and perhaps when
it hurt a little less. He felt so different from Tom and Sandy especially—
they had so much more schooling, and he suspected that they thought
him not as smart. He then felt, he said, "the most unworthy." The similarity of William's and Dave's lives, and eventually Sarah's when she
moved to the farm with Mr. Stevens, helped blend William in. He was
the family memory keeper. Sandy and the others turned to him for information about his mother and their family's life that he could not himself remember (or never knew). William was also the steady oldest.

 The deaths of the other siblings elicited no greater heartfelt emotion
than did Will's final illness and death. Sandy to Sarah: "If you or I, or (I
believe still better) Dave, could take poor Willie in our arms and stroke
his hair and reassure him, I think it would help him greatly when the
Great Terror . . . comes upon him." And after Will's death Sandy wrote
in true Sandy style: "And so he, too, is gone. And that kindly hearted
man, who always dreamed of better things, and sided with the right when
ever he discerned the right."[18]

 Sarah died in 1919, Dave in 1920, Tom in 1921, Sandy in 1933. Some
things about these people changed over their lifetimes. Will and Sandy
became interested in dreams and often relayed bits of them to the others. Sarah turned from a financially inept young woman to a responsible
wife and mother. She went from dressmaker to teacher to county school
board member to active prohibitionist and member of the Woman's
Christian Temperance Union. Her ambitions were no doubt only par-

tially satisfied, but we see little record of that here. Tom and Will turned up for reunions of their Minnesota regiment. Tom's religious fervor did not dim until his daughter's suicide finally led him home in 1920, and he and Carmie retired from missionary work. Tom seemed to become more moderate. Sandy, by contrast, became more rigid and angry. Something in their lives had made Tom a dedicated minister and Sandy a furious antireligionist. When Sarah died in 1919, Sandy sent a detailed description of her final days and her funeral: "Let us be glad that with the closing of the grave she finally escapes from a world of shams,—no sham of them all so disgusting and horrible as Christian religion, Christian ceremonial, and Christian burial."[19]

Their handwriting also changed, of course, from the uncertain scrawl of the young Dave writing to his big brothers at war to the shaky old-woman penmanship of Sarah in her sixties. Their letters gradually contain more memories, more stories of the older days, more "do you remember . . . ?" In a note in 1921, when he was seventy-four, Sandy reflected on his lifelong relations with Tom—one hostile and one dedicated to the same ideas. "We were both wrong in the intermittent wrangle that resulted, lasting for half a lifetime. It is a great mistake for a man to think that 'everybody must sneeze when he takes snuff,'—and both of us made that mistake until age began to cool our blood. However, the sometimes extraordinary heat of the battle was a measure of the depth of our mutual affection." From regrets came remorse and some understanding too. "Not until I looked upon her face in death," wrote Sandy, "did I realize how lonely was her life in youth. She had no sister. The past cannot be changed. Not all the gods together can undo the deed done. Much was my fault that I did not continue through life the intimate brotherly affection with which I regarded her in our prattling childhood. We grew apart, an injury to both. Isolation is a great price to pay for individuality." Sandy concluded: "And so closes Sarah's life in this world, and a great chapter in our own."[20]

It is sad to feel the depth of Sandy's loss as he buried his siblings. We feel, despite his regrets, how much these people shared with each other, how strong were their connections. However much their gender might have assigned them to separate spheres, their family joined them in a powerful and enduring shared sphere.

## Notes

1. Welter, "Cult of True Womanhood"; Cott, *Bonds of Womanhood;* and Smith-Rosenberg, "Female World of Love and Ritual" are the three most important

and best known in this large body of literature. Each was so powerful for me that I even remember where I was when I read each one. Similarly, *In a Different Voice,* Carol Gilligan's work on women's moral development, helped me understand why I hadn't really felt at home in various philosophy courses in particular. I had been able to do the work and I understood the material, but I always seemed to be asking peculiar questions: was Xanthippe really so horrible for asking Socrates to reconsider his decision to drink the hemlock? Didn't his wife and children have some claim on him? Why were being and nothingness so much more important to investigate than friendship or emotions? I had thought simply that I was quirky (and that is probably part of the explanation too), but Gilligan's work encouraged me to think that there might be some method in my quirkiness.

I have, however, come to see the limitations of these various works and their tendency to divide the world too starkly into male and female—and with this work on siblings I'm trying to see some connections between the two worlds. Nonetheless, these works still speak a truth that resonates in both the past and the present.

2. Alexander Christie to Sarah Christie Stevens, Oct. 2, 1873, James Christie and Family Papers, Minnesota Historical Society, St. Paul. Other extensive collections at the Minnesota Historical Society are Thomas and Carmelite Christie and Family Papers and David Bertie Christie and Family Papers. See also Christie, "Sarah Christie Stevens." I have also found very helpful Palmquist, "Journey to Canaan."

In their book, *Women in Waiting in the Westward Movement,* Linda Peavy and Ursula Smith include a chapter on Emma and David Christie. Peavy and Smith show that David often confided in his brother more than in his wife, even in matters that related directly to her, such as David's plan to move the family from Minnesota to Montana. See Peavy and Smith, *Women in Waiting,* 215, for example.

3. Their daughter Agnes's suicide note has survived in the family's papers, and it is painful to read even today. She wrote this note to her brother Paul. See Agnes Christie to Paul Christie, Dec. 30, 191, Thomas Christie Papers.

4. Alexander Christie to Sarah Christie, Nov. 5, 1865, James C. Christie Papers.

5. Thomas Christie to Alexander Christie, March 5, 1864, James C. Christie Papers.

6. William Christie to Sarah Christie, July 11, 1863, James C. Christie Papers.

7. Thomas Christie to Sarah Christie, Jan. 18, 1868; Thomas Christie to Alexander Christie, July 1, 1872; Sarah Christie to Alexander Christie, May 20, 1877, all in the James C. Christie Papers.

8. Alexander Christie to Sarah Christie, Sept. 13, 1872, and Jan. 3, 1876, James C. Christie Papers; David Christie to Sarah Christie, Jan. 9, 1876, James C. Christie Papers; Alexander Christie to David Christie, August 23, 1874, David Christie Papers.

9. Sarah Christie to Alexander Christie, May 20, 1877; Sarah Christie to Annie, July 12, 1869, both in James C. Christie Papers.

10. Sarah Christie to Alexander Christie, June 11, 1870, James C. Christie Papers; Thomas Christie to Sarah Christie, July 1, 1869, James C. Christie Pa-

pers; Alexander Christie to David Christie, April 12, 1898, David Christie Papers; Thomas Christie to Alexander Christie, Sept. 12, 1891, James C. Christie Papers.

11. Thomas Christie to Sarah Christie, Oct. 10 and 26, 1892, James C. Christie Papers; Sarah Christie to David Christie, Sept. 28, 1878, David Christie Papers; Alexander Christie to David Christie, Dec. 8, 1878, David Christie Papers; Thomas Christie to Alexander Christie, June 24, 1870, James C. Christie Papers.

12. Alexander Christie to Sarah Stevens, April 12, 1882, James C. Christie Papers.

13. Sarah Stevens to Alexander Christie, July, 6, 1882, and Aug. 20, 1877; James Christie to Alexander Christie, July 30, 1874; Thomas Christie to Alexander Christie, June 24, 1870, all in James C. Christie Papers.

14. Sarah Christie to Thomas Christie, July 23, 1872, Thomas Christie Papers.

15. Peavy and Smith, *Women in Waiting,* 217–18, 225.

16. Alexander Christie to Sarah Stevens, Aug. 1, 1890, James C. Christie Papers.

17. Sarah Stevens to David Christie, Jan. 30, 1890, David Christie Papers; Alexander Christie to David Christie, Jan. 16, 1890, David Christie Papers; Thomas Christie to Alexander Christie, Feb. 12, 1890, James C. Christie Papers; Alexander Christie to David Christie, March 12, 1890, David Christie Papers; and in the James C. Christie Papers: David Christie to Sarah Stevens, Feb. 16, 1890; Carmelite Christie to Alexander Christie, Jan. 20, 1890.

18. Alexander Christie to Sarah Stevens, Aug. 31 and Oct. 12, 1901, James C. Christie Papers.

19. Alexander Christie to David Christie, Sept. 22, 1919, David Christie Papers. In Minnesota women could vote for members of the school board from 1875 on and could serve on those boards. This was the only vote they were allowed to cast until 1919 with the passage of the Nineteenth Amendment.

20. "Note, Jan. 5, 1921," intended for Thomas Christie from Alexander Christie, James C. Christie Papers; Alexander Christie to David Christie, Sept. 22, 1919, David Christie Papers.

# Epilogue: Except in My Family

My families highlight various "truths" about family life. I've tried to use each family to show a different one. The Putnams show how a family created a culture among its members. They also give us a glimpse into a large family. By contrast, the Arthurs tell a story of a small family in which one member, at least, needed the other intensely. The Channings, a family of multiple divorces and much drama, were warm and expressive with each other. The Janins, another family of divorces, was a family of coolness and detachment. The Curtises were orphaned in their childhoods and spent their adulthoods trying to recreate a family life for themselves, yet the family was split once again, by a suicide. The North-Loomis family made one family out of many families. They found ways to integrate their birth families and their married families to a remarkable degree. The older generation of Blairs shows us a family that organized itself around one of its members and that integrated its and his needs into the family's common purpose. The younger generation of Blairs became estranged when the behavior of one member violated a basic value held by the others. The Christies, finally, show us that males and females within the same family lived within the separate worlds of their genders and the shared spheres of their family life.

Together these families also tell stories of achievement, divorce, suicide, many kinds of marriages, many different ways of relating to each other, many ways of relating birth families and adult families.

My idea has been that these ten families are not necessarily representative. They can't be; they're too similar in ethnicity, in race, in class—despite quite significant and real differences in income. What I have tried to do is look at a variety of families—large, small, urban, East Coast, rural, western, midwestern, loving, fractured, expressive, restrained, extended and nuclear, "traditional," and not quite so.

My point has been that families—even if we look only within these confines—were remarkably different from each other. They organized their collective emotional and social lives together differently from each other.

In contemporary America we have a confused and confusing collective memory of families in the past. One version, usually called something like the "traditional family," describes a family with two parents (married to each other), their biological children (and not too many and not birthed with any fertility or health difficulties). Everyone worked hard and contributed to the common well-being. Couples stayed married. Children outlived their parents—and took care of them when they were old. You know the picture. It's a combination of *Leave it to Beaver, How Green Was My Valley,* and *It's a Wonderful Life.* And most families in the past probably had some of these characteristics. But most examples of families that really fit this mode do come from fiction, whether the pages of a novel or the small or large screen, but not much from the historical record. If we talk about the past without historical information, without specific references and real evidence, we're not talking about the past but the present, about ourselves—but unconsciously. When we're in the realm of the unconscious, we're into the territory of our deepest longings, fears, wishes, hopes—but not history. And isn't this an alluring and seductive idea—the idea that at another time families were not troubled as so many families seem to be today? This vision has a powerful emotional and political currency.

Another version is what most of us live with—our own family stories. In these, unless they've been completely polished up and burnished for our edification, the families may have some characteristics of the "traditional family," but they also had divorces and alcoholics, the bachelor uncle and the maiden aunt who had same-sex "roommates," parents who fought too much, sexual and emotional repression, strict discipline that veered (or plowed) into abuse. In short, most of us have in our heads historical data that make for a more complex, often a more shadowed, picture of families in the past.

So most of us live with a gap between "them" and "us," between those traditional families and our own historical families. What sense can we make of that gap? Three possibilities (and, of course, I'm going to take the third): (1) other families really were like the Cleavers, just not mine; (2) if we just tried hard enough, we could be like the Cleavers—that we're not is our individual/collective fault; (3) maybe the "traditional family" picture could stand a little reality check.

In part, this book can provide that reality check. All the families here are white, middle-class Anglo-Saxon and Protestant families. If any families in the past should fit the traditional mode, it would be these people. But they don't. They're variously big and small, close and conflictual, close and cool, distant but warm, stable, mobile, nuclear, extended, unconventional, happy, and tragic.

I would not argue that American families are all thriving. They aren't. But they never have been. The family is a social institution, and as such it mirrors the society in which it exists. It will adapt to that society, it will be stretched and contracted to be made to fit. It does deserve serious attention and all our best efforts to understand and to care for it. But we cannot correctly diagnose the condition of contemporary American families if we have a false notion about historical American families. Are contemporary families worse off than those in the past? No doubt. Are they better off than those in the past? That's almost certainly true too. If we are going to make good and effective public policy, if we are even going to give ourselves a comparative framework for making personal family policy, we need good, accurate, and varied data. We need to meet some real people from the past. If my head is full of the Christies, Arthurs, Putnams, Janins, Channings, Norths, Blairs, and Curtises, I have some of those real people. I can thereby understand the past better, understand myself better. I have more choices, better choices, and better chances. They're all less perfect than the traditional family, but they're more helpful.

These stories of siblings can also give us one kind of hope as we think about contemporary American families. Perhaps we have put so much emphasis on the relationship between parents and children that we have overlooked and forgotten the importance of siblings. Perhaps we have been so concerned about the breakdown of the parental unit, we have overlooked the resilience of the sibling unit. Of course, not every family has siblings who take care of and care for each other, but enough do that perhaps we could put some of our hope for the family in the connective, sustaining tissue that many siblings in all these families seem to have given to each other.

Every person is an expert on family history. We all have experiences so profoundly personal and primal and compelling that any story of any other family will fall short of the reality of our own. It is difficult—no, impossible—to do justice to the complexity of any family. Every family tells so many stories, and each member tells some different ones. So I offer these siblings to give us information, material for meditation, comparative points. They don't represent the whole spectrum. How much more and what different variations might we add if we got to know historical families who were more varied in ethnicity, race, and class? If we looked at other time periods, other regions, other religions and cultural groups? But even these teach us the folly of ever speaking about "The American Family." Only plurals will do and only conditionals and limits: some, a few, many, or most and only at a certain date in a particular place. I urge us to tell our own stories and to ask more about them and to pursue them. Let us find out about the families in our own pasts and in the pasts of our friends. Find the various and multiple truths. We'll all be better for it.

# Bibliography

Adams, Henry. *The Education of Henry Adams.* Boston: Houghton Mifflin, 1973.
———. *The Letters of Henry Adams.* 6 vols. Cambridge, Mass.: Harvard University Press, 1982–1988.
Adler, Alfred. *Social Interest: A Challenge to Mankind.* London: Faber and Faber, 1938.
———. *Understanding Human Nature.* London: George Allen and Unwin, 1928.
———. *What Life Should Mean to You.* London: George Allen and Unwin, 1932.
Alger, Horatio Jr. *Ragged Dick and Mark, the MatchBoy.* Intro. by Richard Fink. New York: Collier, 1962.
Alpern, Sara, Joyce Antler, Elisabeth Israels Perry, and Ingrid Winther Scobie. *The Challenge of Feminist Biography: Writing the Lives of Modern American Women.* Urbana: University of Illinois Press, 1992.
Ariès, Philippe. *Centuries of Childhood.* London: Cape, 1962.
Bank, Stephen P., and Michael E. Kahn. *The Sibling Bond.* New York: Basic, 1982.
Barker-Benfield, G. J. *The Horrors of the Half-Known Life: Male Attitudes Toward Women and Sexuality in Nineteenth-Century America.* New York: Harper and Row, 1976).
Baydar, Nazli, April Greek, and Jeanne Brooks-Gunn. "A Longitudinal Study of the Effects of the Birth of a Sibling During the First Six Years of Life." *Journal of Marriage and the Family* 59 (November 1997): 939–56.
Becvar, Dorothy Stroh, and Raphael J. Becvar. *Family Therapy: A Systemic Integration.* Boston: Allyn and Bacon, 1988.
Bederman, Gail. *Manliness and Civilization: A Cultural History of Gender and Race in the United States, 1880–1917.* Chicago: University of Chicago Press, 1995.
Belenky, Mary, Blythe McVicker Clinchy, Nancy Rule Goldberger, and Jill Mat-

tuck Tarule. *Women's Ways of Knowing: The Development of Self, Voice, and Mind*. New York: Basic, 1986.

Blackwell, Elizabeth. *Pioneer Work for Women*. New York: Dutton, 1914.

Bowen, Ralph H. *A Frontier Family in Minnesota: Letters of Theodore and Sophie Bost, 1851–1920*. Minneapolis: University of Minnesota Press, 1981.

Boydston, Jeanne, Mary Kelley, and Anne Margolis. *The Limits of Sisterhood: The Beecher Sisters on Women's Rights and Woman's Sphere*. Chapel Hill: University of North Carolina Press, 1988.

Buhle, Mari Jo. "Charlotte Perkins Gilman." In Buhle, Buhle, and Georgakas, *Encyclopedia of the American Left*.

Buhle, Mari Jo, Paul Buhle, and Dan Georgakas, eds. *Encyclopedia of the American Left*. New York: Garland, 1990.

Cancian, Francesca M. *Love in America: Gender and Self-Development*. New York: Cambridge University Press, 1987.

Carnes, Mark C. *Secret Ritual and Manhood in Victorian America* New Haven, Conn.: Yale University Press, 1989.

Carnes, Mark C., and Clyde Griffen, eds. *Meaning of Manhood: Constructions of Masculinity in Victorian America*. Chicago: University of Chicago Press, 1990.

Carroll, Berenice A. *Liberating Women's History: Theoretical and Critical Essays*. Urbana: University of Illinois Press, 1976.

Cather, Willa. *My Ántonia*. Boston: Houghton Mifflin, 1926.

Censer, Jane Turner. *North Carolina Planters and Their Children, 1800–1860*. Baton Rouge: Louisiana State University Press, 1984.

Chafe, William H. *Women and Equality: Changing Patterns in American Culture*. New York: Oxford University Press, 1977.

Chambers-Schiller, Lee Virginia. *Liberty, A Better Husband*. New Haven, Conn.: Yale University Press, 1984.

Chodorow, Nancy. *The Reproduction of Mothering: Psychoanalysis of Gender*. Berkeley and Los Angeles: University of California Press, 1978.

Christie, Jean. "Sarah Christie Stevens: Schoolwoman." *Minnesota History* 40 (Summer 1983): 245–54.

Cicirelli, Victor G. "Sibling Influence Throughout the Lifespan." In Lamb and Sutton-Smith, eds., *Sibling Relationships*.

———. *Sibling Relationships Across the Life Span*. New York: Plenum, 1995.

Clark, Clifford E. Jr. *The American Family Home, 1800–1960*. Chapel Hill: University of North Carolina Press, 1986.

Cmiel, Kenneth. *A Home of Another Kind: One Chicago Orphanage and the Tangle of Child Welfare*. Chicago: University of Chicago Press, 1995.

Conger, Katherine Jewsbury. "Sibling Relationships Across the Life Span." *Journal of Marriage and the Family* 58 (August 1996): 267–84.

Connidis, Ingrid Arnet. "Siblings as Friends in Later Life." *American Behavioral Scientist* 33 (September–October 1989): 81–93.

Connidis, Ingrid Arnet, and Lori D. Campbell. "Closeness, Confiding, and Contact Among Siblings in Middle and Late Adulthood." *Journal of Family Issues* (November 1995): 722–45.

Coontz, Stephanie. *The Social Origins of Private Life: A History of American Families, 1600–1900*. New York: Verso, 1988.

———. *The Way We Never Were: American Families and the Nostalgia Trap.* New York: HarperCollins, 1992.

Cornish, Dudley Taylor, and Virginia Jeans Laas. *Lincoln's Lee.* Lawrence: University of Kansas Press, 1986.

Cott, Nancy F. *Bonds of Womanhood: Woman's Sphere in New England, 1780–1835.* New Haven, Conn.: Yale University Press, 1977.

———. "Mary Beard Ritter." In Sicherman and Green, *Notable American Women.*

———, ed. *A Woman Making History: Mary Ritter Beard Through Her Letters.* New Haven, Conn.: Yale University Press, 1991.

Crane, Katherine Elizabeth. *Blair House: Past and Present: An Account of Its Life and Times in the City of Washington.* Washington, D.C.: U.S. Department of State, 1945.

Crispell, Diane. "The Sibling Syndrome." *American Demographics* 18 (August 1996): 24–30.

Croly, David G. *Seymour and Blair: Their Lives and Services.* New York: Richardson, 1868.

Culler, Jonathan. *On Deconstruction: Theory and Criticism After Structuralism.* Ithaca, N.Y.: Cornell University Press, 1982.

Culley, Margo. *American Women's Autobiography: Fea(s)ts of Memory.* Madison: University of Wisconsin Press, 1992.

Cullum, George W. *Biographical Register of the Officers and Graduates of the U.S. Military Academy,* 3 vols. 3d ed. Boston: Houghton Mifflin, 1891–1920.

Daly, Mary. *Gyn/Ecology: The Metaethics of Radical Feminism.* Boston: Beacon, 1978.

Davidoff, Leonore, and Catherine Hall. *Family Fortunes: Men and Women of the English Middle Class, 1780–1850.* London: Hutchinson Educational, 1987.

Degler, Carl N. *At Odds: Women and the Family in America from the Revolution to the Present.* New York: Oxford University Press, 1980.

De Mause, Lloyd, ed. *The History of Childhood: The Evolution of Parent-Child Relationships as a Factor in History.* New York: Psychohistory Press, 1974.

D'Emilio, John, and Estelle B. Freedman. *Intimate Matters: A History of Sexuality in America.* New York: Harper and Row, 1988.

Demos, John. *A Little Commonwealth: Family Life in Plymouth Colony.* New York: Oxford University Press, 1970.

———. *Past, Present, and Personal: The Family and the Life Course in American History.* New York: Oxford University Press, 1986.

*Dictionary of American Biography.* 20 vols., 8 suppl. New York: Scribner's, 1928–1973.

di Leonardo, Micaela. "The Female World of Cards and Holidays: Women, Families, and the Work of Kinship." *Signs* 12 (Spring 1987): 440–53.

Drake, Michael, ed. *Time, Family, and Community: Perspectives on Family and Community History.* Oxford, England: Blackwell, 1994.

Dubbert, Joe L. *A Man's Place: Masculinity in Transition.* Englewood Cliffs, N.J.: Prentice Hall, 1979.

Dulberger, Judith, ed. *"Mother Donit fore the Best": Correspondence of a Nineteenth-Century Orphan Asylum.* Syracuse, N.Y.: Syracuse University Press, 1966.

Eichenbaum, Luise, and Susie Orbach. *Between Women: Love, Envy, and Competition in Women's Friendships.* New York: Viking, 1987.

Elder, Glen H. Jr., and Charles E. Bowerman. "Family Structure and Child-Rearing Patterns: The Effect of Family Size and Sex Composition." *American Sociological Review* 28 (December 1963): 891–905.

Faragher, John Mack. *Women and Men on the Overland Trail.* New Haven, Conn.: Yale University Press, 1979.

Fehrenbacher, Don E. *The* Dred Scott *Case: Its Significance in American Law and Politics.* New York: Oxford University Press, 1978.

Filene, Peter G. *Him/Her/Self: Sex Roles in Modern America.* Baltimore, Md.: John Hopkins University Press, 1974.

Fink, Deborah. *Agrarian Women: Wives and Mothers in Rural Nebraska, 1880–1940.* Chapel Hill: University of North Carolina Press, 1992.

Floyd, Kory. "Gender and Closeness Among Friends and Siblings." *Journal of Psychology* 129 (March 1995): 193–202.

Foster, Patricia, ed. *Sister to Sister: Women Write About the Unbreakable Bond.* New York: Anchor, 1995.

Frank, Steven. *Life with Father: Parenthood and Masculinity in the Nineteenth-Century American North.* Baltimore, Md .: Johns Hopkins University Press, 1998.

Frederich, Otto. *Clover.* New York: Simon and Schuster, 1979.

Frykman, Jonas, and Orvar Lofgren. *Culture Builders: A Historical Anthropology of Middle-Class Life.* London: Rutgers University Press, 1987.

Gardner, James B., and George Rollie Adams. *Ordinary People and Everyday Life: Perspectives on the New Social History.* Nashville, Tenn.: American Association for State and Local History, 1983.

Gilligan, Carol. *In a Different Voice: Psychological Theory and Women's Development.* Cambridge, Mass.: Harvard University Press, 1982.

Gillis, John R. "Making Time for Family: The Invention of Family Time(s) and the Reinvention of Family History." *Journal of Family History* 21 (January 1996): 4–21.

Gillis, John R. *A World of Their Own Making: Myth, Ritual, and the Quest for Family Values.* New York: Basic, 1996.

Gilman, Charlotte Perkins. *Herland.* Intro. by Ann J. Lane. New York: Pantheon, 1979.

———. *The Living of Charlotte Perkins Gilman: An Autobiography.* Intro. by Ann J. Lane. Madison: University of Wisconsin Press, 1990.

———. *Women and Economics.* Ed. and intro. by Carl N. Degler. New York: Harper and Row, 1966.

———. *The Yellow Wallpaper.* New Brunswick, N.J.: Rutgers University Press, 1993.

Glenn, Norvall E. "A Plea for Objective Assessment of the Notion of Family Decline." *Journal of Marriage and the Family* 55 (August 1993): 542–44.

Goetting, Ann. "The Developmental Tasks of Siblingship over the Life Cycle." *Journal of Marriage and the Family,* 48 (November 1986): 703–14.

Goody, Jack. *The Development of the Family and Marriage in Europe.* Cambridge, England: Cambridge University Press, 1983.

Gordon, Linda. *Heroes of Their Own Lives: The Politics and History of Family Violence, Boston—1880–1960.* New York: Viking, 1988.

Gordon, Michael, ed. *The American Family in Social-Historical Perspective.* 2d ed. New York: St. Martin's, 1978.

Gottlieb, Beatrice. *The Family in the Western World from the Black Death to the Industrial Age.* New York: Oxford University Press, 1993.

Graff, Harvey. *Conflicting Paths: Growing Up in America.* Cambridge, Mass.: Harvard University Press, 1995.

Gray, John. *Men Are from Mars, Women Are from Venus: A Practical Guide for Improving Communication and Getting What You Want in Your Relationships.* New York: HarperCollins, 1992.

Griswold, Robert L. *Family and Divorce in California, 1850–1890: Victorian Illusions and Everyday Realities.* Albany: State University of New York, 1982.

————. *Fatherhood in America: A History.* New York: Basic, 1993.

Gutman, Herbert G. *The Black Family in Slavery and Freedom, 1750–1925.* New York: Random House, 1976.

Hall, Jacquelyn Dowd, James Leloudis, Robert Korstad, Mary Murphy, Lu Ann Jones, and Christopher B. Daly. *Like a Family: The Making of a Southern Cotton Mill World.* Chapel Hill: University of North Carolina Press, 1987.

Hampsten, Elizabeth. *Read This Only to Yourself: The Private Writings of Midwestern Women, 1880–1910.* Bloomington: Indiana University Press, 1982.

Hansen, Karen V. "'Helped Put in a Quilt': Men's Work and Male Intimacy in Nineteenth-Century New England." *Gender and Society* 3 (September 1989): 334–45.

————. *A Very Social Time: Crafting Community in Antebellum New England.* Berkeley: University of California Press, 1994.

Hareven, Tamara K. "The History of the Family and the Complexity of Social Change." *American Historical Review* 96 (February 1991): 95–124.

————. "The Home and the Family in Historical Perspective." *Social Research* 58 (Spring 1991): 253–85.

————. *Transitions: The Family and the Life Course in Historical Perspective.* New York: Academic, 1978.

Hareven, Tamara K., and Maris A. Vinovskis. *Family and Population in Nineteenth-Century America.* Princeton, N.J.: Princeton University Press, 1978.

Hauser, Robert M., and Hsiang-Hui Daphne Kuo. "Does the Gender Composition of Sibships Affect Women's Educational Attainment?" *Journal of Human Resources* 33 (Summer 1998): 644–57.

Heilbrun, Carolyn G. *Writing a Woman's Life.* New York: Norton, 1988.

Herbert, T. Walter. *Dearest Beloved: The Hawthornes and the Making of the Middle-Class Family.* Berkeley: University of California Press, 1993.

Herr, Pamela. *Jessie Benton Fremont.* Norman: University Press of Oklahoma, 1988.

Herr, Pamela, and Mary Lee Spence, eds. *The Letters of Jessie Benton Frémont.* Urbana: University of Illinois Press, 1993.

Hessinger, Rodney. "Problems and Promises: Colonial American Child Rearing and Modernization Theory." *Journal of Family History* 21 (April 1996): 125–43.

Hewitt, Nancy A. "Beyond the Search for Sisterhood: American Women's History in the 1980s." *Social History* 10 (October 1985): 299–321.

Hill, Mary A. *A Journey from Within: The Love Letters of Charlotte Perkins Gilman, 1897–1900.* Lewisburg, Pa.: Bucknell University Press, 1995.

Hill, Mary A., ed. *Endure: The Diaries of Charles Walter Stetson.* Philadelphia: Temple University Press, 1985.

Hinding, Andrea, ed. *Guide to Women's History Sources.* 2 vols. New York: Bowker/University of Minnesota, 1979.

Holt, Marilyn Irvin. *The Orphan Trains: Placing Out in America.* Lincoln: University of Nebraska Press, 1992.

Howe, George Frederick. *Chester A. Arthur: A Quarter-Century of Machine Politics.* New York: Ungar, Company, 1935.

Jabour, Anya. "Masculinity and Adolescence in Antebellum America: Robert Wirt at West Point, 1820–1821." *Journal of Family History* 23 (October 1998): 393–416.

James, Edward T., Janet Wilson James, and Paul S. Boyer, eds. *Notable American Women, 1607–1950.* 3 vols. Cambridge, Mass.: Harvard University Press, 1971.

Jensen, Joan M. *Loosening the Bonds: Mid-Atlantic Farm Women, 1750–1850.* New Haven, Conn.: Yale University Press, 1986.

———. *Promise to the Land: Essays on Rural Women.* Albuquerque: University of New Mexico Press, 1991.

Jones, Jacqueline. *Labor of Love, Labor of Sorrow: Black Women, Work, and the Family from Slavery to the Present.* New York: Random House, 1985.

Kahn, Michael E., and Karen Gail Lewis, eds. *Siblings in Therapy: Life Span and Clinical Issues.* New York: Norton, 1988.

Kaufman, Stuart Galishoff, and Todd L. Savitt, eds. *Dictionary of American Medical Biography.* 2 vols. Westport, Conn.: Greenwood, 1984.

Kerr, Michael E., and Murray Bowen. *Family Evaluation: An Approach Based on Bowen Theory.* New York: Norton, 1988.

Kessler-Harris, Alice. *Women Have Always Worked.* Old Westbury, N.Y.: Feminist Press, 1981.

Kimmel, Michael. *Manhood in America: A Cultural History.* New York: Free Press, 1996.

Klagsbrun, Francine. *Mixed Feelings: Love, Hate, Rivalry, and Reconciliation Among Brothers and Sisters.* New York: Bantam, 1992.

Konig, Karl. *Brothers and Sisters: The Order of Birth in the Family.* New York: Anthroposophic Press, 1958.

Laas, Virginia Jeans. *Love and Power in the Nineteenth Century: The Marriage of Violet Blair.* Fayetteville: University of Arkansas Press, 1996.

———, ed. *Wartime Washington: The Civil War Letters of Elizabeth Blair Lee.* Urbana: University of Illinois Press, 1991.

Lamb, Michael E. "Sibling Relationships Across the Lifespan: An Overview and Introduction." In Lamb and Sutton-Smith, *Sibling Relationships.*

Lamb, Michael E., and Brian Sutton-Smith. *Sibling Relationships: Their Nature and Significance Across the Lifespan.* Hillsdale, N.J.: Erlbaum, 1982.

Lane, Ann J. *To Herland and Beyond: The Life and Work of Charlotte Perkins Gilman*. Charlottesville: University Press of Virginia, 1990.

LaRossa, Ralph. *The Modernization of Fatherhood: A Social and Political History*. Chicago: University of Chicago Press, 1997.

Lasch, Christopher. *Haven in a Heartless World: The Family Besieged*. New York: Basic, 1975.

Laslett, Peter. *The World We Have Lost: England Before the Industrial Age*. New York: Scribner's, 1984.

Lasser, Carol, and Marlene Deahl Merrill. *Friends and Sisters: Letters Between Lucy Stone and Antoinette Brown Blackwell, 1846–1893*. Urbana: University of Illinois Press, 1987.

Lebsock, Suzanne. *Free Women of Petersburg: Status and Culture in a Southern Town, 1784–1860*. New York: Norton, 1984.

Lockridge, Kenneth. *A New England Town: The First Hundred Years, Dedham, Massachusetts, 1636–1736*. New York: Norton, 1970.

Lystra, Karen. *Searching the Heart: Women, Men, and Romantic Love in Nineteenth-Century America*. New York: Oxford University Press, 1989.

McGoldrick, Monica. *You Can Go Home Again: Reconnecting with Your Family*. New York: Norton, 1995.

McGoldrick, Monica, Carol M. Anderson, and Froma Walsh. *Women in Family: A Framework for Family Therapy*. New York: Norton, 1973.

McGoldrick, Monica, John K. Pearce, and Joseph Giordano. *Ethnicity and Family Therapy*. New York: Guilford, 1982.

May, Elaine Tyler. *Great Expectations: Marriage and Divorce in Post-Victorian America*. Chicago: University of Chicago Press, 1980.

———. *Homeward Bound: American Families in the Cold War Era*. New York: Basic, 1988.

Miller, Jacquelyn C. "The Politics of Emotion: The Construction of Middle Class Identity in Late Eighteenth-Century Philadelphia." Paper presented at Organization of American Historians Annual Meeting, March 31, 1995, Washington, D.C.

Miner, Sonia, and Peter Uhlenberg. "Intragenerational Proximity and the Social Role of Sibling Neighbors After Midlife." *Family Relations* 46 (April 1997): 145–53.

Minnesota Commission of Public Safety. "Alien Registration and Declaration of Holdings" for St. Louis County. Division of Archives and Manuscripts, Minnesota Historical Society, St. Paul, 1918.

Mintz, Steven. *Prison of Expectations: The Family in Victorian Culture*. New York: New York University Press, 1983.

Mintz, Steven, and Susan Kellogg. *Domestic Revolutions: A Social History of American Family Life*. New York: Free Press, 1988.

Minuchin, Salvador. *Families and Family Therapy*. Cambridge, Mass.: Harvard University Press, 1974.

Moran, Gerald F., and Maris A. Vinovskis. *Religion, Family, and the Life Course: Explorations in the Social History of Early America*. Ann Arbor: University of Michigan Press, 1992.

Morantz, Regina. "The Lady and Her Physician." In Mary S. Hartman and Lois Banner, eds., *Clio's Consciousness Raised: New Perspectives in the History of Women*. New York: Octagon, 1974.

Morantz-Sanchez, Regina Markell. *Sympathy and Science: Women Physicians in American Medicine*. New York: Oxford University Press, 1985.

Motz, Marilyn Ferris. *True Sisterhood: Michigan Women and Their Kin, 1800–1920*. Albany: State University of New York Press, 1983.

Musser, Emma North. "Memories of a Frontier Childhood." *Overland Monthly and Out West Magazine,* August 1924, pp. 339–40, 364–65, 384; September 1924, pp. 395–97, 412–13; and October 1924, pp. 437–40, 476–78.

Myres, Sandra L. *Westering Women and the Frontier Experience, 1800–1915*. Albuquerque: University of New Mexico Press, 1982.

Nissenbaum, Stephen. *The Battle for Christmas: A Social and Cultural History of Christmas That Shows How It Was Transformed from an Unruly Carnival Season into the Quintessential American Family Holiday*. New York: Knopf, 1997.

O'Day, Rosemary. *The Family and Family Relationships, 1500–1900: England, France, and the United States of America*. London: Macmillan, 1994.

Osterud, Nancy Grey. *Bonds of Community: The Lives of Farm Women in Nineteenth-Century New York*. Ithaca, N.Y.: Cornell University Press, 1991.

Pacey, Phillip. *Family Art*. Cambridge, U.K.: Polity, 1989.

Palmquist, Bonnie Beatson. "The Journey to Canaan: Letters of the Christie Family." Masters' thesis, Hamline University, St. Paul, Minn., 1990.

Parrish, William E. *Frank Blair: Lincoln's Conservative*. Columbia: University of Missouri Press, 1998.

Peavy, Linda S., and Ursula Smith. *Women in Waiting in the Westward Movement: Life on the Home Frontier*. Norman: University of Oklahoma Press, 1994.

Pederson, Jane Marie. *Between Memory and Reality: Family and Community in Rural Wisconsin, 1870–1970*. Madison: University of Wisconsin Press, 1992.

Peterson, M. Jeanne. *Family, Love, and Work in the Lives of Victorian Gentlewomen*. Indianapolis: Indiana University Press, 1989.

Pleck, Elizabeth H. "Gender Role and Relations." In Mary Kupiec Cayton, Elliott J. Gorn, and Peter W. Williams, eds., *Encyclopedia of American Social History*. Vol. 3: 1945–1960. New York: Scribner's, 1993.

Pollock, Linda. *Forgotten Children: Parent-Child Relations from 1500 to 1900*. Cambridge, England: Cambridge University Press, 1983.

Poovey, Mary. *Uneven Developments: The Ideological Work of Gender in Mid-Victorian England*. Chicago: University of Chicago Press, 1988.

Putnam, George Haven. *George Palmer Putnam: A Memoir*. New York: Putnam's, 1912.

———. *Memories of a Publisher, 1865–1915*. New York: Putnam's, 1915.

———. *Memories of My Youth, 1844–1865*. New York: Putnam's, 1914.

———. *A Prisoner of War in Virginia, 1864–1865*. New York: Putnam's, 1912.

———. *Some Memories of the Civil War*. New York: Putnam's, 1924.

Putnam, George Palmer. *Wide Margins: A Publisher's Autobiography*. New York: Harcourt, Brace, 1942.

Putnam, Ruth. *The Life and Letters of Mary Putnam Jacobi.* New York: Putnam's, 1925.

Rabb, Theodore K., and Robert I. Rothberg. *The Family in History: Interdisciplinary Essays.* New York: Harper Torchbooks, 1971.

Raymond, Janice G. *A Passion for Friends: Toward a Philosophy of Female Affection.* Boston: Beacon, 1986.

Reeves, Thomas C. *Gentleman Boss: The Life of Chester Alan Arthur.* New York: Knopf, 1975.

Riley, Glenda. *Building and Breaking Families: In the American West.* Albuquerque: University of New Mexico Press, 1996.

———. *Divorce: An American Tradition.* New York: Oxford University Press, 1991.

———. *The Female Frontier: A Comparative View of Women on the Prairie and the Plains.* Lawrence: University Press of Kansas, 1988.

———. *Frontierswomen: The Iowa Experience.* Ames: Iowa State University Press, 1981.

Rose, Phyllis. *Parallel Lives: Five Victorian Families.* New York: Knopf, 1983.

Rothman, David. *The Discovery of the Asylum: Social Order and Disorder in the New Republic.* Boston: Little, Brown, 1971.

Rothman, Ellen K. *Hands and Hearts: A History of Courtship in America.* New York: Basic, 1984.

Rotundo, E. Anthony. *American Manhood: Transformations in Masculinity from the Revolution to the Modern Era.* New York: Basic, 1993.

Ruggles, Steven. *Prolonged Connections: The Rise of the Extended Family in Nineteenth-Century England and America.* Madison: University of Wisconsin Press, 1987.

———. "The Transformation of American Family Structure." *American Historical Review* 99 (February 1994): 103–28.

Ryan, Mary E. *Cradle of the Middle Class: The Family in Oneida County, New York, 1790–1865.* Cambridge, Mass.: Harvard University Press, 1981.

Rybczynski, Witold. *Home: A Short History of an Idea.* New York: Penguin, 1986.

Scarnhorst, Gary. *Charlotte Perkins Gilman.* Boston: Twayne, 1985.

Schlissel, Lillian. *Women's Diaries of the Westward Journey.* New York: Schocken, 1982.

Schlissel, Lillian, Byrd Gibbens, and Elizabeth Hampsten. *Far from Home: Families of the Westward Journey.* New York: Schocken, 1989.

Scott, Donald M., and Bernard Wishy. *America's Families: A Documentary History.* New York: Harper and Row, 1982.

Scott, Joan W. "Deconstructing Equality-Versus-Difference: Or, the Uses of Poststructuralist Theory for Feminism." *Feminist Studies* 14 (Spring 1988): 33–50.

Shorter, Edward. *The Making of the Modern Family.* New York: Basic, 1975.

Sicherman, Barbara, and Carol Hurd Green, eds. *Notable American Women: The Modern Period.* Cambridge, Mass.: Harvard University Press, 1980.

Skolnick, Arlene S. *Embattled Paradise: The American Family in an Age of Uncertainty.* New York: Basic, 1991.

Skolnick, Arlene S., and Jerome H. Skolnick. *Family in Transition: Rethinking Marriage, Sexuality, Child Rearing, and Family Organization.* Boston: Little, Brown, 1986.

Smith, Daniel Blake. *Inside the Great House: Planter Family Life in Eighteenth-Century Chesapeake Society.* Ithaca, N.Y.: Cornell University Press, 1980.

Smith, Daniel Scott. "Recent Change and the Periodization of American Family History." *Journal of Family History* 20 (October 1995): 329–47.

Smith, Elbert B. *Francis Preston Blair.* New York: Free Press, 1980.

Smith, William Earnest. *The Francis Preston Blair Family in Politics.* 2 vols. New York: Macmillan, 1933.

Smith-Rosenberg, Carroll. "The Female World of Love and Ritual: Relations Between Women in Nineteenth-Century American." In *Disorderly Conduct: Visions of Gender in Victorian America.* New York: Knopf, 1985.

Southwick, Leslie, *Presidential Also-Rans and Running Mates, 1788–1996.* 2d ed. Jefferson, N.C.: McFarland, 1998.

Spence, Clark C. *Mining Engineers and the American West: The Lace Boot Brigade.* New Haven, Conn.: Yale University Press, 1970.

Stearns, Peter N. *American Cool: Constructing a Twentieth-Century Emotional Style.* New York: New York University Press, 1994.

Stearns, Peter N., and Jan Lewis, ed. *An Emotional History of the United States.* New York: New York University Press, 1998.

Steedman, Carolyn. *Strange Dislocations: Childhood and the Idea of Human Interiority, 1780–1930.* Cambridge, Mass.: Harvard University Press, 1995.

Stone, Lawrence. "Family History in the 1980s." *Journal of Interdisciplinary History* 12 (Summer 1981): 51–57.

———. *The Family, Sex, and Marriage in England* (London: Wiedenfeld and Nicholson, 1977.

———. *The Road to Divorce: England, 1530–1987.* New York: Oxford University Press, 1990.

Stonehouse, Merlin. *John Wesley North and the Reform Frontier.* Minneapolis: University of Minnesota Press, 1965.

Stowe, Steven M. *Intimacy and Power in the Old South.* Baltimore, Md.: Johns Hopkins University Press, 1987.

Stratton, Joanna L. *Pioneer Women: Voices from the Kansas Frontier.* New York: Simon and Schuster, 1981.

Suleiman, Susan R., and Inge Crosman. *The Reader in the Text: Essays on Audience and Interpretation.* Princeton, N.J.: Princeton University Press, 1980.

Sulloway, Frank J. *Born to Rebel: Birth Order, Family Dynamics, and Creative Lives.* New York: Pantheon, 1996.

Sutherland, Neil. *Children in English Canadian Society: Framing the Twentieth-Century Consensus.* Toronto: University of Toronto Press, 1976.

Tannen, Deborah. *Talking from 9 to 5: How Women's and Men's Conversational Styles Affect Who Gets Heard, Who Gets Credit, and What Gets Done at Work.* New York: Morrow, 1994.

———. *You Just Don't Understand: Women and Men in Conversation.* New York: Morrow, 1990.

Thorne, Barrie, and Marilyn Yalom. *Rethinking the Family: Some Feminist Questions.* Boston: Northeastern University Press, 1992.

Tilly, Charles. "Family History, Social History, and Social Change." *Journal of Family History* 12 (1–3): 319–30.

Tilly, Louise A., and Miriam Cohen. "Does the Family Have a History: A Review of Theory and Practice in Family History." *Social Science History* 6 (Spring 1982): 131–79.

Tilly, Louise A., and John W. Scott. *Women, Work, and Family.* London: Routledge, 1987.

Toman, Walter. "Basics of Family Structure and Sibling Position." In Kahn and Lewis, *Siblings in Therapy.*

Tosh, John. *A Man's Place: Masculinity and the Middle-Class Home in Victorian England.* New Haven, Conn.: Yale University Press, 1999.

U.S. Bureau of the Census. *Historical Statistics of the United States, Colonial Times to 1970.* Series A 335–349. Washington, D.C.: Government Printing Office, 1975.

Walsh, Mary Roth. *"Doctors Wanted, No Women Need Apply": Sexual Barriers in the Medical Profession, 1835–1975.* New Haven, Conn.: Yale University Press, 1977.

Warren, Andrea, *Orphan Train Rider: One Boy's True Story.* Boston: Houghton Mifflin, 1996.

Welter, Barbara. "Cult of True Womanhood, 1820–1860." *American Quarterly* 18 (Summer 1966): 151–74.

West, Elliot. *Growing Up with the Country: Childhood on the Far Western Frontier.* Albuquerque: University of New Mexico Press, 1989.

West, Elliot, and Paula Petrik. *Small Worlds: Children and Adolescents in America, 1850–1950.* Lawrence: University Press of Kansas.

White, Hayden. *The Historical Imagination in Nineteenth-Century Europe.* Baltimore, Md.: John Hopkins University Press, 1973.

White, James Boyd. *When Words Lose Their Meaning: Constitutions and Reconstitutions of Language, Character, and Community.* Chicago: University of Chicago Press, 1984.

Zmora, Nurith. *Orphanages Reconsidered: Child Care Institutions in Progressive-Era Baltimore.* Philadelphia: Temple University Press, 1994.

# Index

Adams, Clover, 115n.21
Adams, Henry, 115n.21
Adler, Alfred, 7–8
age: authority linked to, 3–4, 62; parents'
  deaths and, 104–5
Alexander, Apolline. *See* Blair, Apolline
  (Apo) Alexander
Alger, Horatio, 106
American Library Association, 21
Andrews, Myra Fithian, 45, 51, 61–62
antislavery advocates, Blairs as, 89–90,
  121
Arizona, Curtises in, 110–11, 112
Arthur, Chester A.: age of, 52n.5; career
  of, 43–44; emotions of, 42–43, 52n.4;
  illness and death of, 41–42, 44, 45;
  marriage and family of, 40–41; papers
  burned by, 44, 53n.12
Arthur, Chester Alan, II: childhood and
  education of, 40–42, 44–45, 53–54n.18;
  illness of, 53n.14; marriages of, 45, 50–
  51; response to father's death, 45, 46–
  47, 104; sister's importance to, 46–52;
  son's attitudes toward, 53n.13; values
  of, 39–40
Arthur, Chester Alan, III, 41, 45, 53n.13
Arthur, Ellen Lewis Herndon, 40–41,
  42–43, 44
Arthur, Ellen (Nell) Herndon: brother's
  importance to, 46–52; childhood of,

41–43; father's death, 45–46, 104; marriage of, 46, 50, 51; values of, 39, 40,
  107
Arthur, Myra Fithian Andrews, 45, 51,
  61–62
Arthur, Rowena, 45
Arthur, William, 40
Arthur family: death of brother, 40–41;
  death of parent, 41–42, 44–45; egalitarianism in, 48; emotions expressed in,
  39–40, 42–43, 46–52, 52n.4, 171; gender in, 41, 50, 66, 70n.28; outline of,
  39; size of, 38; sources on, 52n.1
Ashley, Kate, 95–96
Atkins family: family secrets and, 140; favoritism in, 118–19; gender in, 3–4,
  154–55; in-laws and, 147, 164; parental
  death and, 103–4; photographic record
  of, 19; size of, 1, 5, 174; teaching and
  sharing in, 2, 30
authority, age linked to, 3–4, 62

Barnard College, 18
Barnett family, 1
Beard, Mary, 26
Beloit College, 157, 158
Benton, Thomas Hart, 132, 134–35n.4
birth order: age and authority in, 3–4,
  62; biological vs. functional first child
  in, 53–54n.18; in larger families, 38;

*Annette Atkins,* a professor of history at Saint John's University in Collegeville, Minnesota, is the author of *Harvest of Grief* (Minnesota Historical Society, 1984). She is working on a history of the state of Minnesota.

Typeset in 10/13 Galliard
with Galliard display
Designed by Paula Newcomb
Composed by Jim Proefrock
at the University of Illinois Press
Manufactured by Thomson-Shore, Inc.

University of Illinois Press
1325 South Oak Street
Champaign, IL 61820-6903
www.press.uillinois.edu